Extending
God's Kingdom:
Church Planting Yesterday, Today, Tomorrow

An EMQ Monograph

Laurie Fortunak Nichols,
A. Scott Moreau, and
Gary R. Corwin, eds.

Extending God's Kingdom: Church Planting Yesterday, Today, Tomorrow (An EMQ Monograph)

Edited by Laurie Fortunak Nichols, A. Scott Moreau, and Gary R. Corwin

Cover photos (left) by Steve Evans and (right) courtesy IMB.

Published by EMIS, a division of the Billy Graham Center at Wheaton College, 500 College Ave., Wheaton, IL 60187

Printed in the United States of America.

For information about other resources or publications of EMIS or the Billy Graham Center:
Phone: 630.752.7158
Email: emis@wheaton.edu
Online: www.emisdirect.com
ISBN: 978-1-879089-54-9

Previous Publications in the EMQ Monograph Series:
Engaging the Church: Analyzing the Canvas of Short-term Missions (2008)
Envisioning Effective Ministry: Evangelism in a Muslim Context (2010)

Endorsements

In *Extending God's Kingdom* our friends at *EMQ* have sifted through years of Great Commission lessons to give us valuable insights into church planting. What a great service to the Body of Christ! Thank you, friends, for your excellent work and for giving this back to the Body of Christ.

—***David Garrison***, *missionary and author,* Church Planting Movements

Missionaries eagerly anticipate each edition of *EMQ* to spark creative ideas, engage them in a global dialogue, and encourage them that they are part of a worldwide team of sisters and brothers just like them. *Extending God's Kingdom* gives church planters a one-stop resource to glean the best of the *EMQ* conversation over recent decades. You'll find yourself experiencing "ah-ha" moments of fresh insight, arguing with proposals that provoke you, and stimulated to try exciting new methods. Classic articles are bookended by original pieces by J.D. Payne, Craig Ott, and Tom Steffen that insightfully survey the recent past and expected future of church-planting paradigms. All church planters will want to add this valuable resource to their ministry toolbox.

—***Steve Strauss***, *professor of mission and intercultural studies, Dallas Theological Seminary; former missionary, SIM; former director, SIM USA*

The task of seeing indigenous, biblical church movements among the unreached is too complex and demanding to ignore the careful research, proven ministry insights, and hard-gained wisdom from reflective missionary practitioners over the last decade. This latest *EMQ* monograph offers a wealth of practical help and perspective for all in the mission enterprise. I would strongly urge everyone involved in church planting to make it a field handbook and not just a reference book on your shelf. Better yet, gather your team members and colleagues and energetically engage in discussion and application around these invaluable insights.

—***Daniel Bacon***, *leadership consultant and former U.S. national director, OMF International*

Extending God's Kingdom: Church Planting Yesterday, Today, Tomorrow is an excellent book written not only by theoreticians, but by practitioners on the field as well. It is comprehensive in scope, and addresses most of the contemporary issues in church planting without overlooking the burden of history. As a practitioner, I am concerned about church planting becoming just another theological or missiological gobbledygook; section one of the book addressed my concerns. Ultimately, it is the man or woman of God who is the most important factor in church planting. *Extending God's Kingdom* is a great contribution to the growing library of literature on church planting. I wholeheartedly endorse it.

—***Dr. Damian 0. Emetuche***, *assistant professor of church planting and director of Cecil B. Day Center for Church Planting, New Orleans Baptist Theological Seminary*

Extending God's Kingdom: Church Planting Yesterday, Today, Tomorrow promises to be the best book yet in this *EMQ* monograph series. Laurie Nichols, Scott Moreau, and Gary Corwin have done a superb job in selecting and bunching the articles into six easy-to-read sections. With articles by such practitioners as Ben Sawatsky, Robert Vajko, Johan Lukasse, and Tom Steffen, the volume represents the best of church planting by westerners in the past generation. And the two epilogues by Steffen and Craig Ott are excellent. *Extending God's Kingdom* is an invaluable addition to the church planter's toolbox in the global Church's passion to see the church planted and fully established among every people group in the world.

—**Dr. Monroe "Monnie" Brewer**, *president, National Association of Missions Pastors; international director, Centers of Church Based Training*

In every generation, the Lord gives us challenges that send us back to his word and keep us dependent on him. Ideas about church planting change, grow, and develop. This *EMQ* church-planting volume provides a summation, both valuable and surprising, of current ideas from the experiences of his laborers.

—**Meg Crossman**, *editor,* PathWays to Global Understanding

Table of Contents

Editors

Gary R. Corwin is associate editor of *Evangelical Missions Quarterly* and staff missiologist with the international office of Serving in Mission (SIM).

Laurie Fortunak Nichols is managing editor of *EMQ* and editorial coordinator of the Billy Graham Center at Wheaton College. She is also editorial coordinator of Lausanne World Pulse.

A. Scott Moreau is editor of *EMQ*. He is also professor in the intercultural studies department in the Wheaton College Graduate School.

Article Contributors

Frank W. Allen served with SEND International in the Philippines for more than three decades.

Ken Baker planted churches in West Africa for twenty-four years with SIM, primarily in Muslim regions, urban and rural. He directs Culture ConneXions, a SIM ministry coaching congregations in intercultural relationship and engagement. Ken holds a DMiss from Trinity Evangelical Divinity School.

Shane Bennett is a popular traveling speaker and consultant with Caleb Project.

Scott Bessenecker is associate director of missions for InterVarsity Christian Fellowship, overseeing short-term mission programs. He is author of two books, *The New Friars* (InterVarsity Press, 2006) and *How to Inherit the Earth* (InterVarsity Press, 2009), and edited the newly-released book, *Living Mission* (InterVarsity Press, 2010).

Scott Breslin is a joint member of Frontiers and Operation Mobilization. He has been serving in the Middle East and Europe since 1986, helping ministry teams stay on task, and thrive spiritually. He encourages and equips believers to take up their ambassador/priest role in unlikely workplaces and communities.

Dan Brown served as field director in the international headquarters of Frontiers in England. Previously, he was a church planter for ten years in the Middle East.

Dr. David A. Diaso ministers with Mission to the World, and is involved in church planting and mercy ministries on the San Diego-Tijuana border.

David Dunaetz is a professor of psychology at Azusa Pacific University in California. He spent seventeen years church planting in the eastern suburbs of Paris, France, where he and his wife were blessed by seeing the birth of two churches.

Vergil Gerber was missionary secretary for the Conservative Baptist Home Mission Society.

Dick Grady worked in Indonesia with OC International.

David Greenlee serves as international research associate with Operation Mobilization.

Dr. Todd Jamison (pseudonym) has lived in Central Asia with his wife and four children for the past eighteen years. He facilitates house church planting and leadership training initiatives, as well as business as mission projects throughout the region.

Andy Johnson has been planting churches among the Dagara of Burkina Faso since 2002. He is blessed with a beautiful wife and three children. Andy received his MA in missions from Abilene Christian University.

Mark Johnson and his wife, Kay, are church-planting missionaries with The Evangelical Alliance Mission (TEAM). Mark is also church-planting coordinator for TEAM-Venezuela. They live and work in Caracas, Venezuela, with their sons, Gregory and Ian.

Juha Jones (pseudonym) worked in the Arab world for fourteen years as a bi-vocational church planter (with AWM, now Pioneers International), mentoring teams and mentors. He continues to advise individuals, teams, and businesses internationally on effective reproduction of the kingdom.

Glenn Kendall serves as Africa ministry director for WorldVenture. Previously, he and his wife, Kathy, served in Rwanda and facilitated the planting of hundreds of churches. They have two adult children, both married and serving as missionaries in West Africa.

Rick Kronk and his family spent twelve years church planting among North African Muslim immigrants in France. Since moving to Germany, Rick continues in evangelism, discipleship, curriculum development, and teaching in the areas of Islam and church planting.

Johan Lukasse was president of the Belgian Evangelical Mission in Brussels. Previously, during his 11-year pastorate at Genk, he conceived and developed the idea of starting churches with teams of young people.

Dr. Dwight McGuire (pseudonym) is a media consultant with Pioneers and other organizations. He and his wife, Linda, have served with Pioneers for eighteen years, developing mass media strategies in church-planting movements.

Craig Ott is associate professor of mission and intercultural studies at Trinity Evangelical Divinity School. Formerly, he served in Germany with ReachGlobal (the Evangelical Free Church Mission), where he planted several churches. He is co-author of *Global Church Planting* (Baker Academic, 2011).

J. D. Payne is a national missionary with the North American Mission Board and associate professor of church planting and evangelism at The Southern Baptist Theological Seminary. He is the author of three books, including *Discovering Church Planting: An Introduction to the Whats, Whys, and Hows of Global Church Planting*.

Trent Rowland (pseudonym) led a church-planting team in Asia. He is author of *Pioneer Church Planting: A Rookie Team Leader's Handbook* (Caleb Project, 2001).

Ben Sawatsky has served in various capacities with the Evangelical Free Church Mission since 1961, first as a church planter in Singapore and Malaysia and later as executive director.

Dr. Dietrich Schindler is a TEAM missionary to Germany, seconded to the Evangelical Free Church of Germany as national director of church planting. His most recent book, in German, carries the English title, *The Jesus-Model: Planting Churches like Jesus*. He is married to Jan and they have three adult children.

Floyd and Christine Schneider started Bible studies and planted churches in Austria for years. Floyd has written numerous articles and authored *Evangelism for the Faint-Hearted* (Earl C. Publishing, 1994).

Dick Scoggins trained church-planting teams in the Muslim world with Frontiers and other agencies. His training materials have been used in over a dozen languages. He is the author of a number of books about church planting.

Derek Seipp works in partnership with Saturation Church Planting International (SCPI), coaching and training pastors in church planting and leadership development. He lives in Asia with his family.

Larry W. Sharp has served as vice president of CrossWorld (formerly UFM International) since 1993. He was a missionary in Brazil for over twenty years. In 2007, he started a business as mission consulting firm, which helps kingdom-focused businesses start up in high-risk locations around the world.

Dr. Tom Steffen served twenty years with New Tribes Mission, fifteen of those in the Philippines. He is professor of intercultural studies in the Cook School of Intercultural Studies at Biola University. He is co-author of *Great Commission Companies* (InterVarsity Press, 2003), author of *The Facilitator Era: Beyond Pioneer Church Multiplication* (Wifp & Stock, 2011), and more than half a dozen other books.

Charles Troutman worked with the Latin America Mission. He also served in a number of capacities in Costa Rica.

Dr. Robert Vajko served as church-planting missionary with TEAM in France for twenty-nine years and in Australia for seven. He is now an international church-planting consultant, conducting seminars and training in church planting, church health, and church multiplication. He is also a consultant for Natural Church Development, a ministry to help churches around the world develop greater health.

Dr. Gailyn Van Rheenen served as a church-planting missionary among the Kipsigis of Kenya for fourteen years, taught missions and evangelism at Abilene Christian University for nearly eighteen years, and is the founder and facilitator of church planting in Mission Alive.

Linda Wilson and her husband, Gene, planted French churches in Quebec for eighteen years with Reach Global (the Evangelical Free Church Mission), and served as church-planting coaches to Latin America. She holds a MEd from McGill University in Montreal.

An Epoch of Church Planting

J. D. Payne

All missionaries are a product of their times. History is not simply a thing of the past; it is a dynamic force molding and shaping missionaries of the present. We stand on the shoulders of those who have gone before—both taking delightful drinks from cisterns we did not dig and reaping the problems of the seeds of trouble sown yesteryear. The contents you will find in the chapters that follow are no exception to this rule. They have been influenced by the good, the bad, and the ugly of two thousand years of church history.

In light of our connection to such history, this Foreword is an attempt to provide you with a glimpse of an epoch of church planting, one that follows the dismantling of colonialism and culminates in the present. As we gloss over this time span, I hope to bring to your attention seven significant issues shaping Western expressions of church planting today.

Issue 1: Mission Stations

One of the missionary methods used during colonialism was that of *the mission station paradigm as a means to reach nationals and plant churches* among them. This model (which continued for many years, even after colonialism) was a geographic and cultural bastion of Western civilization in the midst of what was often considered to be an uncivilized and uncultured society. While the Lord was able to work through such an approach, the model reflected a paternalistic endeavor for missionary labors.

Western missionaries, usually locating close to the European military establishments and gunboats and merchants, would establish a missionary compound containing homes for the missionaries, schools, hospitals, and church facilities. While ministry and evangelism took place outside of the station, society within the compound was patterned after the homelands of the missionaries. As nationals came to faith, they would be gathered together as a church, often on the property of the compound and meeting with a building that was reminiscent of a church facility in Europe.

Teaching, preaching, liturgy, and leadership development followed common Western practices. The mission station approach to church planting required not only that the new believers and churches know the scriptures, but that they embrace complex Western church traditions, organizations, and structures in order to serve the Lord in their lands. Both believers and unbelievers came to assume that following Jesus was to be equated with Western cultural expressions.

Issue 2: Indigenous Churches

On both sides of the Atlantic, two contemporaries—working apart from one another—began to advocate for the need for missionaries to plant indigenous churches that were self-supporting, self-governing, and self-propagating (self-extending), and not to reflect a paternalistic approach. These two highly influential men were Henry Venn (1796-1873), general secretary of the Church Missionary Society (London), and Rufus Anderson (1796-1880), corresponding (foreign) secretary of the American Board of Commissioners for Foreign Missions (Boston).

Describing Venn's missiology, Max Warren writes,

> Venn, we must remember, was deeply committed to the goal of a genuinely native church. His great ambition was to see a native church become self-governing under a native bishop. This, so it seemed to him, was much more likely to happen if the church grew naturally with only a very simple organization to begin with than if there was foisted upon it from the start the complex structure that in Venn's time seemed likely to be necessary, once a foreigner was appointed as a bishop (1971, 25).

Anderson, in a similar vein, believed that the chief work of the missionaries was that of planting churches that would not depend upon foreigners, would have their own national leaders, and would multiply themselves (Beaver 1967, 23).

John L. Nevius (1829-1893) was a Presbyterian missionary who served in China in the late nineteenth century. However, it was in Korea where his influence regarding the importance of planting indigenous churches from the very beginning was felt the strongest.[1] Nevius placed great emphasis on raising up national leaders, self-support of those leaders, and not extracting such leaders from their social networks to serve the churches.

Issue 3: The Holy Spirit and Spontaneous Expansion

Shortly after surviving the Boxer Uprising in Peking at the turn of the twentieth century, Roland Allen, Anglican missionary/priest, returned to England and began studying the work of the Apostle Paul.

Allen noted that following his return to the New Testament writings, he came to realize where Western missionaries were falling short in their work by continuing to practice a paternalistic approach to missions and requiring long periods of time before removing Western dependency from the native churches. He argued that it was exactly where the Apostle Paul succeeded in missions that contemporary missionaries missed the mark.

By 1912, Allen published what would become his most popular book,

Missionary Method's: St. Paul's or Ours? It was clear—even from the poignant title—that Allen believed the contemporary church-planting practices were miles removed from that of the apostle. So much so that missionaries of his day (particularly those with the Anglican Church) had a choice to make: either continue with a variation of the mission station paradigm (gradually devolving authority to national churches to be the churches in their contexts without Western domination) or follow the approaches advocated in the Bible (that local churches were to be indigenous from the moment of their birth).

Since Allen believed missionaries practiced paternalism because they feared possible corruption which could become of new churches, he argued that contemporary missionaries had to manifest a missionary faith in the power of the Holy Spirit. For him, it was the only way to overcome the fear of people.

This faith was that the Spirit was able to seal, protect, empower, guide, and sanctify the new churches without forms of Western paternalism. According to Allen, it was only when the missionaries were planting indigenous churches—from the beginning—and manifesting a missionary faith, that the setting was ripe for the Spirit to lead the churches in spontaneous expansion, thus resulting in the multiplication of disciples and churches throughout the society. As long as the missionaries were in control, the Spirit could not be in control and the health and growth of the churches were at stake.

Issue 4: Church Growth Movement

The contemporary Church Growth Movement was birthed in India in the 1950s. Donald A. McGavran, a third-generation missionary, had served for many years in this nation. Over time, he began to wonder why some churches were not growing and others were growing with substantial conversions.

By 1955, he published the movement-producing book *The Bridges of God: A Study in the Strategy of Missions*. Having been influenced by the work of Allen, McGavran was strongly opposed to the mission station paradigm, believing it extracted people from their social networks and hindered the rapid dissemination of the gospel and the planting of churches (McGavran 1955).

He wrote that "...today's paramount task, opportunity, and imperative in missions is to multiply churches in the increasing numbers of receptive peoples of the earth" (McGavran 1970, 63). While McGavran recognized that the missionaries could not control God's sovereignty or the social contexts, he strongly believed that they could change the institutional factors that hindered the advancement of the gospel and church planting. He believed that strategy—or the lack thereof—and methods mattered when it came to the birth of churches.

Issue 5: Contextualized Churches

During the middle of the twentieth century, theologians and missiologists began to change their language from that of "indigenous churches" to "contextualized churches." Some people began to note that local churches could be self-supporting, self-governing, and self-propagating, and still remain very Western in their understanding of themselves as followers of Jesus and how they were to function as churches. It was possible to teach churches to manifest these self's, but teach them how to do so according to the missionaries' cultural preferences.

The result was churches consisting of national believers, but not churches deeply rooted among their cultures. They were not tightly connected to their contexts (i.e., contextualized), again, leaving those outside of the faith to equate Jesus with the abandonment of their people's culture.

Issue 6: Unreached Peoples

McGavran became the founding dean of the School of World Missions at Fuller Theological Seminary in 1965. With the opening of this school, the influence of the Church Growth Movement expanded exponentially across the globe. Concepts such as receptivity, people movements, homogenous units, strategy, and research began to influence church-planting methods in all regions of the world.

One of the first faculty members of the school was Ralph D. Winter. And while Winter's influence on church planting was significant, it was felt the strongest in his advocacy for the hidden peoples of the world and the necessity for cross-cultural evangelism.

It was during the 1974 Lausanne Congress for World Evangelization that Winter presented a paper which would forever change the world of missions in general, and church planting in particular (Winter 1975, 213-241). Leaders from across the world began to recognize the need to reach the unreached people groups, large numbers of peoples who would only be reached by cross-cultural evangelism and church planting. Shortly after that Congress, evangelicals from across the globe began researching and strategizing for planting churches among the unreached people groups.

Issue 7: Church-planting Movements

It was during the last decade of the twentieth century that church growth reports, reflecting professions of faith, baptisms, and newly-planted churches, starting showing high growth rates among different people groups across the globe. David Garrison would describe these as church-planting movements which were understood as "a rapid multiplication of indigenous churches planting churches that sweeps through a people group or population segment" (Garrison 2004, 21).

Over the first decade of the twenty-first century, missiologists would research and attempt to determine the commonalities among such movements, with the desired result of developing strategies and methods that would attempt to help facilitate future movements.

Conclusion

To get a good overview as to what has been happening at the beginning of the twenty-first century beyond church-planting movements, I will direct you to Craig Ott's concluding chapter, "Church Planting and Tomorrow's Challenges." Here, Ott provides us with a glimpse of present realities of the church-planting world. I would only add two items to his excellent chapter.

First, Ott addresses the development of support networks within the United States. I would add that I expect the numbers of such networks to continue to swell in the future. Second, evangelicals will continue to give more and more attention to planting churches among the cities of the world.

Extending God's Kingdom: Church Planting Yesterday, Today, Tomorrow is an outstanding collection of articles on the topic of church planting. This book represents a multitude of both wisdom and experience and the editors have done a great job of taking the "best-of-the-best" from previous volumes of the prestigious *Evangelical Missions Quarterly* and wedding them together in this single work.

Now, let me invite you to prayerfully read through this collection of articles. Reflect on them. Discuss them with others. Apply your findings to your ministry context.

Lord willing, may this book be used to advance the gospel, resulting in the multiplication of disciples, leaders—and yes—future churches among the peoples of this world!

Endnote

1. For a description of what came to be known as the Nevius Method, see *Planting and Development of Missionary Churches* (Nevius n.d.).

References

Beaver, R. Pierce. 1967. *To Advance the Gospel: Selections from the Writings of Rufus Anderson*. Grand Rapids, Mich.: William B. Eerdmans Publishing Co.

Garrison, David. 2004. *Church Planting Movements: How God Is Redeeming a Lost World*. Midlothian, Va.: WIGTake Resources.

McGavran, Donald A. 1955. *The Bridges of God: A Study in the Strategy of Missions*. New York: Friendship Press.

_____. 1970. *Understanding Church Growth*. Grand Rapids, Mich.: William B. Eerdmans Publishing Co.

Nevius, John L. n.d. *Planting and Development of Missionary Churches*. n.p.: The Presbyterian and Reformed Publishing Co.

Warren, Max, ed. 1971. *To Apply the Gospel: Selections from the Writings of Henry Venn*. Grand Rapids, Mich.: William B. Eerdmans Publishing Co.

Winter, Ralph D. 1975. "The Highest Priority: Cross-Cultural Evangelism." In *Let the Earth Hear His Voice: International Congress on World Evangelization Lausanne, Switzerland*. Ed. J. D. Douglas, 213-241. Minneapolis, Minn.: World Wide Publications.

INTRODUCTION

Throughout the Bible we clearly see that God's ultimate plan for the world—the *missio Dei*—has as its primary means of reconciling the world to himself God's initiating and continual developing of the Body of Christ we know as the Church. The Church, however, is neither a disconnected set of discrete "human molecules" nor an amorphous blended blob. Rather, this universal bride of Christ is the net composite of countless individual fellowships and congregations—churches—in every corner of the globe. Every one of these local gatherings is comprised of individual Christians banded together by the love of Christ and their Holy Spirit-fueled desire to glorify God.

While God alone regenerates people and brings them into this universal body, over the past two millennia he has consistently used Christians who have experienced the presence of Christ in their lives as the primary instruments for planting, growing, and developing the individual churches we see scattered everywhere across the planet.

IT IS EASY TO SEE that everything the Body of Christ does—whether directly or indirectly—is connected to God's eternal purpose of building his Church founded on the cornerstone of Jesus Christ.

In light of this, it is easy to see that everything the Body of Christ does—whether directly or indirectly—is connected to God's eternal purpose of building his Church founded on the cornerstone of Jesus Christ. Given that, making resources available to assist believers in this great task as directed and empowered by God should be one of our top priorities.

Over the past several decades *Evangelical Missions Quarterly* has published hundreds of articles focused on planting, growing, and/or building the Church. From this large treasure trove we have carefully chosen the thirty-six that appear in this volume, and supplemented them with pieces commissioned specifically for the book.

As the best of our best, we consider this book indispensable for those engaged in church-focused ministries. Each chapter comes from a cross-cultural servant who, having lived in the trenches, chose to offer the rest of us his or her hard-won insights on methods, models, and strategies. They stem from successes, certainly, but also from that hardest of teachers known as failure.

Together they comprise a mosaic of biblical, practical, and helpful resources which help all of us think and act more biblically and clearly about:

(1) those who plant and nurture churches
(2) the biblical framework for church planting
(3) ideals of what a church plant should produce
(4) strategies for planting churches
(5) partnership in church planting

The case studies in our final section give focused attention on implementing ideas in specific settings.

It is our prayer that God will give you insight and energy as you draw from the well dug by our authors, and that you will be prepared and propelled into the calling God has for you as you participate in his *missio Dei*.

—*A. Scott Moreau, co-editor*

The Church Planter

Before we go out to do what God has called us to do, we must first be the people he has created us to be. Before strategy, activity, and analysis comes character. Any serious church planter (or lay Christian, for that matter) must be serious about displaying the fruit of the Spirit and having a Christ-like attitude in all areas of life. In this first section we look at the church planter— what he or she must keep in mind as one called to those who have not yet heard the brilliant hope of salvation.

J. D. Payne begins with eleven simple guidelines related to the kingdom ethic. **Ben Sawatsky** asks, "What qualities and qualifications should a church planter exhibit?" **Dick Grady** and **Glenn Kendall** share seven general principles for church planters.

Craig Ott goes on to explain that there are at least three types of missionary church planters. **Larry Sharp** calls us back to modeling the fruit of the Spirit, striving to be good at being and making disciples and encouraging those we work with and among to do the same. Writing again, **Kendall** reminds us that our role must be as *facilitator*, not necessarily as leader. **Andy Johnson** reflects on how his role as a father mirrors his role as a church planter. Finally, **Juha Jones** shares four ways church planters need mentoring.

January 2010

Ethical Guidelines for Church Planters

J.D. Payne

Eleven guidelines to allow missionaries to maintain freedom to fulfill their callings, while establishing healthy parameters in light of the kingdom ethic.

Life in the Kingdom of God is life lived by a kingdom ethic. Since life in the kingdom consists of being a slave (Matt. 25:14-30); a good steward (Luke 12:35-48) of the king's resources, as well as making most of the time and opportunities (Col. 4:5; Eph. 5:16); and walking in wisdom (Eph. 5:15), freedom with missionary practices should only be permitted to the extent that proper stewardship, faithfulness, and wisdom are not compromised for a lesser good.

There needs to be a set of contextual ethical guidelines for church planters. The following eleven guidelines allow missionaries to maintain the necessary philosophical and methodological freedom in which to fulfill their callings, while simultaneously establishing healthy biblical and missiological parameters in light of the kingdom ethic. Such a code of ethics is not restricting, but rather liberating, assisting church planters with focus and alignment with the kingdom ethic.

Guideline #1: Since the global need for the gospel is so great, unless God reveals otherwise, we will begin our ministry among people with the greatest need and with a high level of receptivity to the gospel. It is an unethical practice to begin laboring in areas where there is little need for additional evangelicals and low levels of receptivity while there are four billion people in the world with little to no access to the gospel.

Unless there is a strong calling of God to labor elsewhere, the proper approach should be to labor where the receptivity is the highest. (Remember: sometimes the most receptive peoples are those with little access to the gospel.) It is unethical to neglect those asking the question of the Philippian jailer (Acts 16:30) when others are cursing the name of Christ.

Guideline #2: Since the world consists of four billion unbelievers, with two billion who have never heard the gospel, our strategy will involve the use of highly reproducible church-planting methods. Ecclesiology and missionary practices built upon a foundation of paternalism that hinders the birth and multiplication of contextualized churches do not take the global aspect of the Great Commission with the utmost seriousness.

Charles Brock is correct when he notes, "In an age when perhaps more than four billion people do not know Christ in a personal way, it borders on immorality for a planter to plant a church without considering reproducibility" (1990, 25).

Guideline #3: Since biblical church planting is evangelism that results in new churches, we will not prioritize transfer growth over conversion growth by designing ministries that will primarily attract believers. Although crowd attraction and starting a new worship service are not necessarily bad, their manifestations do not necessarily mean the kingdom has advanced. Church planters settling for large numbers of transfer growth is not the pattern of the Apostolic Church.

Guideline #4: Since unity among churches in a geographical area is a powerful witness to the gospel, we will be concerned with other evangelical pastors laboring in the same area as our team, and will take the initiative to meet with them to share our calling, vision, and ethic.

Jesus prayed that his Church would be unified (John 17:11, 23) and noted that the world would know his disciples by their love for one another (John 13:35). Whenever church planters enter into new areas where other evangeli-

IT IS UNETHICAL for a church-planting

team (and the new churches) to receive members from other churches without regard for those churches.

cal churches are present, such church planters need to take the initiative to meet and share their callings and ethical guidelines with the pastors of those churches, making an attempt to live at peace with everyone (Rom. 12:18; Heb. 12:14).

Guideline #5: Since we desire to respect other evangelical pastors in the area, and desire sanctification in the lives of any transfers from local churches, we will have a systematic plan to respond to the transfers who want to become part of the new church.

It is unethical for a church-planting team (and the new churches) to receive members from other churches without regard for those churches. Unless the local church is ungodly in belief or practice, the person should be allowed to become a part of the new work only after being discouraged from leaving his or her church family, and only with his or her pastor(s) and church's blessing, and only if all parties involved believe that the prompting for such a move is from the Lord.

Guideline #6: Since our calling to this ministry, people, and location is from God (and not based on money), we will not end our church-planting ministry in this area simply if our financial support ends, but rather will make appropriate plans for the future of our personal finances. Knowing that the sands in the hourglass of support sometimes quickly run out, many church planters begin well but decide to short-cut the work of the ministry due to lack of funds. Also, external and internal pressures to "produce results" force some to make unhealthy compromises. Long before any such funding comes to an end, church-planting teams must strategize in light of the question, "What if our funding ends?"

Guideline #7: Since the biblical model for church planting is a team approach, and many liabilities come when working as a solo church planter, a team will be developed before the work begins. Whenever church planters "go at it alone" they fail to follow in the model set forth in the scriptures of a team approach. This lone ranger approach to missions creates a dilemma that raises the potential for missiological malpractice. It sets the church planter up for potential burnout and discouragement, and hinders sustained accountability in the ministry.

Guideline #8: Since one of the most critical issues in missionary circles is that of stress on the family, we will not neglect our families for the sake of church planting and will begin our work with a strategy for nurturing our family life while serving as church planters.

SINCE WE ARE KINGDOM CITIZENS, we will not neglect our daily devotional time with the Lord by allowing ourselves to be distracted.

The church-planting family establishes an example for the new believers and churches to follow. Therefore, a church-planting family does not have to be next to perfect—it has to be perfect. If the family falls due to neglect, the ministry falls even harder. A failure to adequately prepare one's family for such labors, and to maintain a healthy ministry that involves the continual shepherding of one's family for their growth in Christ, is reflective of a missionary more concerned with accomplishing the ministerial task of planting a church and not living according to a kingdom ethic (1 Tim. 3:4-5).

Guideline #9: Since we are kingdom citizens, we will not neglect our daily devotion time with the Lord by allowing ourselves to be distracted by the numerous tasks to be accomplished in the ministry. Whenever the demands of the ministry detract from the church planters' devotional times, an ethical dilemma exists. Missionaries cannot substitute time spent on building the church for spending time with the One who promised to build his Church.

Guideline #10: Since the task of missionary work involves effective communication, we will work diligently toward contextualization, rather than bringing our preferred church traditions to the people. Church planters face the temptation to practice paternalism rather than contextualization. Rather than reaching people from the harvest and teaching them how to be the Body of Christ in their local community—thus allowing church structures to develop from the people and grow with the people—many teams create the structures and try to make the people fit into such organization.

Another unhealthy approach that sometimes takes precedence over contextualization is that of pragmatism—the philosophy that whatever works to accomplish the goal is what should be done. The usual result of either of these philosophies is that new churches have no biblical or missiological foundation for the structures, do not own their structures, cannot financially support them, and are not qualified to provide oversight for them.

Guideline #11: Since integrity and accuracy are important when reporting statistics related to our missionary labors, we will strive to report only those numbers and descriptive details which are truly reflective of what the Holy Spirit is doing in our context. The intentional reporting of inaccurate numbers is unethical. It is deceptive and bears false witness against the Spirit. Although all statistical reporting must be done without reproach, particular care must be taken in reporting numbers related to baptisms and actual churches planted. If it is not a church, then don't count it as a church.

Also, accurate reporting must extend beyond the simple reporting of raw numbers—such is especially important in areas not highly receptive to the gospel. Missionaries should provide a "thick description" of what the Holy Spirit is doing among such people. Stories need to be shared. Such stories, particularly when the numerical growth is slow, will encourage both the missionary teams as well as those who read and hear their reports.

The above guidelines comprise a code of ethics for church planters. To my knowledge, such a code does not exist. However, kingdom citizens are called to live according to a kingdom ethic. This divine ethic is not simply concerned with matters of avoiding flagrant sinful acts such as adultery, fornication, lying, and murder, but this ethic touches all of life. For church planters, the kingdom ethic especially speaks to matters related to their missionary practices, philosophies, and methods.

Reference

Brock, Charles. 1990. *Indigenous Church Planting: A Practical Journey.* Neosho, Mo.: Church Growth International.

What It Takes to Be a Church Planter

Ben Sawatsky

What qualities and qualifications should a worker exhibit?

Based on my eighteen years of cross-cultural ministry in Singapore and Malaysia, I believe that church planting is the most strategic cross-cultural ministry today. To plant the church is to join hands with the risen, ascended Lord in an activity of great concern to him. To plant the church is to enter the mainstream of God's plan for the missionary enterprise.

Three New Testament statements reveal Jesus' relationship to church planting. "I will build my church" (Matt. 16:18) reveals Jesus' activity within the church. "Christ loved the church and gave himself up for her" (Eph. 5:25) portrays Jesus' attitude toward the church. Finally, "He walks among the seven golden lampstands" (Rev. 1:1) indicates Jesus' proximity to the church. The first two statements speak clearly of the universal Church, while the last statement speaks of historical local churches.

The Apostle Paul was also concerned with church planting, or, perhaps more accurately, "congregation planting." Wherever he went, congregations began, but Paul did not plant churches during weekend evangelistic blitzes. He spent eighteen months at Corinth and two to three years at Ephesus.

Paul spoke of the ministry of church planting when he wrote, "I planted, Apollos watered, but God was causing the growth" (1 Cor. 3:6). Church planting and "church watering" are on equal terms. The former covers evangelism and other ministries related to the early stages of congregation planting. "Church watering" covers a wide range of ministries, including theological education and discipleship.

Because of the Bible's command and example concerning church planting, we must make this the primary focus of the cross-cultural missionary endeavor. There are two basic types of cross-cultural missionaries. Alongside the "church planters" and "church waterers" are the support missionaries engaged in numerous activities. The problem is that our worldwide, cross-cultural, church-planting task force has dwindled, while our support personnel have ballooned.

One of the reasons for this imbalance is the voluntarism characterizing by much of the modern missionary movement. The mission recruiting net has been cast widely by our saying to young men and women, "Anything you can do, come to us and we'll find a place for you." It would be unthinkable in the business world for a corporation to take in volunteers and then create jobs for them, but is this not what many mission agencies are doing?

There are, of course, other reasons why we have so few church-planting missionaries, such as too few of today's missionaries being discipled in a church-planting atmosphere, or receiving church-planting experience before venturing overseas (see Fisher 1978, 207).

While not viewing necessary and legitimate support personnel as second-class missionaries, we must limit their number to services either not available or affordable in the host country. We should view many support ministries as temporary rather than permanent, and when possible, draw from the ranks of our growing crop of short-termers.

Church planting has become the "in activity" in mission circles. This has led to a tendency to seek legitimacy for every missionary activity by placing it under the church-planting rubric. Church planting is the evangelistic activity which brings into being congregations of believers in Jesus Christ.

This defines church planting, but how do we go about defining a good church planter? What qualities and qualifications should a worker exhibit? Let's look at some of the most important pre-field and on-field qualifications.

Pre-field Qualities and Qualifications

1. A high view of the Church. The church is at the heart of the missionary enterprise. Its role is to select, send, and support cross-cultural missionaries, as spiritual gifts are discovered, developed, and deployed. It is incredible to see young men and women make grand plans for cross-cultural ministries involving huge amounts of money without roots in a local church. Rootlessness at home is reflected in a similar rootlessness of ministry overseas. Too often candidates choose a school, ministry, and mission agency before coming to the local church to pay the bill. The divorce between the local church and mission agency is not only the fault of the mission agency, however. Local churches seem content to allow candidates to choose their own type of ministry and place of training, while the mission agency selects, deploys, and supervises their ministry.

The uniqueness and autonomy of the emerging national Church is also related to a high view of the Church. A missionary to Japan wrote:

> Missionary candidates need to be aware that they are—at least in our case—working in an already established national Church which has some patterns for evangelism fairly well established....Missionary candidates must have strongly impressed on them the fact that things will not be done in just the way they think they should be, and that patience and a willingness to hear and see the nationals' viewpoint is absolutely essential.

Another missionary noted a church relations problem in several parts of the world:

> The current leadership of the Venezuelan Evangelical Free Church feels that local church autonomy is a Western cultural imposition. As in many Third World

countries, authority in Venezuela comes from the top down. Apparently, Venezuelan Evangelical Free Church leadership feels that Free Church policy in Venezuela should follow the cultural pattern.

2. Necessary spiritual gifts. Basic to New Testament patterns and principles of church planting is the universal ministry of all believers. Spiritual gifts qualify every believer to be in this ministry, while training equips the believer for service. Cross-cultural church planters are typically multi-talented people. But cross-cultural church planters need more than skills; they must possess certain spiritual gifts.

• *Apostleship.* In the secondary sense, an apostle is one who is sent. Cross-cultural church planters spearhead and pioneer new work as they enter a new target area to plant a resident witness. Apostleship includes a pioneer spirit and cross-cultural adaptability. With half of the world's people culturally separated from the gospel, we need thousands with this gift.

Apostleship must be tested at home through a good pre-field, cross-cultural experience in this country. However, the American scene can never provide complete preparation for cross-cultural church planting overseas. Nor does much pre-field church work prepare cross-cultural church planters for church planting. Upon arrival overseas, would-be cross-cultural church planters must first recognize their own cultural baggage and then contextualize their church-planting ministry.

• *Teaching and preaching.* Cross-cultural church planters must learn how to teach, lead, and preach. Because of the cross-cultural nature of their teaching ministry, they must be sensitive to the educational modes which are best suited to communicating the truths of scripture in the host culture. Together with their national brethren, they must set about developing a culturally sensitive theology and course of instruction.

• *Evangelism.* Cross-cultural church planters must do the work of evangelism. Church planting and evangelism go hand in hand. Perhaps it would be more accurate to speak in terms of church planting/evangelism. During the initial stages of a new church-planting venture, almost all of the activity is evangelistic.

• *Faith.* For our purpose, faith is the spiritual vision to see something as an accomplished fact well before the natural eyes see anything. This gift allows cross-cultural church planters to see a congregation of believers worshiping, fellowshiping, serving, and witnessing together before such a congregation exists. This gift helps cross-cultural church planters focus on a promise like Matthew 16:18, "I will build my church," without being deterred by obstacles.

• *Leadership.* Leadership was best modeled by Jesus' servant role. He did not lead by self-assertion, self-aggrandizement, or self-adulation. On the eve of his crucifixion, he stated:

> You know that the rulers of the Gentiles lord it over them, and their great men exercise authority over them. It is not so among you, but whoever wishes

to become great among you shall be your servant, and whoever wishes to be first among you shall be your slave; just as the Son of Man did not come to be served, but to serve, and to give his life a ransom for many. (Matt. 20:25-28)

Church planting today is often done by teams of missionaries, national Christians, or perhaps a combination. This allows church planting to be done by individuals with different gifts, skills, and training. With the team approach, each member does not have to possess every gift. Normally, teams have a combination of older, experienced missionaries and new missionaries. This provides the necessary on-the-job training for the new missionaries.

It is best for a team to be working simultaneously with several churches at varying levels of maturity and development. This prevents the missionaries from overwhelming a small congregation and provides a more well-rounded training experience for the newer missionaries.

3. Formal training. Cross-cultural church planters must be trained to cope with the text of scripture and the context of culture. They need skill in both exegesis of the word and the world. Such a difficult task requires the best possible training, preferably an MDiv degree or equivalent.

CROSS-CULTURAL church planters must be able to contextualize the gospel into the host country's culture, preserving the original meaning of the text.

Cross-cultural church planters must be able to contextualize the gospel into the host country's culture, while preserving the original meaning of the text. It is important to be able to craft a Christian apologetic in the context of the country's non-Christian religion. There are no shortcuts in doing this important work. We should also stress ongoing education, including furlough seminars, relevant courses, and perhaps advanced degrees.

4. Stable marriage and family life. The home is the base of operation. By providing for the spiritual, social, academic, and financial needs of the family, church planters serve as models and witnesses in a non-Christian society.

Problems arise as culture shock increases stress on the marriage relationship, with unresolved marital conflicts becoming accentuated and aggravated in the cross-cultural setting. With conflict resolution being more difficult overseas, couples must learn these skills while still at home. It is a good idea for candidates to be married for at least a year before going on the field.

5. Compatibility with colleagues. Incompatibility with fellow missionaries or national colleagues frequently leads to missionaries resigning. A missionary to the Philippines wrote: "All too often, highly qualified and gifted missionaries, with a high degree of training and technical skill, foul out because of inability to work with others and adjust to other people."

On-the-Field Qualities

1. Bicultural. Culture shock is the emotional trauma that results from having much of the familiar removed from us. Cross-cultural missionaries are thrust into a strange environment, where everything from gift giving to keeping appointments is different. Cross-cultural adjustment enables church planters to move freely from their home culture to the host culture and back again with reduced shock.

Becoming bicultural requires sacrifices and a ministry setback in the first term, most of which the missionary must devote to becoming bicultural. Bicultural missionaries have put down linguistic, cultural, and ministry roots. The task of bicultural church planting is to distinguish between what is Christian and what is Western. This enables missionaries to allow the church in the host country to take on a distinctly national shape.

Church planters must be willing to sacrifice pet ideas by allowing the church to become uniquely Japanese, German, or Malaysian. They are not commissioned to produce carbon copies of the home church in America.

2. Simple lifestyle. Cross-cultural church-planting missionaries must be willing to do without some of the material items which have become part of the accepted and, in some cases, expected lifestyle at home. But as the stan-

WITH THEIR LIFE PURPOSE of planting new **congregations** ever before them, cross-cultural church planters realize that to remain in one place too long will keep them from fulfilling their purpose.

dard of living in the Third World rises, material possessions do not put the missionaries out of touch with their national counterparts as they once did. In some cases, our missionaries may even have to consider a higher lifestyle in order to close the material gap.

3. Mobility. The very nature of cross-cultural church planting means that missionaries will spend only a few years in one place. Normally, they will not live in the same house more than one term. Moves tend to become more difficult as the family becomes larger and as church planters grow older. With their life purpose of planting new congregations ever before them, however, cross-cultural church planters realize that to remain in one place too long will keep them from fulfilling their purpose.

4. Strategic mindset. Every field needs at least one cross-cultural church planter who has the mindset of a strategist. This does not mean, however, that the strategy which emerges is the product of his or her mind alone. The best strategists need input from others. It does mean that they are goal and objective oriented. It also means that they can take the lead in developing a plan for church planting evangelism which best suits the host culture. They are able to adapt methods used effectively elsewhere to suit their own church planting situation.

Strategists realize that there is no such thing as either a universal or timeless strategy. A strategy which works very well in Malaysia may run counter to the culture in Japan. A successful strategy in 1991 may well require major modification in 2000. Strategists are sensitive to cultural and time changes. They also must think in terms of strategies rather than a single strategy as different regions of a country will require different approaches. A forgotten characteristic of a strategy is that it reflects the personalities, gifts, and training of the strategists.

5. Flexibility. Flexibility does not mean a willingness to do anything and everything. Jesus had one mission. A similar singleness of purpose must also characterize cross-cultural church planters. They must, however, be flexible in their methods. They must also be flexible enough to assume some responsibility for administrative duties along with their primary task of church planting. It is legitimate for church planters to specialize in church planting, but their specialization must be tempered with flexibility.

Conclusion

The focus of missions today must be church planting. This task is closest to Christ's heart and central to the Great Commission. To properly plant churches, we must take the responsibility of recruiting Spirit-filled candidates exhibiting these important qualities and qualifications. We must see that our churches nurture these qualities, and that mission boards diligently search for qualified recruits, rather than just waiting for whoever comes to their door. With this type of recruiting and nurturing, we will be able to see the gospel spread to every people in our generation, and also know that it is being done in a way honoring to our Lord and most likely to produce the fruit we are all seeking.

Reference
Fisher, Ron. 1978. "Why Don't We Have More Church-planting Missionaries?" *Evangelical Missions Quarterly* 14(4):205-211.

Seven Keys to Effective Church Planting

Dick Grady and Glenn Kendall

*Survey finds seven strategy principles that successful church plant-
ers follow, whether they work in responsive or resistant places.*

What sets apart successful church planters from the rest of the crowd? That's what many missionaries and mission boards would like to know. Do they use different methods? Are their personal lives different? Are they limited to certain parts of the world, to certain agencies?

To find out, a survey was sent to one hundred missionaries chosen as successful by their boards. It was returned by eighty-five church planters from all geographic areas. From their responses, we developed seven strategy principles that successful church planters follow, whether they work in responsive or resistant places.

1. More effective church planters spend time in prayer. The more time spent in prayer, the more effective the church planter. Regardless of field difficulties, those who prayed more tended to be more effective. The most effective church planters average four hours and fifteen minutes more in prayer per week than their less effective colleagues. We hesitate to quantify prayer, yet we know prayer is effective. The current movement of concerts of prayer could usher in a new wave of conversions around the world.

2. More effective church planters use broadly-based evangelistic efforts. The most effective church planters had a greater tendency to use outreach methods that provide a large number of contacts in a given community. Those who enter a new cross-cultural situation and devise a method for sharing the gospel with a large number of people may then identify from this large group those who appear to be spiritually hungry. They invest productive time in discipling those who are more interested.

Starting the process and finding spiritually-interested people is best accomplished by some form of community-wide evangelistic campaign, with lots of noise, excitement, and activity, using many people. Traditionally, this meant nightly meetings with a well-known, gifted speaker. But successful church planters are not limited to that method.

They often use a variety of tools, including films, videos, door-to-door witnessing, surveys, public meetings, book tables, literature distribution, singing groups, drama, media campaigns, parades, special church services, extended prayer meetings, and so on.

Evangelistic methods aimed at a narrow range of people become wider if carried out by a sufficient number of people. For instance, a home Bible study group is not a broad-based method. But if multiple Bible study groups are started in a target community, then the outreach is extended, leading to greater overall results.

This principle supports the current use of church-planting teams. More people together in ministry are better able to carry out broad-based evangelistic methods.

3. More effective church planters are flexible in their methods. The most effective church planters demonstrate a high degree of creativity in their outreaches. They identify and use culturally relevant ways to communicate.

Each method has a target audience. Some methods hit one class, educational level, or even gender or age group better than others. Using a variety of methods extends the range of potential successes. The broader pool makes it more likely that people in families, clans, and groups will respond individually and simultaneously to the gospel. This increases the chances for a people movement.

WHILE CREATIVITY and flexibility are beneficial in evangelism, rigidity in doctrinal position, at least initially, produces better results.

More successful church planters combine flexibility with broad-based efforts. They coordinate multiple, broad-based methods. Evangelizing in multiple ways simultaneously compounds their effectiveness. Each method appeals to and attracts a different cross-section of the population, building up the effort to find those who are interested.

These church planters seek to use numbers of people for bursts of intensive outreach. Nearby church people, fellow missionaries, distant national Christians, international teams, and short-term workers make the contacts for later follow-up.

4. More effective church planters are committed to a doctrinal position. While creativity and flexibility are beneficial in evangelism, rigidity in doctrinal position, at least initially, produces better results. The most effective church planters appear to be very tight in their theology. The specific position itself is not as important as strict adherence to it.

It seems that in establishing new believers, it is best not to get into doctrinal controversies, but to instead transmit core beliefs. Possibly by focusing on the major point of reaching additional people, rather than taking time and energy to thrash out all the pros and cons of various theological debates, churches grow faster.

A "this is what we believe, take it or leave it" attitude, while not the best for developing theological creativity, does allow for concentration on the basics. Greater theological diversity, especially at the beginning, can delay expansion. Energy expended in defining and learning the finer points of theology, and then choosing a doctrinal position, is better used in reproduction.

5. More effective church planters establish greater credibility. There is a high degree of correlation between missionaries who emphasize activities to increase credibility and who plant more churches. Credibility is established in two ways, by meeting social needs and by building relationships with community leaders. These steps of themselves do not make church planters more effective. But as church planters incorporate social work and building relationships into their total ministries, people respond.

Social work is not the primary focus of effective church planters, but one of many activities done by the more effective ones. They do not say, "First, we will fill your stomach and then you will be willing to hear our message." Rather, they say, "We will proclaim our message. If you want to have your stomach filled, that is possible, too."

Social activity and gospel witness go on simultaneously. One does not depend on the other. Often, national Christians do the social work while others witness. Local people participate as they will. Social ministries, of course, produce additional contacts. Non-Christians get to know Christians and the church building in non-threatening, need-based encounters. They see the church as credible, as part of the community, not an outside agency. They become more open to the gospel.

Building relationships means getting to know political, religious, government, military, and other community leaders. After getting to know as many of them as possible, effective church planters develop a few deeper friendships. This reduces suspicions and helps alleviate future problems.

For example, new Christians were having a Christmas celebration in a moderately hostile Muslim area of Indonesia. A low-level official came to shut it down. But the national church planter had developed a close relationship with this official's superior. He arrived and asked if there were any problems. The lower-ranking man bowed out and the Christians said everything was fine. What could have been a disaster was avoided because of the care taken to establish a friendship.

6. More effective church planters have an ability to identify and then work with people who have a loosely structured religion. Where the religious structure is fairly loose, church planting tends to be more successful. This finding corresponds to the principle that says church planters ought to work among more open people first. As they respond, church planters can build on multiplied contacts provided by new Christians among more resistant people.

Successful church planters in the survey were either finding sectors of society more open to change, or were using evangelism and making converts in ways that allowed people to become Christians and retain the essence of their culture, while putting a Christian stamp on it. This confirms what Donald Mc-Gavran has taught that "resistance arises primarily from fear that 'becoming a Christian will separate me from my people'" (McGavran 1990, 191).

For example, more people tend to respond to the gospel when they have recently moved. Some of the more effective church planters worked with people who had just migrated into land recently opened by the government for settlement.

Other successful church planters found large new housing projects more open to the gospel for the first five years. Once people had settled in and developed new habits, they were no longer as open. They had built a new web of social contacts, so they had more to lose by joining a Christian group than when they first arrived.

7. More effective church planters have an ability to incorporate new converts into evangelistic outreach. Consistently, the more effective ones quickly involved new believers in ministry and evangelism, even though they had minimal training. The survey uncovered three positive results from this practice.

First, *new convert evangelism takes advantage of natural bridges for sharing the gospel while the new convert still has the greatest number of non-Christian friends.* The longer people are Christians, the fewer non-Christian friends they tend to have.

Second, *as new believers do evangelism, they develop a stronger commitment to the gospel.* They become insiders, part of a new family. Even if forced to cut the ties with their old relationships, they can see new friendships developing.

Third, *as they share their faith, new believers immediately are hit with questions about what they believe.* Rather than destroying their faith, this forces them to study and learn more about it. As they study the Bible and learn from more experienced Christians, their faith and knowledge grow. Their quest for maturity is need-driven.

Case Study

To show how these principles work, we selected the story of church planting by the Association of Baptist Churches of Rwanda (AEBR), where Glenn Kendall worked with the Conservative Baptist Foreign Mission Society for thirteen years. During his time there the association grew from 1,100 members to over 17,000 baptized adult believers.

1. Prayer. The AEBR outreach emphasized prayer, not just daily prayer, but four weeks a year of special prayer: between Palm Sunday and Easter, the week before Pentecost, during a week of special summer meetings, and the week before Christmas. Almost all churches observed these weeks. Most groups met early in the morning; some met throughout the day; some in late afternoon.

Sending churches mobilized prayer, especially in the early days when larger churches sent their pastor or church leader to participate in evangelism and church planting in new areas. They prayed before and during the campaign.

Participants prayed together each morning; those doing house-to-house evangelism prayed before and often during those visits.

The eight missionaries were prayer warriors. They enlisted prayer from their sending churches. At semi-annual missionary meetings, the first day was devoted exclusively to prayer.

2. Broad-based evangelism. Even though door-to-door evangelism was the heart of the campaign, it became a broad-based outreach because so many people did it. Our goal was to have everyone in the community know we were there. Those who were spiritually hungry often sought out Christians to hear the gospel. When campaigners went to homes, they were often told, "We were waiting for you to come."

3. Flexible methods. As campaigns progressed, workers found additional ways to present the gospel to different segments of the population. In each of the later campaigns, they gave out ten thousand gospel tracts and sold books, Bibles, and scripture portions. This appealed to the more educated people in a media-poor society.

For the first campaign in Uganda, a choir from Zaire ministered. Musically and rhythmically gifted African young people flocked to hear the choir and

DURING A CAMPAIGN IN ZAIRE, workers conducted their first parade. Townspeople flowed behind the sound system and campaign people. Many stayed to hear the gospel.

followed them around. Music was like a magnet.

During a campaign in Zaire, workers conducted their first parade. Townspeople flowed behind the sound system and campaign people. Many stayed to hear the gospel.

Possibly the most effective method was the *Jesus* film. Translated into the local language, it drew thousands to nightly showings, each in a different place. People even stood through the rain to watch it. Showings were advertised ahead of time. This medium attracted a majority of men.

Each method added to the cumulative impact of the campaign. Methods that worked best were discovered by trying ideas often generated by people beyond the immediate leaders.

4. Doctrinal rigidity. The AEBR is very rigid in doctrine. The church often has one position on each issue and that's it. The association has one church constitution and one church covenant. This helped in church planting. People accepted the church's beliefs. Later, those who were interested went on to learn about various other positions. Theological debate did not slow AEBR's expansion, which was unhampered by doctrinal controversies.

5. Credibility. Like stubborn customs officials, missionaries at first resisted all the social programs the church leaders wanted them to do. After persistent pressure from both the church and the government, missionaries agreed to go ahead, provided that expansion be the primary mission of the churches.

The AEBR launched a literacy campaign; at its peak, 13,500 people were learning to read. It started a school system (twenty thousand in primary and one thousand in post-primary education), health centers, clean water projects, enterprises like brick-making. The projects consumed much energy and resources, but the gain was worth it.

People coming to reading classes were not afraid to enter the churches. New water sources not only saved church families hours of water hauling every day, but made the churches the center of community activity. The schools were training a future generation of leaders.

These programs gave points of contact for many people, drew them in, and integrated the churches naturally into the community. Being part of the church became a normal, expected part of life.

6. Loosely structured religious base. The first cluster of churches started by the AEBR was in a new migration area, land recently opened for settlement. Land was easy to get, there was little competition from other churches, and the people were quite responsive.

The second cluster was in another place where some previously started churches had died out because of legal complications. The AEBR made the required legal changes and saw about three thousand people added to the church.

The third cluster area was picked because of its strategic location on a ridge about halfway between the first and second clusters. The ridge was a traditional trade route. People had settled there years ago and were better off economically. They were much less open to the gospel.

This area still lags behind other, even newer clusters. It was chosen for geographical reasons, not because of receptivity of the people. They were well-established in their social and religious structures. Campaigners knew this, but ignored it as a criterion.

7. Using new converts in evangelism. By using new believers in ministry, the cluster church-planting model generates many new leaders. Early in the campaign, leaders looked for new converts willing to take leadership training. At the end of the 10-day campaign, and with only a week of training, new Christians were given leadership in the new groups of believers. They were supervised and spent one day a week in training.

Contrary to some views, this early, supervised training and ministry produced quality leaders. Many dropped out, of course, but with four or five from each group in training, there were enough.

It was also discovered that waiting to baptize people until after they are thoroughly trained does not help to keep them in the church. In fact, a long training process before baptism tends to discourage them. People seemed much more open to training once they were on the inside. Church growth was aided by both quick acceptance into membership and leadership.

Resistant People

Because the mission boards were asked to select effective church planters to participate in the survey, returns were heavily weighted toward those who work among animistic people. These missionaries see a greater ingathering, so that's why they were chosen by their boards. The survey has a higher percentage of these missionaries.

Armed with the seven principles discovered in his survey, Dick Grady set off to work with a resistant people, the Sundanese of Indonesia. Did the principles apply there as well? Yes, except for one. Working with Muslims, it was not wise to use methods designed to hit the masses and draw in many people in an open way, lest the wrath of Muslim religious leaders be incurred and the chances for church planting threatened. Even so, it is possible to use broad-based methods by mobilizing national Christians to share their faith in more low-key ways. Above all, he found that prayer is the most important principle.

Reference
McGavran, Donald. 1990. *Understanding Church Growth*. Grand Rapids, Mich.: William B. Eerdmans Publishing Co.

Matching the Church Planter's Role with the Church Planting Model

Craig Ott

Three types of missionary church planters can be identified: the pastoral church planter, the apostolic church planter, and the catalytic church planter.

In recent years, a number of church-planting strategies and models have been produced and promoted. This is a welcome development, which has not only stimulated discussion, but also moved church-planting practice beyond the "open shop" approach, which took little account of culture, reproduction, and long-term developmental considerations.

A less discussed issue relates to the role of the missionary church planter. In training, observing, and consulting church planters, I've become convinced that if the church planter does not have a clear understanding of his or her role, he or she is likely to undermine the best methods and models. The church planter's self-understanding must match the church-planting model.

Essentially three types of missionary church planters can be identified, which correspond to three broad approaches to church planting: the pastoral church planter, the apostolic church planter, and the catalytic church planter. Each has a different self-understanding, will go about investing his or her time and energies differently, is faced with particular opportunities and challenges, and is suited for a different situation.

The Pastoral Church Planter

The goal of the pastoral church planter is quite simply to begin a new church and pastor it until it can call and pay its own pastor. The missionary can then move on and plant another church. The method is straightforward. Initially, evangelistic efforts are necessary to gather a congregation of new believers. But once a core of believers has been gathered, this church planter tends to shift into the pastoral care giving mode, focusing energy on preaching, teaching, counseling, and various other pastoral duties.

If the church continues to grow, it is often through new members who are already believers—this is called *transfer growth*. The church is considered "planted" when it can call and pay a pastor to replace the missionary pastor.

This is no doubt the most common variety of church planter both in home and foreign missions. I adopted this approach (albeit unconsciously) in the first churches I planted. I simply wasn't aware of any other approach. Even missionaries who are committed to church multiplication and lay mobilization almost automatically slip into the pastoral mode. There are a number of reasons for this.

Most seminaries train pastors, not evangelists, or church planters; thus most seminary-trained church planters feel comfortable with this role. Most Western books on church planting assume this method. This is the model of ministry which we have observed and come to appreciate in our home churches, and which has been adopted in many, if not most, denominations abroad.

Most of us have never experienced or observed an alternate approach. The members of the church plant often expect this of the church planter: "Be our pastor! That's what you are trained and paid for." Because the missionary church planter usually has not only more training but also more time than lay church members, it is only natural that he, and not they, bear the load of pastoral ministry. This problem is all the more aggravated if several full-time missionaries are serving in the same church plant.

This model of church planting works well under three conditions: (1) high potential for rapid church growth, either because the people are responsive or through transfer; (2) affluence, where the new church can finance its own

IF CHURCH GROWTH IS SLOW and local **resources are limited,** the church will have difficulty calling and paying a replacement for the missionary church planter.

pastor; and (3) where there are trained national believers available to call as pastor. This is why church planting in North America has been generally successful using the pastoral church planter model.

Unfortunately, these conditions are absent in most places where foreign missionary church planting is happening. If church growth is slow and local resources are limited, the church will have difficulty calling and paying a replacement for the missionary church planter. The longer the missionary remains in this role, the more the church becomes dependent on him.

Sometimes, the missionary church planter remains faithfully at the location for ten or even twenty years, hoping that one day a national pastor can be called to replace him. Usually, frustration sets in sooner. The only solution appears to be for the mission to financially subsidize the calling of a national pastor—if one can be found—so that the missionary can finally move on. This only increases the dependency, which is most difficult to break. Multiplication of such churches is very difficult and rare.

The conviction which underlies the pastoral church planter understanding is that a church must have a fully-paid, expertly-trained pastor to be considered a legitimate, planted church. Such a pastor may be desirable in many situations, but this is certainly not a biblical requirement to being considered an established church. The churches planted in the New Testament were virtually all lay-led.

Indeed, mission history up to our own day has demonstrated time and again that the most dynamic church-planting movements were lay-led and not encumbered by the "how can we pay a pastor" dilemma.

Furthermore, because the pastoral church-planting missionary assumes that one day a professionally trained pastor will replace him, minimal effort is invested in training and empowering the laity for genuine pastoral ministry. Finally, believers in the church plant can become "spoiled" by having a full-time missionary pastor. The missionary pastor has set a professional standard which is difficult to follow. Nationals may feel inferior, because they believe that they cannot minister as well as the missionary, and they fear that the church cannot survive without a trained paid pastor.

This thinking is perhaps the single most unnecessary hindrance to church planting and multiplication in most parts of the world today. Not only are missionary resources tied up at one location for many years, but a professional attitude toward ministry is instilled, which inhibits full mobilization of local lay believers.

The Apostolic Church Planter

The self-understanding and approach of the apostolic church planter is radically different from that of the pastoral church planter. This church planter models himself after the Apostle Paul—thus apostolic—who rarely allowed himself to become pastor of a church he planted. Instead, he focused on empowering the local believers to minister, who would as laymen carry on and expand the work after his departure.

Sometimes local believers would be included in Paul's itinerant missionary team, thus instilling vision for multiplication and mission at the very inception of the young churches. Dependencies were avoided from the outset. With this model the question "Who will replace the missionary pastor?" never arises, because the missionary never becomes the pastor. It is assumed that the nationals can pastor themselves if provided with adequate teaching and models.

This approach has been advocated in a number of current church-planting models, perhaps most cogently by Tom Steffen in *Passing the Baton: Church Planting that Empowers*. Steffen was a church planter among the Ifugao in the Philippines. Observing that truly "three-self," multiplying churches were not being planted by his mission agency, he developed a five-stage "phase-out" approach to church planting which he successfully implemented. This model maps out how the missionary must continually change his or her role from learner to evangelist, to teacher, to resident advisor, to itinerant advisor, and finally to absent advisor.

Some suggest that the missionary work in two or three areas simultaneously, thus reducing dependency and forcing local laypersons to develop their churches and ministries. Tent-making church planters also have an advantage in this regard. Because they are not able to serve the church full time, the church tends to become less dependent on them.

This approach demands radical rethinking on the part of most church-planting missionaries. From the outset, nationals must be trained to do all essential ministries—evangelism, preaching, teaching, counseling, etc. The missionary must surrender the desire to have "up front" ministry. His or her primary role is behind the scenes, equipping others. The lay sermons will probably not be as homiletically polished or theologically astute as those the missionary could preach. But the reward will be the development of a truly empowered local leadership, which will serve the church well after the missionary has departed.

The missionary is constantly working him or herself out of a job, performing a ministry only so long as necessary to train a national. Indeed, apart from evangelism and initial follow up, if a national is not available and willing to be trained, the ministry should probably not be initiated. This makes for a

THE MISSIONARY BECOMES IMPATIENT and presses forward, initiating new programs, taking on more ministry responsibility hoping that the nationals will "catch up" with a little time and maturity.

slower start, but, I believe, a more solid finish for the church plant.

While most church planters will agree with this approach in principle, difficulties arise when national believers seem to lag in their willingness or ability to bear the responsibility of ministry. The missionary becomes impatient and presses forward, initiating new programs, taking on more ministry responsibility hoping that the nationals will "catch up" with a little time and maturity.

The opposite usually happens: the nationals become increasingly dependent on the missionary, increasingly feeling inadequate to minister and convinced that the missionary has no confidence in their abilities. Worst of all, they learn that if they just wait long enough, the missionary will plant the church and run the program without them. The church is viewed as the missionary's project apart from their contribution.

While on a consulting trip, I sat in on the meeting of the leadership of a small new church plant in an Eastern European city. They were discussing how they might move from semi-weekly to weekly church services. The main obstacle was the lack of a preacher for the additional services. The language skills and background of the missionary made it impossible for him to preach more than two Sundays a month. The natural tendency of the group was to request from the mission another missionary or to look for other outside resources to meet the need. As we began to brainstorm for alternatives, it soon became apparent that several of the lay leaders would preach if the missionary were to assist them in their preparation. A solution was found, which guarded against increased dependency, while at the same time promoting mobilization of the laity and their ownership of the ministry.

The strengths of this model, however, should not blind one to the challenges inherent in it. This missionary church planter must change location frequently, which is difficult for families and long-term relationships. Few missionaries are trained in such an approach, and few are really willing to restrain their ministry or slow the advancement of the church for the sake of developing lay ministers and ownership.

There are situations, especially in resistant areas, where local believers just aren't suitable for leadership or are unwilling to bear responsibility. Especially where new believers are illiterate, nomadic, or come from radically non-Christian worldviews, the process of developing leaders and churches may be long and tedious. The early departure of the missionary can result in major problems in the new church, as the Apostle Paul experienced with the church in Corinth. Nevertheless, this is the approach which Paul used and which has been used in most rapidly expanding church-planting movements in responsive parts of the world.

The Catalytic Church Planter

A third understanding of the church-planting role is that of the catalytic church planter. A catalyst creates or effects a chemical reaction among other elements. The potential was latently there, but the catalyst sets it in motion. The catalytic church planter is a church planter who plants a church, and remains as pastor or resource person in that church to become a catalyst or facilitator for church multiplication.

Considerable energy and resources are usually invested in establishing and strengthening the initial church plant with the goal that it will become a "beach-head" or "launching base" for numerous additional church plants in the region.

The "mother-daughter," "hiving-off," or "cell division" approach to church planting is among the most effective methods for rapid church multiplication. Such movements, however, rarely develop apart from catalytic leadership. Churches need visionary, motivational, and specially gifted leaders to move them from maintenance to multiplication. Apart from such leadership most churches evolve quickly into a maintenance mode, and fail to reproduce. Ideally, a national pastor or laymen provide such leadership, but there can be a place for a missionary church planter to play this catalytic role.

Rick Warren is an example of a catalytic church planter. He pioneered the planting of the Saddleback Valley Community Church twenty years ago. Although Warren did not himself directly plant or pastor any other churches, under his leadership Saddleback went on to plant twenty-six new churches. He was no doubt a significant catalyst used of God to ignite that multiplication of churches.

Such catalytic church planters are rare among nationals, and even rarer among foreign missionaries. Mobilizing such a church-planting movement demands exceptional gifts and vision. Indeed, perhaps the greatest weakness of this model is the tendency for a church planter to overestimate his ability to provide this kind of leadership, investing much time and energy while failing to, in fact, reproduce churches. Furthermore, the church-planting movement may become very dependent on the catalytic ministry of the missionary, which then ceases when the missionary departs.

But a catalytic church planter needn't have the dramatic gifts or success of a Rick Warren to be effective. There is much to be said for remaining with a church plant until it has successfully launched its first daughter church, thus setting a pattern which can be continued after the missionary's departure. Nor is it necessary that the mother church have thousands of members before it can launch a movement. Even in the moderately resistant cities of Germany, church-planting movements have emerged largely through visionary, catalytic leadership in churches with less than two hundred members.

Which Role Is Best?

At first glance, the apostolic model might appear most biblical, because it is closest to Paul's method. A better standard, however, for measuring a method is its compatibility with broader biblical principles and its ability to reach biblical goals of church planting such as spiritual health, multiplication, indigenization, and stewardship of resources. Judged in this way, any of the three models might be the best model depending upon the church planter, the setting, and God's sovereign working in the church plant.

As indicated above, the pastoral model works best in responsive and relatively affluent populations where the likelihood of the church growing and being able to quickly call and pay a pastor is great. The catalytic model is best suited for urban areas of moderate responsiveness and with potential for multiple church planting in the region. However, the church planter must be exceptionally gifted and able to make a long-term commitment. The apostolic model is most versatile and suited for both rural and urban settings, affluent and poor populations, and seems to be the approach which God has most greatly blessed in facilitating rapidly growing church planting movements throughout the world. But this approach demands long-sighted patience and significant rethinking and retraining of most missionary church planters.

In all events, it is essential for the church planter and each member of a church-planting team to be aware of the various options, to be unified in their choice of an appropriate model, and to consistently implement the model, being aware of pluses and pitfalls. These considerations will often need to be made in consultation with the national Church or local believers to avoid misunderstanding and ensure realistic expectations.

In most cases, this will demand a reassessment of the missionary's role and self-understanding. The effectiveness of any church-planting model will largely depend on the church planter's willingness and ability to adapt his or her role to fit and facilitate the model.

Are We Really about Church Planting?

Larry Sharp

*Instead of strategy, we need to concentrate more on modeling the
fruit of the Spirit, striving to be good at being disciples, making
disciples, and encouraging national Christians to do the same.*

We in the mission community think of ourselves as being in the
church-planting business. But somehow I often wonder if we are de-
ceived. Jim Collins' book *Good to Great* inspired me to think about what we
are good at and what we are deeply passionate about. What really is our *raison
d'être*?

When I think about the myriad church "forms" in the world, even among
mainstream evangelical missions, I wonder if the focus on church planting has
detracted from our real business. Are not the commands of Jesus to "make disciples," "preach the word," "follow me," "feed my sheep," "be my witnesses?"
These are the mission activities which produce "men for God from every tribe
and language and people and nation" (Rev. 5:9). As John Piper reminds us,
"The goal of missions is the gladness of the peoples in the greatness of God…
worship is the fuel and goal of missions."

Of course we know that the Body of Christ is an important institution with
the task of providing fellowship, leadership, teaching, and ministry. Disciples
assemble in churches as part of that act of obedience, but the church is not an
end in itself. The goal is obedient, transformed worshipers.

It is interesting that Paul did not give strategic plans for church planting
as we strategists would have done. Instead, he focused on the qualities of elders and a few simple points about church order. Only one of twenty-three
qualities of an elder in the epistles to Timothy and Titus is skill related. What
impressed Paul about the believers in Thessalonica was their modeling of the
gospel, not their strategic, end-in-view, church-planting model. The biblical
metaphors for the church are defined in terms of lifestyle and purpose, not in
terms of structure and strategy.

Jesus gave neither strategic road maps nor resources for fulfilling the Great
Commission; he simply stated that his disciples are to "make disciples," and
that "I will be with you." Christ made it clear that he will build his Church
(Matt. 16:18).

There does not seem to be a clear definition of "church" in the New Testament. The church is both form and function. It is phenomenon and creeds,
institution and community, organization and organism, visible and invisible.
Jesus simply wants followers.

The church looks different everywhere, and that is the way it should be because the church should naturally fit into any given culture. Missionaries who define themselves as traditional "church planters" have difficulty avoiding transplanting their culture's idea of church.

But if they simply teach the word, make disciples, and encourage those disciples to "do church" in their own contextually appropriate way under the guidance of the Holy Spirit, they will avoid the many pitfalls of church planting. If church planting becomes the work of national believers, missionaries don't have to pass a baton; the baton is in national hands from the beginning.

I recently visited a "simple church" in a Dani village high in the mountains of eastern Papua, Indonesia. A Dani church leader said, "Thanks for sending Jack, who is the Lord Jesus to our village." A generation ago, this warring culture of fear and death had never heard the name of Jesus. Jack translated the Bible, taught it faithfully, and lived like the Lord Jesus. Today, there is a contextualized Dani church worshiping the Creator of the universe.

I propose that modern missionaries should evangelize, equip new believers to be disciple-makers, and then stop. I do realize that the term "church planting" is not going away. But could we at least honorably live out the real meaning of "planting?"

The verb "plant" means to set in the ground to grow. On the farms of the Canadian prairies where I gained my first work experience, we planted grain for the wheat harvest. That meant to set in the ground to grow. We returned periodically to fertilize, cultivate, and spray for weeds. Farmers do very little with their crops between seeding and harvest!

Church "planting" should look roughly the same—setting the gospel in the ground and following up with periodic teaching, encouragement, and prayer. By the power of the Holy Spirit (the rain and sun for the seedling church), a mature church develops. If this is what is meant by "church planting," then I'm in favor of calling ourselves "church planters."

A missionary who hangs around too long is equivalent to a wheat farmer who stays in the wheat field from May to September, digging around the tender plants, telling seeds how to adjust to the potassium in the soil, explaining the increasing sunlight until June 21, and then promising rain. Did not the apostles in Acts just "plant" rather than devise and implement an end-in-view church-planting strategy? They built people, not churches.

We talk a lot about our church-planting priorities. How about instead of church movements with long- and short-term strategies, we concentrate more on modeling the fruit of the Spirit in our adopted cultures? How about instead of being good at planting churches, we strive to be good at being disciples, making disciples, and encouraging nationals to do the same? Maybe in another generation, people will consider us to be in the Jesus-planting ministry.

Missionaries Should Not Plant Churches

Glenn Kendall

Our goal as missionaries must be as facilitators of new churches instead of leaders.

We had last seen Bob and Ann fifteen years ago at our graduation. They had gone to a tough mission field: few evangelicals and not much response. Now, at lunch together, they described their struggle. Little did I know then that within six months I would see their field for myself.

As I worshiped with some sixty people meeting in borrowed facilities in that urban metropolis, and heard Bob preach, I couldn't help wonder why it had taken a decade and a half to get this far. But I never questioned their dedication to the task.

Next morning, quite by chance, I bumped into Jeff, another college friend and fellow missionary whom I thought was in another part of the world. But no, four years ago he had come to this same city and in that time had started two churches and was working on a third. Membership far surpassed Bob's, especially surprising in what has always been considered a resistant field.

As Jeff and I talked about this, some strong philosophical differences emerged between him and Bob, differences that produced startingly different results. Let me briefly describe their differences.

Bob set out to plant a church and he succeeded, albeit slowly. Because none of his people had training or experience, Bob did most of the preaching and leading. His people generously affirmed his ministry. They weren't ready to assume his role and he wasn't eager to give it up. He had invested fifteen years in this church and didn't want to release control too soon and risk a failure.

Jeff, on the other hand, facilitated the starting of churches. He motivated and trained people to do it. He wasn't up front every Sunday. He encouraged new Christians and developed leaders from the beginning. He would not start church services unless he had nationals to lead them.

Jeff's ministry expanded as he drew out leaders to take over. Bob's ministry dragged on. He thought it would take another ten years before he had responsible leaders.

As I have since reflected on biblical and historical models, as well as on Bob and Jeff, it seems to me that our goal must be to be facilitators of new churches instead of leaders of them. For example, Jesus seemed to concentrate on a few men whom he wanted to be leaders. He trained them for future ministry and got them into it quickly. He lived with them and invested himself in them. But my friend Bob did not set out to develop leaders. He gathered people around him for worship.

The Apostle Paul followed Jesus' pattern. He traveled from place to place, staying for a few months to a few years, leaving behind trained leaders to carry on the work. True, Paul was an evangelist, but he also concentrated on training reliable leaders. That seemed to be the reason for my friend Jeff's success.

In my own field, we have seen remarkable success. National missionaries sent by the churches I serve do both evangelism and leadership training. The growth in new churches is impressive: our association of 28 groups and 1,000 members in 1975 today numbers 335 groups with 17,000 members.

Amos is one of our church planters. When he started out, he knew he had to stress evangelism and leadership development. He knew he could not plant one church and stay around to pastor it. He knew he had to find capable men to train and they could teach the others. But Amos failed. In four years he started one church, which even today is not strong. Thank God others caught the picture of being facilitators. They brought into being several new churches with hundreds of believers.

In Kigali, Rwanda, it's been said that our city is probably the hardest place in sub-Saharan Africa to plant a church. But our records prove otherwise. On average, our churches have doubled their membership each year over the past five years. Certainly, some people are more responsive than others, but after comparing Bob's ministry and Jeff's and ours, it seems that our methods and philosophy have a lot to do with responsiveness.

Dr. Ray B. Buker Sr. makes a telling observation based on his fifteen years in Burma. The great Adoniram Judson, who founded the Church among the Burmese, discouraged ordaining Burmese pastors and opposed offerings in the churches. Consequently, says Buker, there was no growth. "When I arrived, the Burmese Church numbered five thousand; fifteen years later, it still numbered five thousand," he says.

However, the different results among the Karens was striking. They had to develop their own political leaders while their churches grew and spread. They ordained their own leaders, took offerings, built churches and schools, and for many years had no missionaries. Today, they have the strongest church in Burma "because they founded and developed their own churches," according to Buker.

Admittedly, missionaries like to be the whole show. It's hard to turn things over. Not only does the Protestant work ethic drive us, but when we get overseas, we are impelled to work hard to be sure that we are accomplishing something. Yet, our strong desire to run the church mitigates against the goals we set for ourselves.

Philip Thornton wisely observed that "any strategy that places missionaries in key positions of leadership and later seeks to transfer that leadership to national hands is not one that will attract strong, natural leaders" (1984, 241). But that's exactly what missionaries like my friend Bob do, and they think they are following good church-planting strategy.

Missionaries trying to pastor new churches run into a host of problems. The church will usually develop along the foreigner's leadership style. The foreigner, no matter how culturally sensitive, will always be a foreigner. Inevitably, he will draw people interested in a foreign type of church.

Then, when a local pastor comes in, attendance often slips because some people will go to another foreign-style church. People wrongly conclude that the new leader is incapable and that the church wasn't ready for local leaders. But if they go back to missionary leaders, then the whole process will be set back.

Foreign leadership invariably inhibits the number of new churches because there are only so many missionary pastors to go around. Instead of recruiting more missionaries to plant churches themselves, mission boards should seek a few church growth facilitators, missionaries who can train and encourage nationals to train others to start churches.

Here are some ways that missionaries can be facilitators of church growth:

1. Evangelism and leadership training must be top priorities. Bible training without evangelism produces a sterile church. Evangelism without training opens the doors to syncretism, cults, and false teaching. When a missionary reports "quality growth," that may mean few or no conversions. But how can a church have quality growth when no one responds to the gospel? Reproduction is a necessity of life. The church that doesn't reproduce will die.

2. Set big goals. Planning for a people movement is different than planning to start one church. Keep your eyes on the bigger task. Aim to complete the task.

3. Work in two or three areas or ministries at the same time. This really helps to get new churches started, because you will be the advisor, not the kingpin. Working two or three places at the same time forces you to be away from them and gives room for national leaders to grow. You will strangle the new leaders unless you build into your plans time to be away.

4. Work hard to build relationships. This means mutual commitments, unselfish assistance, room for creativity, and building a team on trust.

The missionary can either deter or facilitate church growth. All of us have great ambitions and desires, but sometimes our best-intentioned efforts prevent us from seeing the kind of results we might otherwise see. We should not plant churches; we should facilitate church growth.

Reference

Thornton, W. Philip. 1984. "The Cultural Key to Developing Strong Leaders." *Evangelical Missions Quarterly* 20(3): 234-241.

The Toddler's School of Missiology:
Everything I Needed to Know about Church Planting I Could Have Learned from My Children

Andy Johnson

How child rearing and church planting reveal similar lessons.

My wife and I live among the Dagara people of southwestern Burkina Faso. Being a relatively new father of two (a son adopted from our host country and a daughter born to us), I daily find myself reflecting on how I am raising my children. Additionally, as our team of four families has passed the midway point of our initial commitment to the Dagara, I have also found myself considering what it means to plant churches among this people group. Oddly enough, many of the lessons I have begun to learn in the one apply to the other. Below are five of these.

Lesson #1: Not Everyone Wants to Follow My Schedule

Parenting. My son is an amazing sleeper. From the time he came into our lives, he has slept through the night and has taken two naps daily. Our newborn daughter, however, was an entirely different story. Over the course of her first few weeks, she quickly settled into a regular pattern, albeit not the one we would have chosen: one night, she would sleep three to four hours at a stretch; the next, she would not sleep for more than fifteen minutes at a time.

Church planting. This lesson applies universally when it comes to church planting. I sometimes feel I should write a modified suggestion of James' words in James 4:15 at the top of every page in my daily planner: "If it is the Lord's will, Monday...If it is the Lord's will, Tuesday..." I am regularly frustrated by what happens to my finely-tuned schedule. For instance, the Dagara have 3-day long funerals. When we first began ministry, I would become quite irritated when I rode into a village, sweaty and tired, only to find a funeral in progress—an event which inevitably translated into no teaching time for me. After all, I had scheduled this lesson series to end a month from now.

With time, I began to understand that these funerals were an opportunity for me to show respect, cement relationships, create new ones, and show that Christians are compassionate and care about more than their daily planners. Many Christians even use these funerals as an outreach opportunity. During a funeral, while various pagan rituals are going on, Christians will gather together to sing, to ask for God's mercy, to take up a collection to help the family defray the costs of the funeral, and to pray for those who do not yet know the Lord.

Lesson #2: Lifelong Patterns Are Difficult to Change

Parenting. Our son was four months old when we brought him home from the orphanage. Over the course of his young life he had understandably grown accustomed to a certain way of life. My wife and I had been told at the orphanage that he was an unusually calm, easy baby. In fact, through the hustle and bustle of making it back to our home, he indeed was quite calm.

Once we arrived and settled in, however, he began screaming any time he was alone with the two of us. After trying all the standard tactics, it dawned on us that he only screamed during quiet times. With forty other children in his orphanage, he was accustomed to noise of one kind or another every minute of every day. Loud music calmed his crying fits and brought on sleep. As an active toddler today, if there is not enough noise to suit him, he gladly supplies it himself.

Church planting. The process of salvation happens in an instant. There is that moment when our sins are forgiven and the Holy Spirit comes to dwell in us. Beyond that, however, our lives are a continuing process of redemption. As Paul told the Philippians, we can be confident that "he who began a good work in us will carry it to completion" (Phil. 1:6). This requires much patience on our part; however, I am slowly realizing that it requires even more patience on God's part as he watches his children work out what it means to be saved. Paul did, after all, tell those same Philippian Christians that God's good work would not be finished next week, but only on the day of Christ.

One of the most challenging and most rewarding aspects of our work is walking alongside new Dagara Christians as they discern how to honor God within their culture. Marriages, how they plant their fields, what they do at funerals, how they treat their children—all these must be reconsidered. It is a slow, painful process that sometimes seems to involve four steps back for every five forward. Despite that, God is redeeming his people.

Lesson #3: Being Adopted Provides Equal Sonship

Parenting. Our son had been with us a couple of months when I found myself preparing to feed him a banana for the first time. I was suddenly struck with panic, afraid I would send him into anaphylactic shock. I am mildly allergic to bananas, and I was worried he could have inherited my food allergy. Several minutes later, it dawned on me that the likelihood of my adopted son inheriting my food allergy was slim to none. This was indicative, however, of how he had become my son. I no longer thought of him as my adopted son. He was, simply, my son.

Church planting. All Christians have been adopted by the Father in Christ, and are heirs together with him, true children, complete with all the rights of sonship. All of us are branches that have been grafted into the tree. We were all dead in our sins, but are now made alive in Christ. Although I know these things, at times I have struggled to trust this when it comes to the Dagara Christians. Given the fact that we have more training and more experience interpreting God's word, the very same Spirit that indwells the members of our team indwells the newest Dagara Christians. We must remember that, as heirs of the promise, the Dagara are gifted by the Spirit just as we (the missionaries) are. Increasingly, I am trusting them to be led by the Spirit.

The village church of Mutori had an interesting problem in that while there were more than twenty women in the church, only one man had come to the Lord. They committed to asking the Lord to call the men of Mutori to the Body of Christ. After a period of prayer, they believed the Spirit led them to throw a party to commemorate their baptisms. They felt called to invite the entire village at the cost of spending every last bit of money the church had collected.

My immediate reaction to "wasting" the entire church treasury on one party was to dismiss it as a terrible idea and poor stewardship. Feeling led to trust, however, our team kept silent and watched with anticipation the results of this rather unique evangelistic outreach. While the party did in fact take all the church's money (and more on top of that!), it also served to increase their standing in the village and to rekindle interest in what God was doing in their village. The financial burden of this party was well worth it, as this church now counts among its members not only more than twice the original number of women, but also a number of men. As he has on so many occasions, the Spirit proved to be already living and active in these newly adopted children of the Father.

Lesson #4: Live in the Present

Parenting. I have often wished my son were just a little older. When he was so little that he could not even hold his head up, I found myself looking forward to watching him sit upright. When he began crawling, I wanted him to walk so he would not get so dirty (a fact which illustrates how little I knew about toddlers). Now, as he learns to speak, I am wishing fluency on him. So many parents have warned me not to blink—that before long I will be dropping my son off at college or walking my daughter down the aisle. Yet, I still find myself nudging them onward to the next milestone. I have begun intentionally living in the now, enjoying my son's almost-intelligible baby talk and getting excited when my daughter turns her head toward my voice.

Church planting. I believe I have the best job in the world. Every morning, I wake up in an exotic (well, at least, different) place, with the job description of planting churches and telling those who have not heard about Jesus his good news. I get to ride my bike to work. I live an hour from elephants in the wild. I have a 4-wheel-drive truck in a place where I actually need it from time to time. On good days, it is hard for me to believe I get paid (albeit not well, but paid nevertheless) for what I do.

Despite that, I have recently found myself obsessing about the end of my time in Burkina Faso. Our team has been very intentional about keeping our eventual phase-out in mind. We have never sunk our tent pegs too deep. Additionally, this past September marked the midway point of our initial commitment to the field. The end is hopefully at least five years out, and yet I am already job hunting!

One of my goals for the coming years is to relish what a great thing it is to plant churches. I will remember that look in someone's eyes when, for the first time, it dawns on him or her that even he or she can be forgiven. When I am there for someone once named "The gods' love" to publicly change her name to "God loves," I will live in that moment. When an old man draws water from a well (most definitely woman's work) to fill a 55-gallon drum in order to be baptized during the dry season, I will not think about my next career move. And when I see thirty people get on their knees in order to be baptized in six inches of water and mud, I will thank God for putting me there for such a time as that.

Lesson #5: I Knew More about Parenting and Church Planting before I Started Doing Them

Parenting. Prior to having children, I would often return home after a party or church activity and pontificate to my wife about what a poor job so and so was doing with his kids. When I saw a boy who would not eat his veggies or who hit another child, I judged the parents for not knowing what I, in my child-free brilliance, already knew. Now, however, it is my own son trailing sand throughout my in-laws' house because he stuffed his diaper full at the playground when I was not looking. My pride and joy is now the one running up to his playmates at church, hugging them gently, kissing them on the cheek, and shoving them to the ground. It is my boy, the one who will carry on the Johnson name for future generations, whose favorite, most comfortable position involves his thumb in his mouth and his forefinger in his nose. As it turns out, I did not know nearly so much as I thought I did.

Church planting. Leaving university life, equipped with my lovely bride at my side and my MA in missions in my back pocket, I felt confident I knew what I was getting into. Now, six years into full-time ministry, I feel as though I am finally beginning to get a handle on the things that I need to start learning! This turnaround is due not to forgetting what I knew back then, but rather to the Lord developing two things in me: humility and trust.

First, I have begun to understand that truly humble people do not have a low self-image. They do not go through life convinced they are incompetent or unable to get anything done. It is not about a low self-image; rather, it comes down to no self-image. Truly humble people have no self-image because they focus entirely on the character of God. They focus so much on becoming Christ-centered that their personal opinions of themselves fade into the background as of no importance.

Second, I am learning to trust God. Despite saying most of the things I am supposed to say about this mission being the Lord's, as I left for the field, it was something I was going to do. It did not take long, however, for it to dawn on me that this task was far too great for me and that there was no way I or my team could possibly get this done.

Thankfully, following close on the heels of that panicky revelation, came the assurance that the work is the Lord's. He calls us to be faithful, but promises to do the heavy lifting himself. According to the promises in his word, he will fight for us—we need only to be still. We need not let our hearts be troubled; we trust in God and can also trust in Jesus, knowing that he goes before us to prepare our places in eternity. It is thrilling to know that some of those places are now prepared for Dagara children of God. Perhaps, when my time to return home finally comes, I will be blessed by the Lord to have my place prepared next to one of my good friends and brothers in Christ from Burkina Faso.

Four Ways to Mentor Church Planters

Juha Jones

Four ways in which church planters need mentoring—and how they correspond to four eras in a church planter's life.

In principle, I would be willing to mentor someone** in church planting; however, I don't have time, and anyways, we never got mentored, so surely it can't be that important." I hear this refrain in the Arabian Peninsula where I live and work; however, I suspect it is heard wherever there are busy tent-making church planters. The reality is the current generation of mission-minded workers is expressing the need for mentoring. And yet the demand for mentoring does not stop with the newbies; veterans on the field are expecting more mentoring as well.

Most organizations already have some form of mentoring in place, whether they call it mentoring or not. Still, increased expectations will place stress on all our current systems for mentoring, because at its core, mentoring is a very personal and people-intensive task. The increased demand for mentoring does not come just from within the ranks of traditional missionaries: we are seeing more Christians on the field who are not with traditional agencies, but who are nonetheless wanting to "do more for God." Some have come to the field intentionally to get involved; others hear God's call while they are on the ground. As a community of God's people, we need to be finding ways to transfer wisdom to upcoming workers so that God's diverse community can join in the worship that is mission.

When we stop to think about what people need when they ask for mentoring, we realize they are often asking for very different things. To aid with our listening, I suggest four ways in which church planters need mentoring. These roughly correspond to four eras in a church planter's life.

1. Vision Mentoring: Developing Motivation

Imagine a Filipino worker in Riyadh who is worshiping secretly each week with others. God speaks and a new worker is mobilized. The details aren't clear yet; however, the motivation is there. Maybe the whole church has caught the vision. Maybe the church is not in Riyadh, but in Rayleigh. The problem is the same: they need to understand what God is saying so that they can take his word seriously.

At this early stage, the individual or group needs a mentor who is able to inspire vision. Intrinsic to this is the ability of the mentor to show how the vision can be implemented. What is the practical outworking of this vision?

The mentor will also need to know how to motivate the team to learn. The mentor's primary task is to help the individual or group understand that they need to learn both information and skills as well as continue to develop their character.

The length of the initial vision mentoring could be as short as a weekend; however, it is more likely to be six months to a year as the individual or group digests the enormity of their call and starts to count the cost. Although some quarters have condemned mission agencies for slow recruitment processes, there is a useful side-effect for the candidates in that they have time to get their minds around what they are doing. Mobilization is going to happen more quickly in the current generation (whether on the field or off); however, that just means we will need to be more intentional about the initial vision mentoring. It will likely mean we will have to do repeated vision mentoring as the individual acclimates to one level of cost and needs to be taken further in the process of dying to self.

Vision mentoring can be an intimate process; however, the crucial element is that the mentor has the gifts to speak into the newcomer's life with inspiration and authority. Some will regard giving vision for learning and enculturation as an exciting task. Although it can be, we will need to keep before us a key proverb: "Suffering produces perseverance, perseverance, character, and character, hope."

2. Skill Mentoring: Developing Ability

People don't just need vision; they also need to develop the skills to be effective in the community. In the Arab world these skills include Arabic, Islamics, cultural fluency, and ministry skills. Skill mentoring needs to be carried out by experienced, skilled practitioners. In the Arabian Peninsula in Arab World Ministries (AWM), we encourage new personnel to join an Equipping Team specifically for the purpose of developing those skills (usually alongside language study).

The Equipping Team is usually led by two experienced couples who are active in ministry and can therefore mentor the newcomers. While initial, full-time language study may be for as little as two years, the process of skill mentoring is likely to last longer, usually at least four years.

The mentor will ensure that information transfer is taking place and skills are being developed with some fluency. Some of the skills are more cognitive than expressive. For example, the mentor will need to effectively transfer frameworks that help make sense of what is going on. These frameworks will be used and refined as the person's character matures.

One crucial framework provides the ability to understand diversity and conflict appropriately. It answers questions regarding other workers (i.e., "What is our basis for trusting each other?"). This framework needs to be established early so that people can keep coming back to it when conflict arises. A second framework will be necessary for understanding the local community with its complex relationships. (This is a topic for another article.) Suffice it to say that without relational and cultural fluency, linguistic fluency will be of little use.

The third major framework is required to handle the ethical issues. It will be vital that the people have the ability to recognize when they have made ethical mistakes in the local culture and in their ministry. Without the ability to recognize mistakes, there is little readiness to turn to God for correction.

While the majority of this skill mentoring should occur in the early years, all workers will continue to receive skill mentoring in a variety of areas. Through the skill mentoring process, the experienced mentor will need to keep another key proverb in mind: "Knowledge puffs up, but love builds up."

3. Peer Mentoring: Developing Application

Not all mentoring is done by more experienced people. Much is done by peers. In church planting, most of the specific development of individual ministries is done through peer mentoring, as fellow team members give feedback and input into each other's lives.

In the Arab world it is likely that this stage will take the worker to the 10-year mark in his or her service on the field. In AWM, this is often the main function of a church-planting team once the person has finished his or her full-time language study. While vision mentoring could be likened to preaching and exhortation, and skill mentoring can be likened to teaching, peer mentoring is primarily about discernment and encouragement (especially to persevere). The first involve intensive input from senior mentors (usually the team leaders).

The main source of input for stage three is the ministering community (team) itself. There may be a ministry team leader; however, in healthy teams, most of the help will come from one another. The emphasis here is on how an individual's or group's ministry should be worked out in the local community. It will require discernment by the ministering community with occasional input from roving leaders.

The main objective at this stage is to understand each part of the Body of Christ and how it should interact with the other parts. That way, the ministering community can rejoice in the God-given diversity and exploit it for God's glory. For example, one person might have a ministry that involves ploughing the ground in advance of other church-planting teams to come in and be fruitful. By now you should be able to find your own key proverb for these mentors.

4. Mature Mentoring: Removing Barriers

While peer mentoring is likely to be required throughout ministry, the intensity of input is likely to diminish as the individual or group becomes established in specific ministries. However, this does not mean that no mentoring is required. Rather, it means that the issues of character will be coming to the fore. Some of those issues will relate to the character of the individuals or ministry group. Other issues will relate to the character of the church being planted.

This is not the time to send a mentor with information; instead, it is a time to send someone who can guide the individual or group to address the issues. It is a time to send a retired or mature worker to encourage reflection on the root causes of the problem and to encourage the person to press on through the pain of character development. This is best done by people who have already seen the pain and pressed on through it themselves. This is more of a pastoral role.

The mature mentor needs to visit regularly for an extended period each time. He or she will come alongside, look at the ministry issues, and comment on what is happening. He or she is not there to provide information or didactic teaching, but to help overcome the personal and community barriers to ministry.

These month-long visits must be repeated in order to build a high level of trust and achieve a level of correction. This gives the mentor permission to address heart behaviors, to speak deeply into situations, and where necessary, to say when the workers are working against their ministry interests. Repetition will come with multiple visits.

As we look for mature mentors, we may need to look in less obvious places. A mature mentor may not be the public speaker or the up-front leader. It may be the wife of a leader who has spent her life politely helping her husband see his own self-deception. We have many great resources sitting at home, praying in retirement. We need those grandparents to visit and remind us what we are really doing. We need their wisdom and proverbs applied appropriately to our communities so that God's Church is planted to thrive.

Biblical Guidelines for Church Planting

Paul. **The model church planter.** What can we learn from him and other New Testament early church planters? As we seek to be relevant and effective in our evangelism and discipleship, we must temporarily put aside cultural, social, and linguistic issues and begin with what scripture is saying in regards to church planting. After all, the spontaneous, Spirit-led growth of the early Church is a great example for us today. In this chapter, we look at what scripture can teach us as we seek to build God's Church globally.

Vergil Gerber begins by sharing the New Testament blueprint for starting and organizing local churches overseas. **Scott Bessenecker** then looks at lessons from the Apostle Paul's church-planting methods and concludes that we can still trust God to raise up essential components of an indigenous church.

Derek Seipp shares five lessons related to church multiplication strategies learned from the Apostle Paul. Finally, **J. D. Payne** takes a biblical examination of eight aspects from the life of Barnabas.

October 1969

A New Testament Blueprint: Starting and Organizing Local Churches Overseas

Vergil Gerber

While great stress today is laid on money and methods, men and women are still God's means of reproducing responsible churches.

The Church in New Testament perspective is neither incidental nor accidental. Establishing the goal toward which all missionary purpose is to be directed, Jesus enunciated with incisive language: "I will build my Church and the gates of hell shall not prevail against it" (Matt. 16:18). Fulfillment of the missionary mandate, therefore, is to be measured in terms of church dimension (Matt. 28:19-20).

The evangelistic task falls short of its objective unless it relates individual conversion to the local community of the redeemed. According to Elton Trueblood:

> To be an effective Christian it is not enough to be an individual believer. Men are never really effective unless they share in some kind of group reality. Inadequate as the fellowship of the church may be, in many generations, including our own, there is not the slightest chance of Christian vitality without it. New life normally arises from inside. (1961, 21)

The church is both the goal and the agent of dynamic reproduction. On the day of Pentecost the first church in Jerusalem added three thousand to its embryonic fellowship of 120 members. These in turn reached out into the metropolitan community gaining favor with people. And day after day the Lord added to their number people who were being saved (Acts 2).

The early *koinonia* was much more than a local fellowship as an end in itself. The root meaning of the Greek word is "to have in common, to share with others." Barnabas and Paul received the right hand of fellowship (*koinonia*) at Jerusalem in order that they might go to the nations (Gal. 2:9).

It is in this missionary dimension that Peter Beyerhaus and Henry Lefever define the church as being "at one and the same time the community of the redeemed and the redeeming community" (1964, 110).

This mission to reproduce herself in every nation is the dominating motif of the Book of the Acts—the acts of the early Church. Her spiritual dynamic is the *dunamis* of Pentecost. This dynamic quality in the Person of the Holy Spirit is promised to the disciples for the explicit purpose of multiplying nuclear cells around the world (Acts 1:8).

"The Great Commission derives its meaning and power wholly and exclusively from the Pentecost event" (Boer 1961, 47). "Restlessly the Spirit drives the Church to witness, and continually churches rise out of witness" (1961, 161). Dynamic, living cells multiply into hundreds of congregations in Asia, Europe, Africa, and around the world. The Book of Acts is the historical record of first-century church multiplication through missionary witness and in the power of the Holy Spirit.

There are two parallel truths which, if properly understood, lay the foundation for starting and organizing local churches overseas:

1. Only God can do this. The church is the life of God in action. All life originates with God. Its unique characteristic is its reproductive quality. It cannot be self-contained. Spiritual reproduction, whether on the individual or collective level, is intrinsically and uniquely the work of the Holy Spirit. Neither methods nor men, however good, can reproduce the life of the church. This is the Spirit's ministry.

THERE IS NO SUCH THING as instant church.

No miracle drug or promotional stimulant can eliminate the hard labor of bringing churches into existence.

2. While men are wholly dependent upon the Spirit for the reproduction of life, in paradoxical contrast God has made himself wholly dependent upon men for the building of his Church. According to Melvin Hodges, "God's methods are men, and we are the men! Methods are no better than the men behind them; and men are no better than their contact with God" (McGavran 1965, 32).

There is no such thing as "instant church." In this twentieth century, when everything comes in instant "how-to-do-it" packages which guarantee maximum results at minimum effort, churches are still born out of travail of soul. No miracle drug or promotional stimulant can eliminate the hard labor of bringing churches into existence.

Even after two thousand years of Christian experience and evangelistic know-how in the ecclesiastical science of church birth, there is still no easy formulae nor simple how-to-do-it package plans for church reproduction. Winston Churchill's pungent words, "blood, sweat, and tears," serve to remind us that the Church too is born of blood, sweat, and tears—the blood of Christ, the sweat of discipleship, and the tears of prevailing prayer.

Although God has left it to men to build his Church, he has not left to trial and error the construction of that Church. Too often we start with missionary activity rather than the missionary objective. We recruit volunteer workers rather than craftsmen. We equip them with scaffolds and tools and material resources. And we send them out. But we neglect to provide them with the necessary know-how for building, or with a clearly-defined plan for starting and organizing churches overseas. As if churches were of secondary importance—a sort of by-product of Christian mission.

For any other career we require specialized training. What would happen if we required a major in church extension and a year's internship in church planting before graduating missionaries or sending them to the field? According to T. Stanley Soltau, "It is highly important that missionary candidates be well-acquainted with the goal of mission work in terms of an indigenous church and with the New Testament principles by which this goal can be attained" (1954, 18-19).

No one would think of building a building without a well-defined plan of construction to follow. It is not enough to provide materials and hire workmen. A building starts with an architect's concept of the end result to be achieved. Once that objective is agreed upon, a careful plan of construction is drawn up. This blueprint is then carried out in detail by experienced laborers. All three are vital to its success.

These three come through with remarkable clarity in the pages of New Testament history. Robert Coleman refers to this biblical blueprint as "The Master Plan of Evangelism" (1964). What he sees in the pattern laid down by our Lord and his early followers is a detailed blueprint for numerical multiplication of visible, local fellowships in every nation. Let's look at it.

Well-defined Mission

On the Day of Pentecost (Acts 2) we see a responsible church growing out of witness. Filled with the Holy Spirit, the first Christians began to speak not in unintelligible babble, but in effective communication. And men from every nation under heaven received their witness. The result: three thousand were baptized and added to the Jerusalem fellowship. Many others carried the seeds of the Church to foreign soil.

What clearly emerges is a newborn church with all the characteristics of what Beyerhaus and LeFever call "responsible selfhood" (1964, 21). From its inception, individual and corporate responsibility can be seen in:

- **Organizing.** They were immediately baptized and added to the new fellowship (Acts 2:41).
- **Educating.** They continued in the teaching of the apostles (2:42).
- **Sharing.** They sold their possessions to take care of their material needs (2:45).
- **Reproducing.** They gained favor with all the people and the Lord added daily people who were being saved (2:47).

This self-determining and self-continuing nature of the Jerusalem church gives striking evidence of well-defined mission. At the same time the church's mission was yet to be accomplished. As Alexander McLeish points out in his Princeton lectures, the establishing of a responsible church is not only central to the existence of the faith, but to its proclamation to the world: "The object of its existence is to expand its fellowship to all nations" (1952, 11).

He views the calling into being of the new fellowship as the agent for world-wide missionary purpose. Turning the pages of the historic blueprint, we see the fulfillment of this purpose in churches being reproduced in Judea, Galilee, Samaria, and most of the then-known world. How was it accomplished? What specific methods produced this phenomenal first-century expansion? For an answer to this we follow the pattern laid down by the greatest of all New Testament missionaries, the Apostle Paul.

Well-planned Methods

Paul's methods were directly related to his predetermined mission. All of his missionary activity contributed to that end goal. "His was no vague effort to meet universal need which so often inspires what we loosely call 'evangelism'" (McLeish 1952, 18). He concentrated on the creation and care of churches.

Let's begin with his relationship to the Antioch church. Paul started by becoming a responsible member (Acts 13:1). As a Christian, he recognized that he was responsible to the church and for the church. Responsible churches are made up of responsible members. This principle is vital to effective evangelism. Accepting Christ as Savior means accepting him as Lord. And this means responsible church-relatedness.

This "cost of discipleship" as Dietrich Bonhoeffer calls it, stands out in the New Testament blueprint in sharp relief against the easy believism of modern evangelism. "Cheap grace is the deadly enemy of the church....Christianity without discipleship is always Christianity without Christ" (1967, 45, 64). The first step in starting and organizing local churches overseas is to "make disciples" (Matt. 28:19)—Christians who are responsible to the church and for the church. If we fail here, we will inevitably fail in establishing the church.

Paul, along with Barnabas and others, spent eleven years developing the responsible selfhood of the Antioch church. From the beginning, Paul recognized the centrality and autonomy of the local fellowship. He placed himself under its direction and discipline. It was to the church that the Spirit finally spoke: "Separate unto me Paul and Barnabas for the work whereunto they are called" (Acts 13:2). It was the church that sent them forth on their first missionary journey. It was to the church that they returned to report (14:27).

Here is a principle of inter-responsibility: *the missionary responsible to the church; and the church responsible for the missionary.* Furthermore, the church is both independent and interdependent. Paul and Barnabas were sent by the church at Antioch to the Jerusalem church to report on their missionary work.

Hearing the report, the latter took official action on the report (Acts 14:25, 27), making certain recommendations that had far-reaching effects on the founding of new churches in other places.

McLeish observes, "This acknowledgment of the church at every stage of his work has, for a man of St. Paul's independence of mind, a very special significance for us" (1952, 8). These two principles of interrelationship stand out with clarity:

1. Missionary responsibility to the church—church responsibility to the missionary
2. Church independence—church interdependence

Paul's carefully-planned methods for starting and organizing churches concentrated on the population centers of Iconium, Lystra, Derbe, Antioch, Pisidia, Pamphylia, Perga, and Attalia (Acts 14). The cities were his target. He went where the greatest number of people were. At times, he preached in the synagogues; at other times, in the marketplace or the open air. Sometimes, he concentrated on individuals; at other times, on the masses.

But his strategy was always to concentrate on the areas of greatest potential

PAUL NEVER SEEMED HURRIED. He took the time needed to develop responsible converts into a responsible fellowship.

for church growth. Although preaching and witness planted the seed, this was never an end in itself. It was always followed by in-depth instruction with the view of making responsible disciples (Acts 14:21).

Paul never seemed hurried. He took the time needed to develop responsible converts into a responsible fellowship. In Corinth, he spent a whole year and a half (Acts 18:18). In Ephesus, he needed three years (20:31). In Rome, he stayed two years. In every place when the church was sufficiently mature he encouraged them to appoint leaders (*presbuteros*), committed the newly-organized group to the Lord in prayer, and moved on to another place (14:23).

The simplicity of church government in New Testament practice is not accidental. As J. B. Phillips says, "This surely is the church as it was meant to be. It is vigorous and flexible, for these are the days before it ever became fat and short of breath through prosperity, or muscle-bound by over-organization" (1955, vii). Paul clearly outlined for Timothy, a young church planter and convert of his in whom he had invested considerable time and training, the qualifications necessary for the two offices of the church (i.e., bishop-elder-pastor and deacon [1 Tim. 3]). The need for these arose as a result of the phenomenal growth of the church at Jerusalem and its resultant problems (Acts 6).

Gustav Warneck (1834-1910), who has often been called the founder of the scientific study of missionary principles, distinguishes three stages in the process of building a responsible church (1964, 49):

Stage 1: Gathering of individual believers
Stage 2: Forming them into congregations
Stage 3: Joining of local congregations into a communion

This is in keeping with the principle of interrelationship which we observed in Antioch-Jerusalem churches (i.e., the interdependence of the early fellowship).

Although many twentieth-century missionaries look for a building as the first step in the development of a church, even before the preaching of the gospel, the New Testament lays little or no stress upon a building as the necessary means to the formation of a church. Erroneously, we speak today of "the church on Main and Walnut Streets." But the New Testament leaves no room for such interpretation. The Greek word literally means "called out ones" and is used in the scriptures to denote the assembling of believers together in a certain place, or the designation of a specific fellowship of believers in a particular place.

We read of "the church of the Thessalonians" (1 Thess. 1:1), or the church meeting in the house of Nymphas (Col. 4:15). It is true that Paul often began his initial efforts preaching at the local synagogue of the Jews, but this is never considered a church in the New Testament. For many years, the early believers met in homes and never possessed any special buildings for their gatherings (Rom. 16:5; 1 Cor. 16:19; Col. 4:15; Philemon 2).

"There is no clear example of a separate building set apart for Christian worship within the limits of the Roman empire before the third century" (Lightfoot 1868, 241). Paul concentrated his efforts not on buildings, but on men. Men are God's method.

Well-trained Men

It all started by Jesus calling a few men to follow Him....His concern was not with programs to reach the multitudes, but with men whom the multitudes would follow. Remarkable as it may seem, Jesus started to gather these men before He ever organized an evangelistic campaign or even preached a sermon in public....The initial objectives of Jesus' plan was to enlist men who could bear witness to His life and carry on His work after He returned to the Father. (Coleman 1964)

Jesus' selection of disciples was done with the utmost of care. Prior to the selection of the twelve, he spent all night in prayer (Luke 6:12-16). These men at first do not impress us as being outstanding church leaders, but what is evident is their willingness to learn. And Jesus concentrated his teaching on these few:

> Here is the wisdom of His method....the fundamental principle of concentration on those He intended to use....The necessity is apparent not only to select a few laymen, but to keep the group small enough to be able to work effectively with them. (Coleman 1964, 24)

Paul likewise concentrated on potential leaders (i.e., Timothy, John, Mark, Aquilla and Priscilla, Philemon, etc.). In writing to Timothy he underlined "and the things that thou hast heard of me among many witnesses, the same commit thou to faithful men who shall be able to teach others also" (2 Tim. 2:2). Here is the "each one teach one" philosophy of mission: making reproducing Christians who in turn will make other reproducing Christians. Here is the mathematical solution to world evangelism (i.e., the principle of multiplication rather than simple addition).

While great stress today is laid on money and methods, men are still God's means of reproducing responsible churches. Melvin Hodges has said it this way:

> We can study methods of church growth and write books about indigenous church principles, all of which is well and good; but we will never have anything like New Testament churches and New Testament growth until we get something like New Testament men with New Testament experience. I do not know how this affects you, but it challenges me to the depths of my being. God's methods are men, and we are the men!

References

Beyerhaus, Peter and Henry Lefever. 1964. *The Responsible Church and Foreign Mission*. Grand Rapids, Mich.: William B. Eerdmans Publishing Co.

Boer, Harry R. 1961. *Pentecost and Missions*. Grand Rapids, Mich.: William B. Eerdmans Publishing Co.

Bonhoeffer, Dietrich. 1967. *The Cost of Discipleship*. New York: The MacMillan Co.

Coleman, Robert E. 1964. *The Master Plan of Evangelism*. Westwood, N.J.: Fleming H. Revell.

Lightfoot, J. B. 1868. *St. Paul's Epistle to the Philippians*. London and Cambridge: Macmillan Co.

McGavran, Donald. 1965. *Church Growth and Christian Mission*. New York: Harper & Row.

McLeish, Alexander. 1952. *Objective and Method in Christian Expansion*. London: World Dominion Press.

Phillips, J. B. 1955. *The Young Church in Action*. New York: The Macmillan Co.

Soltau, T. Stanley. 1954. *Missions at the Crossroads*. Wheaton, Ill.: VanKampen Press.

Trueblood, Elton. 1961. *The Company of the Committed*. New York: Harper & Row.

Paul's Short-term Church Planting: Can It Happen Again?

Scott Bessenecker

The author looks at lessons from Paul's church-planting methods, makes cultural comparisons, and concludes that we can also trust God to raise up the essential components of an indigenous church.

Roland Allen, in *Missionary Methods: St. Paul's or Ours?* looks over the panorama of churches established by Paul with wonder and incredulity: wonder that so many growing indigenous churches over such a broad territory could be established in just ten years; and incredulity that so many in missions today consider the feat impossible to repeat (Allen 1962, 3).

What factors contributed to Paul's success? How did he plant so many churches, made up of very different people groups over a large geographical area, in so short a time? Most importantly, can his success be duplicated today?

I believe there is, indeed, a basis for expecting, in the twentieth century, results such as Paul experienced. After briefly surveying and drawing lessons from some of Paul's church-planting methods, I would like to draw attention to three primary areas of comparison between his day and ours—cultural conditions; spiritual conditions; and potential "entry points" for gospel witness—and show that we, like Paul, can trust God to raise up the essential components of an indigenous church in time frames ranging from one month to one year.

Paul: Short-term Missionary Par Excellence

Paul was, in essence, a short-term mission leader. Like many present-day short-termers, he took missionary teams from place to place, seeking to proclaim the gospel along the way. It was not uncommon for him and his traveling companions to see a church begin to grow out of a stay of just two months. Moving on, usually because of persecution, they would repeat their pattern of ministry while the Lord continued to raise up church after church.

Paul's First Journey: April 48 to September 49

Several years after God had told Paul he would evangelize the Gentiles (Acts 9:15), and after he and Barnabas had spent several years in ministry at Antioch, the Spirit of God singled out these two men as missionaries—during a worship service at the Antioch church. That church included both Gentile and Jewish believers, and as such was well-equipped to fan into flame Paul's calling to the Gentiles.

Indeed, it would have provided a working prototype of the sort of church Paul was setting out to plant. If we are to see results today similar to those that Paul experienced, we must not short-circuit the process of calling, community confirmation of the call, and Spirit-anointed commissioning.

Paul, Barnabas, and John Mark sailed from Antioch to Salamis, on Cyprus, where they "proclaimed the word of God in the synagogues of the Jews" (Acts 13:5). This probably means that they expounded the Old Testament scriptures in light of their Christian fulfillment. The team then traveled to Paphos and saw the conversion of the proconsul, Sergius Paulus, who probably was familiar with the Jewish scriptures. Then, after just two months in Cyprus, they sailed to Asia Minor.

After their arrival on the mainland, they traveled through Pamphylia, where John Mark left them, and on to Pisidian Antioch, one hundred miles farther north, where once again they spoke in the synagogue. This time, their synagogue preaching led to their being run out of town—but not before a core group of believers had been established.

We do not know why John Mark left the team, nor why Paul turned northward. Some have suggested illness (see Gal. 4:13). Whatever the case, God used the circumstances to direct their travels.

The pattern continued: synagogue entrée, preaching the word, curiosity and acceptance giving way to confrontation and persecution, ending with the establishment of a small group of believing Jews and Gentiles while Paul and Barnabas were forced out of town. After four or five months in Iconium they left the new church and moved on to Lystra, but were followed by angry Jews from Iconium and Antioch, who stirred up trouble for them in Lystra as well. Paul was stoned, recovered, and moved on with Barnabas to Derbe, where they "made many disciples." They had spent a total of three and a half months in Lystra and Derbe.

By this time, it was June of 49, more than a year since they left their home church. Groups of believers had been won in Pisidian Antioch, Iconium, Lystra, and Derbe. Paul and Barnabas spent the summer retracing their steps to encourage the new Christians, appoint leaders, and teach in each place.

Paul's Second Journey: April 50 to September 52

The first few months of the second missionary journey (April to June 50) were spent visiting the earlier church plants, including the churches in Lystra and Derbe. There, Paul and Silas met Timothy. Although Timothy may have been a Christian for only a year or two, and probably had had no formal leadership training, Paul felt he was ready for mission work.

Paul's bringing Timothy onto the team highlights several important keys to short-term church planting. First, Paul was active in his promotion of national leaders. Second, in this case, a young person of potential was identified—

someone with many years of service ahead of him. Third, Paul did not confine Timothy to a lengthy "home" education program but actively employed him in mission work right away.

This accomplished two things: it educated Timothy in the "school of hard knocks," and it very quickly propelled the young local church into world evangelization, forestalling any provincial, inward focus. Additionally and more practically, Paul now had an ethnic Greek to help him reach the Gentiles.

Finally, note the absence of the "Lone Ranger" mentality. Paul always traveled with a team. This allowed for a multiplicity of gifts and mutual encouragement. His traveling companions were as invested in the work as he was. Paul's success at quickly planting churches surely could not have happened alone.

The short-term church-planting team tried to travel north and east, deeper into the heart of Asia, but apparently God had Europe on his heart. Three mystical encounters led to a change in itinerary (Acts 16:6–7). They ended up in Philippi for "some days," where within two or three months they saw a church

PAUL'S WORK IN THESSALONICA led to a riot, after which he and Silas were wisked off to Berea. We can only imagine that Paul was quite concerned for the infant church amid such persecution.

established. And once again, there had been the predictable church-planting cadence: entrance through a Jewish gathering (in this case, God-fearing Gentile women), conversion of mostly Gentiles, followed by persecution.

On to Thessalonica, where after three weeks in the synagogue a church was apparently formed (Acts 17:4). Note here the special mention of women. Although Paul always began at the synagogue, it was often those on the fringe of society (women and Gentiles) who responded first.

Paul's work in Thessalonica led to a riot, after which he and Silas were whisked off to Berea. We can only imagine that Paul was quite concerned for the infant church amid such persecution. After an effective ministry of less than a month in Berea, Paul left Silas and Timothy and went to Athens. F.F. Bruce proposes that Paul may have written 2 Thessalonians before he left, intending for Timothy to deliver it to Thessalonica to encourage them.

Paul enjoyed several weeks of ministry in Athens then moved on to Corinth sometime in mid-March of 51. By perhaps May, Silas and Timothy rejoined him. Timothy brought word from Thessalonica which encouraged Paul and warranted another letter—1 Thessalonians.

Looking back on the church in Thessalonica, we see that it was planted in the span of about three months. Shortly after a hasty departure by the foreign missionaries, the church was sent a letter by way of an ethnically Greek missionary-in-training with whom they had some relationship. This young man spent probably about three months with the believers and then caught up with the foreign missionary (Paul) and brought him news of the church. The foreign missionary, anxious for the church's establishment, was relieved to have good news and replied with another letter to further establish and build up this church not yet even a year old.

It is amazing to note the level of affection in Paul's letters to the Thessalonians (see 1 Thess. 2:17–20; 3:6, 9). Deep and meaningful relationships can be developed in short periods of time. Short-term church planting need not be seen as promoting shallow and ineffective relationships.

Paul stayed in Corinth eighteen months, during which he began a missionary-in-training program with fellow tentmakers Priscilla and Aquila. With these two co-workers he went to Ephesus, where he left them after staying only a week or two. Apparently the training had been effective, because Priscilla and Aquila helped to educate Apollos, and they probably established the church in Ephesus and perhaps in other places as well.

Paul's third journey would involve mainly revisiting churches planted on the first two journeys. What do we learn from Paul's "short-term church-planting journeys?"

1. We must trust God to call mature people who will wait on that calling until, in the context of community confirmation, they are released into ministry with the assurance of the Holy Spirit's backing.

2. The commissioning church should be one in which the church planters have labored and learned, and one that can serve as a prototype for the churches they will plant.

3. Redirection due to undesirable circumstances may be God's sovereign way to bring us in touch with the right people at the right time.

4. The short-term missionary must carefully look for a point of entry for witness, then be prepared for both enthusiasm and antagonism.

5. We should revisit the churches we establish, to give them additional guidance and help them establish leadership.

6. Our relationship with the churches we plant should be so good that we will want to stay in touch with them, even years later.

7. Each new church should be a bridge to additional churches, as missionaries and new believers move deeper into unreached territory.

8. We should identify young leaders among new converts and involve them in our ministry.

9. We should work with teams, including men and women, who can provide examples of church life even as they plant new churches.

10. People of stature and influence may not always be attracted to our message. Often those people who do not completely fit in with our target people group will respond.

Cultural Comparisons between the First Century and Today

But what, we might ask, does Paul's day have in common with the twentieth century? Actually, there are several similarities—things which helped advance the gospel in the first century and which may help short-term church planters today.

1. Language: English vs. Greek. Paul's success was due in part to his ability to communicate fluently in a language spoken by the vast majority of the people he sought to reach. As with Greek in the first century, English today is the most widely spoken language in the world.

2. Travel: Roman roads vs. modern air travel. The world in the first century was shrinking through the expansion of trade by land and sea. Likewise, travel today is fast, cheap, far-reaching, and widely available. It would be difficult to prove that Paul's church-planting success was due to any advantage over us in the area of travel.

3. Hellenization vs. westernization. When Paul interacted across Asia and Europe with peoples of varying cultures, part of what helped him communicate and develop relationships was the predominance of Hellenistic culture. In our time, for better or for worse, the whole world is being westernized.

CHRISTIANITY WAS BORN into a world where mystery religions were flowering. The mystery religions were indicators of an inward hunger not being satisfied.

Someone accustomed to city life could conceivably get along well on brief stays in almost any country on the planet. What's more, the philosophical underpinnings of Western thought are accompanying many of these changes. Like the Hellenization of Paul's day, this is often a veneer-like surface over a dramatically different heart culture, but it does allow for enough familiarity to begin a dialogue.

4. Spiritual conditions then and now. Christianity was born in a world where mystery religions were flowering. The mystery religions were indicators of an inward hunger not being satisfied. "Their appeal seems to have been the assurance of immortality which they gave to their members, combined with a fellowship which many craved in a world [of] uprooted individuals"[3] (Latourette 1953, 25).

Today, the New Age movement is quickly becoming a global phenomenon. Groups like Planetary Citizens boast a long roster of leaders and host New Age conferences involving hundreds of worldwide organizations (Groothius 1986, 118). I believe that the appeal of the gospel will be high among those New Age dabblers disenfranchised by westernization, even as first-century crowds groping for an experience with the divine through the mystery religions responded to Paul's message.

Religious persecution was a major reason Paul's stays were so short in several cities. There are at least two reasons to believe that this persecution may have actually helped new churches become established more quickly. First, where sin abounds, grace abounds all the more. God in his mercy sustained the church by intervening in special ways, giving strength and numerical growth in the face of martyrdom. Second, opposition to the persecution galvanized the fellowship of believers and tested the tenacity of their faith.

Similarly today, short-term ministries often seem most effective in establishing strong new churches precisely in areas where, because of persecution, longer-term ministry is not possible.

5. University and synagogue. The university campus is often the open door to a hostile environment today, just as the synagogue was for Paul. Like the Diaspora synagogue, the university is a gathering place for people from many ethnic backgrounds, all drawn by a quest for learning. Like the synagogue, it also exerts substantial influence on society. If we hope to see results like Paul's, we need a platform like the synagogue where the message will gain a hearing. The university is just such a platform.

Contemporary Case Studies

In addition to the principles we have learned from Paul's church-planting journeys, we have looked at several aspects of first-century Mediterranean life that parallel current world trends, and which may suggest greater opportunities for success in short-term church planting. Two contemporary case studies suggest that such success is indeed possible.

Kiev Linguistic University. In 1990, InterVarsity Christian Fellowship sponsored an exchange program between Kiev Linguistic University and Inter-Varsity members, during which thirteen Ukrainian students and faculty professed faith in Christ (Evenson 1994). One of the student missionaries spent the next year in Ukraine encouraging the young believers. Here is an example of a budding church emerging in response to a short evangelistic visit.

But could such a young group of Christians survive? Yes, they showed quickly how well they grasped the essentials of the gospel. The following year seven of them attended a conference sponsored by Sun Myung Moon, and without exception they all realized the error of his teachings. They even led one of the other attendees to Christ.

In 1994, thirteen Ukrainian Christian student leaders, most of whom had come to faith as a result of a short-term mission, took part in an internship program to become student ministry leaders. Most of them now travel regularly to begin new student fellowships.

American students who were part of these efforts often returned for longer terms to support the growing student group. Many others kept a correspondence relationship with their counterparts to encourage them in their walk. These activities reflect the church-planting strategy of Paul and his companions.

Central Asian University.[1] Mark, an American student from Dallas, led Yousef, a Central Asian student, to Christ, and together they led a short-term evangelistic effort in Central Asia, resulting in four new believers. Within two months, Mark and three other American college graduates had moved to Central Asia to work with Yousef in establishing these young believers. Today, a group of thirty attend a Christian fellowship at their university, and two, besides Yousef, are evangelizing other areas.

Both of these examples suggest that deep relationships, solid conversions, and competent leaders can emerge out of short-term programs.

Conclusion

This examination is in no way meant to denigrate longer term church-planting efforts. In many places, missionaries must grow deep roots for the gospel to flourish. I have tried to show, however, that short-term church planting is possible and can be very fruitful—if the New Testament criteria are met.

Endnote

1. Names of locations and people have been changed. Information is based on the author's personal knowledge of those involved.

References

Allen, Roland. 1962. *Missionary Methods: St. Paul's or Ours?* Grand Rapids, Mich.: William B. Eerdmans Publishing Co.

Evenson, James. 1994. "Building Indigenous Christian Student Movements in the Former USSR." InterVarsity Christian Fellowship.

Groothius, Douglass. 1986. *Unmasking the New Age.* Downers Grove, Ill.: InterVarsity Press.

Latourette, Kenneth Scott. 1953. *A History of Christianity, Volume 1: to A.D. 1500.* San Francisco: Harper Collins.

Written by the Hand of Paul: Church Planting Naturally

Derek Seipp

Five lessons learned over ten years of using various multiplicative strategies.

For almost ten years I have rigorously worked overseas toward the goal of church multiplication. For much of that time we worked on a team crossing denominational and organizational lines to train, envision, and encourage churches to multiply. After eight years, we saw at least sixty new churches, but we also witnessed several derailments and a few crashes. Although I wish those derailments had never occurred, I believe we learn only through a combination of success and failure. We sat down with local leaders to discuss lessons learned and some of the shortcomings in multiplicative strategies. As for what we learned through the successes, we found that these principles were already written plainly by the hand of Paul.

I preface these thoughts with an acknowledgment that church growth is tied to the Holy Spirit, cultural realities, and regional church histories. What works in one place may not be applicable to another. The Church itself remains the "mystery" Paul so eloquently described.

First, we learned that *multiplication is but one of many biblical strategies for fulfilling the Great Commission.* Church planting, as such, is not taught in the Bible, yet it is what happened. This is not pitting discipleship vs. church planting, but merely acknowledging an intrinsic both/and relationship.

In Acts 19 it appears that Paul changed his methodology for church planting in Ephesus, a change which resulted in some degree of church multiplication. Starting with twelve disciples, in only two years all of Asia heard the gospel, and, as some theologians believe, the seven churches of Revelation were planted. These churches became pillars of the Christian community. In his letter to the Ephesians, Paul calls the believers back to a DNA he had previously strived to implant within them—most likely while at the lecture hall of Tyrannus. This DNA focuses primarily on the Church being the agent for restoring lost people to their creator.

Second, we learned that *multiplication, or even church planting itself, is not the goal. God's mission is explicit: to restore people back into a relationship with him.* Church planting is secondary, and multiplication is just one of many strategies toward that end. As Acts shows, however, new churches should be a natural result. Let me assure you that I am still on the church multiplication bandwagon. I have just radically changed my methodology.

Third, we learned that *multiplication is an incomplete and possibly deceptive barometer of success*. Church after church that held multiplication as the primary measurable outcome often made decisions that unwittingly derailed the process. Many churches came back together again. Other leaders felt pressured to perform while ordinary believers felt disconnected to their pastor's multiplication strategies. Other churches multiplied several times, then stopped. Many leaders were overwhelmed after several years.

You may argue they did not adequately think through their decisions or give themselves to the vision. "Evaluate everything with respect to our vision," we say proudly. True, but through reflection, we, fourth, learned that *a primary focus on church planting leads to an unbalanced expression of the gospel*. Where success did happen, we learned that leaders correctly focused on creating a new lifestyle, one that produced a powerful result. They correctly placed the

WE SEE HIS LETTER to the Ephesians as a plea for believers to return to living out a purpose-filled lifestyle, linked to God's mission for the lost, while tied with an empowering leadership structure.

mandate on a relationship with God, and personally/corporately joining him on his mission. When this happened, churches multiplied out, and exhibited what I now call an "Ephesians lifestyle"—a modern-day implementation of the values and principles that Paul taught to the Ephesians (and letters to Timothy, the worker in Ephesus).

We see his letter to the Ephesians as a plea for believers to return to living out a purpose-filled lifestyle, linked to God's mission for the lost, while tied with an empowering leadership structure. These three ingredients were the same influences we saw that caused churches we worked with to multiply naturally, rather than through a forced strategy.

Finally, we learned that *imparting a lifestyle to ordinary believers is much more difficult and time consuming than simply holding church multiplication training*. Although these churches still taught multiplication, they spent more time focusing on the whole body of believers, helping them actively live in the world in a way that is tied to God's mission while continuously empowering and releasing people into ministry opportunities. This is what we all saw reflected so clearly in Paul's writings, and I believe that when it happens, we have prepared the soil for the Holy Spirit to do a church-planting miracle.

Putting Together a Church-planting Team? Look to Barnabas

J. D. Payne

A *biblical examination for church-planting teams of eight aspects from the life of Barnabas.*

I want to challenge you to look at Barnabas in a different light—one in which he is understood as a model for contemporary church planters, complementing what we have already learned from the model of Paul. The following is a biblical examination of eight "Barnabas Factors"—aspects from the life of Barnabas that should be present in your church-planting team members.

Although these factors are not exclusive to Barnabas, they do offer us a fresh and significant perspective when it comes to critical characteristics that should not be taken for granted. This article concludes with an assessment guide to assist in selecting team members based upon the factors.

Factor 1: Walks with the Lord

Barnabas was sold out to Jesus. Walking uprightly with the Lord enabled him to know how to live in relation to God, other team members, and unbelievers. It is most unlikely that the Holy Spirit would have ordered Paul and Barnabas to be set apart (Acts 13:2-3) if they did not walk faithfully with the Lord. Such a lifestyle allowed the Spirit to work through them to accomplish the miraculous.

Barnabas' godly lifestyle made him loveable (Acts 15:25), trustworthy and reliable (Acts 11:28-30), and able to manifest an attitude of encouragement—thus, giving him the name "Son of Encouragement" (Acts 11:23). His walk with the Lord gave him wisdom to know how to engage unbelievers (Acts 1:8; 11:24), boldness for evangelism (Acts 13:45-46), and perseverance when faced with discouragement and persecution (Acts 13:50-51).

Factor 2: Maintains an Outstanding Character

Other believers recognized his outstanding character. Luke noted that he was "a good person, full of the Holy Spirit, and full of faith." He was so well respected by the apostles in Jerusalem that they had no problem extending to him the "right hand of fellowship" (Gal. 2:9). He was also recognized as one who should represent the Jerusalem Church while investigating the birth and growth of the Antioch Church (Acts 11:22). The Antioch Church also recognized his outstanding character when they trusted him and Paul to carry an offering to the Jerusalem Church to assist with the famine relief (Acts 11:27-29).

In Lystra, he and Paul could have avoided persecution by acting as if they were Zeus and Hermes (Acts 14:10-13), but they refused to take glory away from the Lord. When the Jerusalem Council gathered to debate the necessity of circumcision for salvation, the entire assembly paid close attention to the words of Barnabas and Paul (Acts 15:12). These two men not only were influential regarding the outcome of the meeting, they were also selected to represent the Council in Antioch (Acts 15:22), being referred to as "beloved" men (Acts 15:25-26).

Factor 3: Serves the Local Church

Barnabas had an excellent track record of serving the local church. In addition to his encouragement, he also served the church through his participation and submission. Of all the members of the Jerusalem Church, Luke singled him out and introduced him as the Son of Encouragement, who sold his tract of land and gave the proceeds to the apostles to distribute to the needy (Acts 4:32-37).

Long before he was serving as a church planter, he was setting the example of a faithful and sacrificial church member. He also submitted to the church's desire to send him to Antioch following the birth of the church in that city (Acts 11:19-23). Such an act on his part would have demanded great sacrifice of personal security, money (for travel), and time.

Factor 4: Remains Faithful to the Call

Barnabas was given numerous reasons to abandon his ministry. He experienced opposition by Elymas (Acts 13:8) and persecution by the Jews (Acts 13:45, 50). After he and Paul arrived in Iconium, they soon found themselves the target of a group of citizens desiring to stone them (Acts 14:5). Later in Lystra, he witnessed the stoning of Paul (Acts 14:20). In spite of all the verbal and physical abuse for the sake of the gospel, Barnabas remained faithful to his calling. He continued on the missionary journey with Paul, and after their separation even led a second missionary journey with John Mark (Acts 15:39).

Factor 5: Shares the Gospel Regularly

Barnabas was intentional and verbal in his evangelism. He and Paul lived according to a definition that biblical church planting is evangelism that results in new churches (Acts 14:21-23). It is not a coincidence that just after Luke noted that Barnabas was a "good man, and full of the Holy Spirit and of faith," he recorded that in Antioch, "considerable numbers were brought to the Lord" (Acts 11:24). Five points must be made here.

1. Barnabas' evangelism was done with intentionality. He and Paul did not wait for opportunities to verbally share the gospel, but rather sought out such opportunities in every city they entered.

2. Barnabas' evangelism was done with boldness. Luke recorded while in Antioch of Pisidia, "Then Paul and Barnabas boldly said, 'It was necessary that God's message be spoken to you first'" (Acts 13:46).

3. Barnabas' evangelism was done with tenacity. After experiencing opposition and persecution in Antioch of Pisidia and Iconium, he and Paul fled to the towns of Lystra and Derbe (Acts 14:6). Instead of cowering in fear, Luke wrote, "...and there they continued to preach the gospel" (Acts 14:7).

4. Barnabas' evangelism was done with a preference toward receptive people. Although the purpose of this church-planting team was to take the gospel first to the Jew and then to the Gentile, Barnabas and Paul were not slow to depart from unreceptive areas. Again, turning our attention to Antioch of Pisidia, when they were expelled from the district, they shook the dust off of their feet against the people and traveled to Iconium (Acts 13:51).

5. Barnabas' evangelism was done with a follow-up orientation. An examination of the work of Barnabas and Paul on the first missionary journey (Acts 13-14) reveals that these men did not conceive of fulfilling the Great Commission as making converts, but rather making disciples. The gathering of the new believers together into local churches and appointing elders over them is additional evidence for this fact (Acts 14:21-23).

Factor 6: Raises Up Leaders

Barnabas saw the potential in others to become leaders in the kingdom. With Stephen's death and Saul's rampage still fresh in the minds of the Jerusalem Church, no one was willing to accept Saul into the fellowship after his conversion. Barnabas, however, took a calculated risk and reached out to him, brought him to the apostles, and vouched for his changed life (Acts 9:27). Barnabas' actions resulted in the church embracing Saul (Acts 9:28). Also, after observing the great work of the Spirit in Antioch, Barnabas decided to locate Saul in Tarsus and bring him to Antioch to help in building up the church (Acts 11:25-26). Barnabas was willing to take a chance with Paul as a leader.

Barnabas was also willing to extend a second chance to John Mark. Even when Paul was not willing to give John Mark a second chance (Acts 15:37-38), Barnabas saw potential in this young leader and took him to minister in Cyprus (Acts 15:39). We later learn from Paul's letters that his attitude became more favorable toward John Mark (Col. 4:10; 2 Tim. 4:11; Phile. 24). I like to think that John Mark's time with Barnabas on his second missionary journey assisted him in his growth as a leader, which contributed to a change in Paul's attitude.

In addition to Barnabas' influence on the leadership development in the lives of Paul and John Mark, he was active in leadership development by appointing leaders over the newly-planted churches (Acts 14:23).

Factor 7: Encourages with Speech and Actions

One of the first things that usually comes to mind when we think of Barnabas is that he was an encourager. In fact, we often speak of a person who has significantly supported or encouraged our ministries as being a "Barnabas" to us. Clearly, Barnabas encouraged with both his words and deeds. His actions were substantial, sacrificial, helpful, and exemplary among the Apostolic Church. In addition to selling his property for the church (Acts 4:37), he also gave up comfort and safety when he traveled to Antioch (Acts 11:22), where he remained an entire year (Acts 11:26) to help the new church, and traveled a multitude of miles on his journeys for the kingdom.

Factor 8: Responds Appropriately to Conflict

Barnabas experienced conflict with Paul on at least two occasions. The first occurrence was related to the John Mark incident (Acts 15:36-40). Following the conflict, he and Paul each began a second missionary journey, with Barnabas taking his cousin, John Mark, and Paul teaming up with Silas. Although Luke recorded that the two men had a "sharp disagreement" (Acts 15:39), he did not attempt to attribute the division to either the sin of Paul or of Barnabas. The only exceptional note he recorded was that Paul and Silas were "committed by the brethren to the grace of the Lord" (Acts 15:40).

The second occurrence of conflict clearly revealed that sin manifested itself in Barnabas' life. In Paul's letter to the Galatians, he mentioned his conflict with Peter regarding Peter's hypocrisy (Gal. 2:11-13), and illustrated the severity of the matter by including that "even" Barnabas was led astray by the hypocritical actions (Gal. 2:13). Although we do not know the details of this matter regarding Paul's encounter with Barnabas, obviously such sin in the life of Paul's former traveling companion created such conflict in his heart that he felt it was worthy of mention.

Conclusion

In this article, I have pointed to Barnabas as a healthy model for contemporary missionaries. Since I believe it is helpful for missionaries to have a tool to assist them with the selection and development of church-planting teams, I have included a subjective guide to help meet this need (see pages 78 & 79).

Barnabas Factors Standard of Excellence Guide for Team Development[1]

Please note this is simply a guide to assist you in team development. Your evaluation of an individual is subjective. However, since you are the team leader, your subjectivity is important. Make prayer a priority. The best way to assess a person in light of these factors is to be in community with the individual over a period of time. If this is unlikely, evaluate the individual and speak to someone who has been in community with the person. If neither of these two are an option, then a prayerful, extended period of conversation with the candidate is another route.

On the following scale, rank each candidate in light of each Barnabas Factor:

Low				Medium				High	
1	2	3	4	5	6	7	8	9	10

The following are some questions to help you with your evaluation:

Factor #1: Walks with the Lord
- Is this person loveable, wise, trustworthy, and reliable?
- Does this person have a good attitude about God, life, and serving on this team?
- Can this person provide a clear, verbal testimony of a conversion experience?
- Does this person persevere during difficult times?

Factor #2: Maintains an Outstanding Character
- Does this person have good speech, a gentle spirit, and is he or she faith-filled?
- Does this person manifest good actions and the fruit of the Spirit?
- Does this person trust God for his or her provisions and plans?
- Does this person rob God of his glory?
- Does this person truly trust God to do the impossible?

Factor #3: Serves in the Local Church
- Is this person an active member of a local church?
- Is this person passionate about the local church and use his or her gifts to build up the church?
- Does this person work alone or does he or she exhibit servant leadership and is a team player?
- Does this person make sacrifices for his or her church and submit to the leaders of that church?

Factor #4: Remains Faithful to the Call
- Is this person faithful to the Lord and committed to the Great Commission?

- Will this person be faithful to the team?
- Does this person have a clear call that is similar to that of the team?
- Will this person remain faithful to his or her calling, even if not invited to serve on the team?

Factor #5: Shares the Gospel Regularly

- Does this person have a history of regularly sharing the gospel?
- Is this person intentional and zealous in his or her evangelism?
- Does this person desire to make disciples and not just converts?
- Can this person verbally share a clear and concise gospel presentation?
- Does this person share the gospel even when people are not receptive?

Factor #6: Raises up Leaders

- Does this person have a mindset to multiply leaders?
- Does this person take wise and strategic risks?
- Is this person's attitude and lifestyle a good example for new believers?
- Is this person willing to grow as a leader?
- Does this person want to spend most of his or her time working with a few leaders rather than with the crowds?

Factor #7: Encourages with Speech and Actions

- Does this person speak the truth?
- Does this person encourage others with both speech and action?
- Is this person helpful?

Factor #8: Responds Appropriately to Conflict

- Does this person have a healthy understanding of conflict?
- Does this person respond in love when wronged by others?
- Does this person hold grudges?
- Does this person exhibit love, humility, and a Christ-like attitude during times of conflict?

RANKING	SCORE	ASSESSMENT
Low	8-24	It is not recommended that this person be on the team.
Medium	32-56	You may want to consider inviting this person for the team, but only with reservations. Provide guidance in the areas where this person scored low. This person may bring some significant struggles to the team.
High	64-80	Invite this individual to the team. He or she strongly manifests the Barnabas Factors. But remember, a high score is no guarantee for effectiveness.

Endnote

1. Adapted here from Appendix Two in *The Barnabas Factors: Eight Essential Practices of Church Planting Team Members.*

Reference

Payne, J. D. 2008. *The Barnabas Factors: Eight Essential Practices of Church Planting Team Members.* Smyrna, Del.: Missional Press.

Section 3

The Church Plant
(what it looks like)

When we close our eyes and envision what a successful, God-centered, missional church plant looks like, what do we envision? As it is happening, what key things are being done such that it appears to be blessed by God? Some may first consider a church plant to be a building or structure, but at the core, it is the people of God coming together in Acts 2 style. In this section, we hear from six veteran missionaries sharing their vision of what a healthy church plant looks like.

Trent Rowland and **Shane Bennett** discuss ten church-planting "events" in which missionaries must demonstrate competency in order to last and be effective. **Robert Vajko** helps us understand key factors reproducing churches do right.

Ken Baker delineates the difference between church planting and kingdom building. **Johan Lukasse** shares practical suggestions for teams working in difficult areas. Finally, **Linda Wilson** addresses issues women in missions face.

Qualifying for the Pioneer Church-planting Decathalon

Trent Rowland and Shane Bennett

Ten church-planting "events" in which missionaries must demonstrate competency in order to last and be effective.

In 1992, the gold medal hopes of the United States track team (as well as the financial hopes of their sponsor, Reebok) were firmly pinned on one superb athlete, Dan O'Brien. Through the first seven events in which he competed, he was on world-record pace. When it came time to qualify for the decathlon, though, he failed to clear his opening height in the pole vault. Hopes started to fade. In the end, O'Brien didn't even make the team.

To participate in the decathlon, an athlete must qualify in each of the ten events the contest includes. It is not a sport just for the superstars or absolute best in a particular event. Decathlons are for those who can do better than most in a combination of many events. Since O'Brien's pole-vaulting skills were relatively strong, he didn't attempt a vault until the bar was fairly high. Then he missed on all three tries and his hopes of a gold medal were buried in the sand pit where the bar fell.

In the lives of fellow church planters in parts of Asia, we're beginning to see similarities to O'Brien's setback. The pathways to ministry in certain areas are more defined than they were a few years ago, but they are by no means thoroughfares. The bar is high. Only the tenacious actually make it to the field. Those who do make it usually arrive with several strong abilities and gifts. Trouble arises, however, when church planters who excel in some areas fail to even qualify in others.

It may seem simplistic, but we've identified ten church-planting "events" in which missionaries must demonstrate a measure of competency in order to last and be effective. There may be others to consider. Fail to meet the minimum standard in any one of these ten areas and you may find yourself returning home, as many have before you. Achieve the minimum standards, and you have a good chance of making the team.

Event No. 1: Language and Culture Learning

The third time you reach the point of despair and seriously consider giving up, you're probably approaching the "end of the beginning" of this agonizing and essential process. A thousand urgent issues and important items will rise up to distract you. You must not abandon the fundamentals.

Minimum standard: Plan to spend most of your first two years working on this event. Don't give up until locals stop telling you how well you speak. Aim for fluency in the local heart language. This poses difficulties in the unreached world where language schools, skilled teachers, and bilingual books are rare or non-existent. But that doesn't change the necessity to master the local language, both speaking and writing.

Common mistakes: Looking for a jump-start, many begin to minister in English, through translators, or use a less appropriate trade language. Why not have a policy of no ministry except in the local language?

Mothers caring for young children or home-schooling have the biggest challenge. They'll have to have a slower learning pace and need facilitative help from their husbands, teammates, and agencies. But if they don't learn it in the first few years, they probably won't. Staying long term only gets harder for those who cannot easily communicate.

Event No. 2: Identification with the Host Culture

John's Gospel begins with "The Word became flesh and dwelt among us." Paul applies this principle to himself and to us in 2 Corinthians 9:22 when he says, "I have become all things to all men." For us, God took on flesh. For the Gentiles, Paul let go of his Jewish privilege. For unreached people groups, we're called to relinquish our rights to our home cultures and its lifestyle to become like those whom we endeavor to reach.

Minimum standard: Tom and Betty Sue Brewster have thrown down the gauntlet for our generation of church planters. They've admonished us not to ease into the new culture, but to jump in with both feet. Bonding, they say, happens much better when we immerse ourselves in the local scene. Spend your first several months living with a local family. This was so important for us. We strongly recommend this, and have seen it reap rewards in the lives of the team members who've followed us to our city.

Having bonded, or at least begun the process, we must continue on in our effort to identify with our hosts. With Jesus and Paul as models, Hudson Taylor set a fine example for us in living a life of identification with his chosen people. Taylor worked hard to dress, speak, and act the part of an honorable Chinese man. For most of us, identification is likely to include some measure of simplification of our lives, decreased reliance on technology, and increased reliance on relationships.

Common mistakes: Obviously, this issue is more complicated than simply, "Live on the level of the people you're trying to reach." Identifying with your host culture can be complex and likely will be difficult. There are often many subcultures that present conflicting models.

While not trying to address all the issues, I would like to point out two areas that threaten our most sincere intentions. A reluctance or refusal to give up your home culture is the first. God calls all of us to some measure of sacrifice. Those who take the gospel to a new culture, and in doing so let go of their grip on their home culture, sacrifice more than most of us can imagine.

Second, we must be careful to treat as righteous what our host culture sees as righteous. Don't get nervous here. I'm not saying, "Serve idols, if your host culture believes that to be righteous." It's more like, "Don't serve Spam if your host culture views pork as unclean." Behave as honorable and reverent men and women.

Event No. 3: Tentmaking

Like most things in life, this event calls for balance. Because most unreached peoples live under governments who decline to issue missionary visas, tentmaking has increasingly become the strategy of choice. Missionaries around the globe have responded by starting businesses, teaching English, and engaging in other occupations in addition to their ministry as church planters.

Minimum standard: Find a balance between work and ministry which ensures long-term credibility and viability in your city, while allowing sufficient time for evangelistic friendships, language and culture learning, and team relationships.

Common mistakes: We may feel the necessity to invest so much time and energy to maintain our visa and establish credibility that we become a "residential non-missionary," unable to make contact with the target group, learn their language, or establish relationships with them. On the other hand, if we don't take our tentmaking role seriously enough, we may fail to honor God through our efforts. This could also result in local friends and authorities smelling a front for an undeclared purpose which they fear is spying, or worse.

Event No. 4: Staying Focused

Many issues and responsibilities vie for the attention of a beginning (or veteran) church planter. Missionaries often find themselves in areas where great needs abound—needs they have the resources to meet. Compounding that are the extra stresses of living in a cross-cultural setting and the tendency of Christians everywhere to hold meetings. You've got to work hard to focus on what you are there to do. This is further exacerbated by the failure of many missionaries to articulate a clear and measurable plan for ministry.

Minimum standard: Write down what you will do and how you believe God wants you to go about doing it. Determine your goals and prayerfully place them on a timeline.

Common mistakes: Without a clear-cut, compelling strategy, we can float from one good thing to the next, failing to accomplish work of long-term value. Or we might try to do every good thing, which will make us mediocre at all of them. Realizing this, we are tempted to despair. Our physical limitations further complicate the situation, leading to exhaustion. Don't lose sight of your goals.

Event No. 5: Evangelism and Discipleship

Non-believers almost always become mature followers of Christ through the costly life-on-life investment of Christian friends. This means that a key part of a church planter's life will be telling the story of Jesus, persuading people to follow, and helping them grow strong in the faith.

Minimum standard: When plotting your weekly schedule, consider how many hours are both available for, and scheduled as, relationship building and sharing the gospel. What time is devoted to one-on-one discipling of believers? Guard this time.

Common mistakes: Greg Livingstone, founder of Frontiers, once said, "We talk about resistant lands. Sometimes I think it's a matter of 'little sowing, little reaping.'" We can mistakenly think, or hope, that fluency in the local tongue and good contextualization will automatically result in established churches. We may, because of timidity or distraction, do everything but talk to folks about Jesus. We fill our hours with work, get tired, and wonder why we aren't seeing churches planted. Don't forget why you've come.

Event No. 6: Contextualization

While it's lovely to think, "Beneath our skin, all people are really just the same," in reality, beneath our skin, we're all so radically different that it's amazing we haven't completely killed each other yet. These differences between people groups reflect the wonderful complexity and creativity of God. When we consider the hurdles the gospel has already overcome, they speak of his great power and commitment to his purposes. Church planters must keep in mind these differences and work with them to maximize their efforts.

Minimum standard: Church planting decathletes must have the wisdom and capacity to conform their presentation of the gospel to the minds and life experiences of the people they are ministering to. But it's not enough to simply speak appropriately (even as complex as that may seem); they also must envision a contextualized church that grows up thoroughly biblical and thoroughly like the target group. And they need to determine to rely on the insight of the Holy Spirit through the lives of early local believers.

Common mistakes: We may think through our presentation carefully while we diligently learn the heart language, but fail to think about what a relevant church for our target people will look like. Failing to consider this, we are prone to default to working toward the church models we grew up with, except for the nice buildings and Xerox machines.

When we do give thought to contextualizing the church, we may be susceptible to two additional errors. The first could be called "my way or the highway." We fix on a particular degree or style of contextualization and will neither budge nor waver, even in the light of clear wisdom and veteran experience. The second could be called "the latest and greatest." We're susceptible to jumping on the latest trend, moving from one plan to the next as fast as we hear about them. Ask God for wisdom in this.

Event No. 7: Emotional Stability

Some of the world's greatest history makers, missionaries included, have gone insane. Today's church planters have, in addition to chemical treatments unavailable to our ancestors, two tools to help us stay closely linked to reality. The first is more a freedom than a tool. It's now okay to consider how you're dealing with the stresses life is throwing at you. *It really is*—even for the most spiritual of missionaries. Second, today's emphasis on church planting in teams allows individuals the increased strength of a like-minded cadre.

Minimum standard: To succeed in this event, pay attention to, but don't obsess over, your mental health. At a minimum, ask yourself this question: "Is there one person on my team who is honestly helping me assess my mental health?" Further, aim to grow in your ability to receive from your team and to edify them in return. The Bible is full of admonitions and advice, warnings and threats in this area. God is very concerned about the way we relate to one another. In fact, Jesus told his disciples that others would recognize them by their love for each other.

Common mistakes: Lack of balance is the defining characteristic of failure in this event. Some individuals, usually men and often team leaders, decide they don't need anything from their comrades. Moreover, they don't even need comrades. This approach, seldom seen in the Bible, can wreak havoc on a team and is dangerous for the individual.

On the other side is the team member who has enslaved him or herself to his or her feelings. Try as he or she might, his or her comrades cannot emancipate that person. This makes life difficult for the team and can sidetrack, or hinder, the work of the team. Teams can also face trouble when they lack common agreement as to what it means to be a team. Take pains to articulate these issues early in team formation.

Event No. 8: Marriage

A disclaimer: Not all church planters among the unreached are married, and those who aren't have unique concerns all their own. However, most are, or will be, or will serve on teams with married people.

As *the* most intimate and intense relationships in a situation characterized by intimate and intense relationships, marriages on a church-planting team need special attention. Marriage has a unique capacity not only to bring joy and stability to church planters, but also to cause havoc and even disqualification for otherwise gifted missionaries.

Minimum standard: On the vast sea of good marriage advice, three things come to the surface as especially important for the church-planting couple. Fail to heed these at peril of sinking! Make your relationship a priority: plan time for it. This may mean time taken from worthwhile ministry activities. Listen to each other: This will also take time. Living and working in a new culture stresses people in ways that cannot be communicated in a single brief conversation.

Finally, avoid competing with each other: One of you is bound to be better at learning the language, as well as the rest of these events. You will both struggle with almost everything to different degrees at different times. Do your best to carry one another through the dark times.

Common mistakes: What if one member of a couple begins to feel he or she simply can't continue on the field? God values your marriage above your contribution to a ministry. Drop back, pray, re-evaluate, and make the necessary adjustments.

Event No. 9: Endurance

When my seventh-grade gym class held a pentathlon (same as a decathlon, but only five events), hardly anyone signed up to run the mile. It wasn't hard to figure out why: the mile hurt, and for longer than the other events. Today, short-term missions are the rage. While I'm all for short-term missions, one reason for their popularity is the presence of a return ticket. Staying is hard, but essential. Churches that last are rarely planted quickly. This is especially true for the remaining unreached peoples.

Minimum standard: Plan to stay at least five years. In many places, this is the minimum amount of time required to learn the language and minister well enough to disciple early converts. A church in Phoenix, Arizona, approaches endurance this way: to protect the investment they'll make in the members of their church-planting team, they only accept candidates who are confident that God is calling them to give ten years of service on the team. Team members understand that once on-site, there is ample grace to leave the team if things simply aren't working out. The result is that people go with the mindset to stay.

Common mistakes: Many of us and our organizations have followed the lead of our culture in redefining "long term" as "more than six months." We (at least those of us in the U.S.) also live in a time when an amazingly high value is placed on having multiple, attractive options. It doesn't take a rocket scientist to realize that a decision to spend three years learning Tadjik, for example, severely limits one's options, and not only for those three years. How many different things can one do with a mastery of Tadjik? Not many, certainly, but such a person can do a few things better than most others in the world.

Church planters need to avoid falling prey to these cultural patterns. Even though we have sufficient funds for an unscheduled trip home (and there's never been more money available for missions than today), we need to face the pain and loneliness and press on with the work. Planned endurance increases our likelihood of working with solid teams that will plant reproducing churches.

Event No. 10: Prayer

Prayer serves as the anchor event of the church-planting decathlon. It calls forth from God the grace, wisdom, and strength needed to compete successfully in the other events.

Minimum standard: Carve time out of your ministry schedule for personal and team prayer. Guard this time. Pray for your work, but also continue to pray for the rest of the world.

Common mistakes: When the battle heats up, we sometimes focus our blame on something other than the real source of our problems, such as our team, the agency, or the local, municipal, regional, provincial, or federal government. Remember whom Paul says we're really fighting against (Eph. 6:12) and pray accordingly.

Without becoming timid and mousy, we must avoid being either arrogant and cavalier toward evil, or naive and rationalistic. The balance can be difficult to find. Keep in mind the model of Jesus, whose attention was overwhelmingly directed toward the Father, with only occasional directives to demons.

Conclusion

This article is not a treatise on how one person can act as the whole Body of Christ. God has given us teams to work with so others might cover areas where we are weak, and our strengths can cover the weaknesses of others. Nor is it a call to focus on well-roundedness so that we do nothing really well. Unreached people groups will not become Christian through comfortable mediocrity. Excel in your strengths, but mind your potentially disqualifying areas. Meet these minimum standards so you can qualify for and stay with the team.

I invite you to do the following: Read this article with someone who knows you well. Ask that person to tell you which five events he or she believes to be your strongest, and which three have the potential to sink you. Ask the person how you might be further released in your areas of strength and how you might grow in your areas of weakness.

A final note: Rarely does disqualification last forever. After failing to make the 1992 Olympic team, Dan O'Brien went on to win his next eleven decathlons.

Why Do Some Churches Reproduce?

Robert Vajko

Research helps us understand fourteen things that reproducing churches do right.

It is amazing how learning and growth take place as we find ourselves in certain contexts. Our experience in a church-planting ministry in France for nearly thirty years taught us this lesson. In God's sovereignty, my wife and I were assigned by our mission to take responsibility for a church that had been planted by another missionary. Through that experience, God began to teach us what church multiplication really involves. So much seemed to happen spontaneously. I began to grasp in a new sense what missionary Roland Allen means when he states:

> This then is what I mean by spontaneous expansion. I mean the expansion which follows the unexhorted and unorganised activity of individual members of the Church explaining to others the Gospel which they have found for themselves; I mean the expansion which follows the irresistible attraction of the Christian Church for men who see its ordered life, and are drawn to it by desire to discover the secret of a life which they instinctively desire to share; I mean also the expansion of the Church by the addition of new churches. (Allen 1962, 7)

Why do some churches move toward multiplication while others never reproduce themselves in daughter churches? My answer to this question came out of quantitative and qualitative research during my doctoral study of reproducing churches. As I began to reflect on what had happened in our experience, I wanted to see what others had found out about church reproduction. I focused on denominations and churches in France that were effective in daughter-church planting: the Assemblies of God, the Brethren, one Baptist church, and the Alliance of Independent Churches (AEEI in French).

As I worked through what was to be a project for daughter churches, certain common qualities became evident. In all, I identified the following fourteen qualities of reproducing churches. I do not intend to suggest that all reproducing churches have or will have all of these fourteen features, but the more a church has of these qualities, the more likely it is to multiply itself.

1. A vision for reproduction. A reproducing church's goal is not just to see their own church grow, but to plant new congregations. Pastors of reproducing churches seem to look at their region and envision new churches being born all around. One French pastor, when asked about the principal elements that encouraged daughter-church planting, replied, "The desire to evangelize, a burden greater than just seeing our city reached." A missionary church planter I interviewed said that a "lack of vision" was the reason many churches were not planting new churches. The elder of one church responsible for planting six daughter churches and two granddaughter churches echoed the same words.

The question might be asked, "Is this vision something that some pastors have and others lack?" I believe I saw the answer to this question during a seminar in Switzerland where the vision for church multiplication was shared. One Swiss pastor who caught the vision was used by God to encourage the planting of five daughter churches. In a similar church-planting and multiplication seminar in Taiwan, a pastor from Taichung caught the vision and at the end of the seminar, committed himself and his church to plant a number of new churches in that city. They have planted one daughter church and are now desirous to plant another.

2. Willing to take risks to start new churches. Reproducing churches are willing to trust God to provide as people leave to start new ventures. One pastor interviewed seemed to rejoice in people leaving and beginning new works. He did not fear that his church would be weakened. His church planted six daughter churches.

The importance of taking risks was one of the lessons I had to learn. Although I longed to see our churches multiply, I found myself feeling fearful as the vision of church multiplication began to catch on. The people who were leaving to begin new church plants took their money and spiritual gifts with them. God had to teach me to take the risk and trust him to provide—which he did.

3. A spirit of self-giving that compels them to make great sacrifices. Non-reproducing churches in many cases seem to be so wrapped up in what they are doing in their church that they do not consider thinking about helping new churches begin in other regions. One pastor interviewed in my research stated that an "egocentric" attitude was an obstacle to daughter church planting.

Churches defined by a spirit of self-giving seek not to build empires within their own walls but to give up some members in order to start other churches. Reproducing churches do not have to be large. One pastor interviewed said that a church should not start a daughter church without a "critical mass." But he added that for him a "critical mass" was eighty to one hundred people. The spirit of self-giving in this church meant that it multiplied itself by giving of itself to start daughter churches.

4. Growing themselves. A growing church is not always willing to plant daughter churches, but my research showed that growing churches tended to reproduce more willingly than static churches. One striking example of a growing church multiplying itself was that of a church in the twentieth arrondissement of Paris which increased so vigorously that it ended up planting six daughter churches and two grand-daughter churches.

It needs to be said, however, that even a church not experiencing strong growth can plant a daughter church. There are examples of slowly growing or non-growing churches planting a church. My wife and I were involved in a church plant in Australia where a church experiencing difficulty in growing was willing to make the sacrifice to plant a daughter church. However, the principle is still generally true—the more a church experiences dynamic growth, the more it will be able to plant new churches.

5. Know how to plant daughter churches. Reproducing churches are ingenious at finding old and even new methods for starting new churches. For example, one church multiplied itself by finding halls in apartment complexes that could house new congregations.

6. Sensitive to the Spirit of God. Reproducing churches are sensitive to the Spirit of God moving them to the "spontaneous" expansion that Roland Allen describes. This might be called the Acts 13:2 characteristic—"While they were worshiping the Lord and fasting, the Holy Spirit said, 'Set apart for me Barnabas and Saul for the work to which I have called them.'" I remember

IN REPRODUCING CHURCHES, finances are not central to the planting of a daughter church. They do not say, "We cannot plant a daughter church because we do not have the funds."

vividly a dynamic convert that had a Spirit-given vision for reaching out and planting a new church in a needy area. The only explanation for his vision came from the working of the Spirit of God in his life. I believe that this supernatural element is not to be minimized lest we end up with "techniques" to plant daughter churches and forget the importance of clearly wedding the strategic and the supernatural.

7. Finances are not central. In reproducing churches, finances are not central to the planting of a daughter church. They do not say, "We cannot plant a daughter church because we do not have the funds." When conducting this research, it was fascinating to speak with a pastor in Grenoble, France, whose church had planted six daughter churches. I asked him how much money had been given to start those churches. "Nothing," he replied.

I have discovered that as soon as a group bases its church multiplication on how much money is available, they stop planting churches. This does not mean that in other church multiplication movements, finances were not given to the daughter churches, but this financial help was not central to the planting of new churches. In a recent book, Ralph Moore, founder of the Hope Chapel Movement, states that one of the main hindrances to church planting is "full-time remuneration for pastors" (Moore 2002, 102).

8. Care for the training of their own church planters. Rather than depending upon a more formal educational model, reproducing churches train their own church planters. Formal education may divorce the trainee from his church and its vision of multiplication. This was particularly evident among Pentecostal groups and Brethren assemblies. The Grenoble pastor mentioned above started his own Bible school within his church to train workers.

When leaders enroll in a formal educational institution, they tend to look at their education as an entrance into a more established church where they can be adequately cared for financially. Leaders trained within a church more often catch a vision that will make them willing to sacrifice in order to see a new church started. They understand the centrality of the local church and the joy of church planting. A missionary who planted a church in the southern suburbs of Paris was able to see two of the men he trained plant daughter churches because he trained them in the context of the local church rather than sending them off to seminary.

The authors of a guide to church multiplication discuss the question of bringing in pastors who had formal training: "They stopped their churches

REPRODUCING CHURCHES seem to have a **"Pauline vision"** for regions, rather than one town or city. Paul often spoke of regions when he talked about evangelism and planting churches.

from reproducing—every time. We had to fight the old battles all over again! We learned it the hard way: for church multiplication, train your pastors within the movement itself; do not import them" (Patterson and Scoggins 1993, 94). These authors do accept the possibility of using formal residential education with the caveat that such education incorporates "practical internships" (1993, 95).

9. Leadership base multiplied. Reproducing churches are characterized by what I call a "leadership overflow"—having too many leaders for one church. As I studied one large Brethren assembly in eastern France, I discovered that they planted new churches as they found their elders bumping into one another. When I speak with church leaders about starting new churches and they tell me they cannot do it because they do not have leaders to start new churches, I typically reply, "Then you need to develop and train more leaders than you need."

10. A Pauline vision. Reproducing churches seem to have a "Pauline vision" for regions, rather than one town or city. This is somewhat related to the first characteristic mentioned in this article, but it merits a separate mention. It is interesting to note that often Paul spoke of regions when he talked about evangelism and planting churches. This is where missiological research drives us back to scripture. Allen points out that Paul, in his evangelistic church-planting strategy, looked at provinces and areas rather than one individual church (Allen 1962). The reproducing church must have what might be called a "regional vision."

In a number of the interviews I conducted, the concern for a region and not just one church plant was manifested either in words or actions by leaders of reproducing churches and leaders of daughter churches.

11. Receptive areas sought. Reproducing churches are more effective in planting new churches when they put people into receptive areas rather than into more resistant areas. Of the six daughter churches planted by the church in Grenoble, one had a very difficult time because it was planted in a difficult area. A church planted in St. Quentin, France, was able to plant two daughter churches as it sought out receptive areas.

This receptivity may come about as a family or families in a given area form a core group to plant a new church. Their influence and ministry can be used by God to open hearts and doors. One church in the Paris suburbs had four families move to a rapidly-growing satellite city to plant a strategic new church.

12. Homogenous populations targeted. There has been a lot of debate over the homogeneous unit principle in church growth, but one thing is certain—church plants are at least initially more successful in homogenous settings. Once established, however, a greater heterogeneity can come about. A number of churches in the Paris area discovered this process as they multiplied churches among the French-speaking Antillian population.

13. Creativity is encouraged. Reproducing churches encourage creativity in the daughter churches that they plant. Most daughter churches copy much of what they have learned in their sponsoring church. This is not inherently problematic, but the new church does better when creativity is permitted and encouraged. Daughter churches multiply best when they are not harnessed with a burdensome yoke of duplication. This was evident in one church plant where the new pastor developed some very inventive ways of evangelism. He rented a roller skating rink for youth evangelism; sponsored a boat ride on the Seine River where people could invite their friends; and encouraged special events in his church to address pertinent needs in his area.

14. Clear principles. Reproducing churches have clear principles that they follow when planting new churches. These principles are not always expressed in explicit propositions but the vision of church reproduction is embedded in the very fiber of the church and its leaders. Reproducing churches have a built-in theology of multiplication.

Churches that are a part of a fellowship of churches tend to reproduce themselves more than independent churches. My study of reproducing churches showed that the most reproductive churches, not surprisingly, were a part of a movement that encouraged reproduction. In a book dealing with the growth of the church in the Philippines, the authors state:

> Horizontal mission structures—unless they, like the Bible Societies, remain strictly service oriented—find that their evangelistic and church-planting goals are reached better if they plant clusters of congregations which have close fellowship with each other, i.e., denominations. (Tuggy and Toliver 1972, 115)

David Garrison's book on church-planting movements shows that one of the keys to rapid reproduction is interchurch cooperation:

> In Church Planting Movements, both leadership development and every-member discipleship are built into the ongoing structures of church life—along with a passion for starting new churches... Rapid reproduction starts with the DNA of the first church. (Garrison 2004, 195)

Garrison posits that a church-planting movement "has its own internal momentum" (2004, 196). Dynamic growth occurs when a collection of churches share a common vision and momentum.

Conclusion

These fourteen discoveries could help churches avoid sterility and be the keys to effective church planting. It would be a mistake to assume that if these principles are followed in a rigid way, church multiplication will spontaneously occur. More research needs to be done to determine how these fourteen characteristics work out in other cultures and sub-cultures. I have a hunch, however, that further research will demonstrate that the more these principles are alive in a church, the more there will be the "spontaneous expansion" of churches for the glory of God.

References

Allen, Roland. 1962. *The Spontaneous Expansion of the Church.* Grand Rapids, Mich.: William B. Eerdmans Publishing Co.

Garrison, David. 2004. *Church Planting Movements.* Midlothian, Va.: WIGTake Resources.

Moore, Ralph. 2002. *Starting a New Church.* Ventura, Calif.: Regal.

Patterson, George and Richard Scoggins. 1993. *Church Multiplication Guide.* Pasadena, Calif.: William Carey Library.

Tuggy, A. L. and R. Toliver. 1972. *Seeing the Church in the Philippines.* Manila, Philippines: O.M.F. Publishers.

Vajko, Robert J. 1996. "Principles for the Design and Implementation of a Working Strategy for the Multiplication of the TEAM-related Churches in France by the Daughter Church Method." DMiss project, Trinity Evangelical Divinity School.

April 2009

Church Planting and Kingdom Building: Are They the Same?

Ken Baker

Church planting involves the structural growth of the Body of Christ; however, kingdom building expands the concept of Christ-like character built upon a biblical interrelating of the Body of Christ.

In the late 1980s our mission challenged us to partner with another couple to reach a resistant people group in northwest Cote d'Ivoire. Fresh from several doctoral courses on contextualization, I was inspired toward the nascent incarnational approach. In this solidly Islamic region, our approach was to live as much like the local population as possible, learn language and culture, then look and pray for a breakthrough.

One specific activity was to open a reading room near the local market in our small town. In true contextualizing practice, we styled this room, and our personal interactions, with a Muslim perspective in view—floor mats, discreet literature shelves, a prominent place for the scriptures, shoes off at the entrance, appropriate vocabulary, etc.

After quite some time there was virtually no response. We had made some friends; however, there was not the inquisitiveness we had experienced elsewhere in the country and region. Were we not sufficiently contextualized? What were we missing? Actually, the barrier was more basic.

There was a Christian church in the area (the only one for 150 miles in any direction) whose congregants consisted of transplanted believers from the animistic south. They were government employees posted in our region, and they had a poor reputation in the area, mainly due to shady business practices involving a couple members (as well as the traditional north/south rivalry).

Despite our low-key profile, there was no way as westerners we could avoid the Christian label. Even though we sought to promote a "teacher of faith" status, the people knew our reality. So, by default, we were linked to the local church. No matter the sincerity of our cause and approach, our ministry to the indigenous people was dead in the water.

Setting Out to Help Transform the Local Church

We soon realized that without transformation in the local church there would be no gospel breakthrough in that area. So we modified our approach. My wife and I began to focus increasingly on the church (there was no pastor, just transient lay leadership) with extensive teaching and discipleship.

Gradually, this church body, made up of seven different ethnic groups (with French as the common language), was transformed toward humility through a new understanding of grace. They evolved in faith and understood their calling to all peoples, specifically their Muslim neighbors. As their vision grew, so did a group of indigenous believers through the life testimony of the Christians from this church. By God's grace, this group maintains a faithful witness despite intense social and political upheaval in recent years.

As a result of this experience, I began to learn three fundamental, and complementary, lessons about church planting.

1. Every church-planting context is unique. While there is a range of similarities from one area to another, each setting is unlike any other, even from village to village in a specific region and/or people group. The particular mix of people (indigenous or expatriate), and their personal experiences and exposures, have a unique role in the way in which the gospel message is received and spread.

2. Assumptions cannot guide the process. Going back to the story above, on the "broad strokes" level, we assumed we knew why we were there, how we should proceed, and what the result would be. In my experience, the presumptions church planters bring in the areas of motivation, process, and outcome directly impact the flow of ministry efforts—positively or negatively.

3. The process of planting a church, or even launching a church-planting movement, is not the same as kingdom building or "building God's household." I can already sense the reaction to such a claim as mere semantics; however, I seek to make a point about the difference between kingdom structure and character. When a family moves from one place to another, the preliminary ritual prior to the move itself involves "house hunting" in the new area. The intent is to find a dwelling, a structure, which will serve as family lodging.

Conceptually, this family is not looking for a "home," just a house. However, they intend for it to become a "home." This is the difference between structure and character. A house has the potential to become a home, but this process involves time, relationship, intimacy, and character. Similarly, unless church planting endeavors to understand the less tangible concept of character, it is just structure—a frame—not God's intended kingdom expression.

People Groups, Mission, and Kingdom Building

Let me paint a different picture of mission and kingdom building. Planting a church is not a "straight line" endeavor; instead, it is a winding path which can double back without warning, promising an array of surprises along the way. Whenever we presume to have the formula, we tend to take less time weighing the decisions we make along the way. As I noted above, assumptions about the mission process play a significant role in shaping outcomes.

One such area involves methodology. Increasingly over the last thirty years, the focus on people groups, and the desire to see church movements develop among those who are unreached, has been the holy grail of church-planting endeavors. This people group focus grew out of a reaction to the general mission practice in preceding generations where geo-political boundaries were the standard for grouping churches into associations or denominations. One of the watershed moments was an address at the 1974 Lausanne Congress by Ralph Winter, entitled "The Highest Priority: Cross-cultural Evangelism," which popularized the "hidden" people focus.

In tandem with the emphasis on people groups, there arose an innovative theory—the homogenous unit principle—which proposed that church growth is based on people who are alike gathering together. In other words, "birds of a feather flock together." This is the principle of "attraction"—when given the freedom to choose, people will congregate with those most like themselves (Winter 1998, 406).

This theory spawned the "target audience" approach, which has dominated evangelistic ministry since the 1980s. Domestically, it is expressed through the marketing strategy of identifying a "demographic slice" of society (seekers, post-

NOT ONLY ARE THEORIES often unreliable, but they can actually be misleading when they reach the status of assumption.

moderns, ethnic groups, etc.), then tailor-shaping a ministry program or church so as to "attract" this group. Abroad, attraction theory has been expressed through identifying and targeting individual people groups. In church-planting practice, this has meant concentrating exclusively on one people group in order to maximize gospel impact. This ministry methodology works to a degree, but is this kingdom building?

Throughout my church-planting career, I have seen missiological theories play out in real-world contexts, either by participation or by observation. Yet, rarely, if ever, do outcomes follow an expected script. Not only are theories often unreliable, but they can actually be misleading when they reach the status of assumption.

Looking Deeper at the Unreached People Group Movement

Looking back on nearly twenty-five years of church-planting experience in five distinct areas (in three different countries, urban and rural, animistic and Islamic), I have noted certain overreaching assumptions, particularly in the unreached people group movement (UPGM). This is not to imply that I have a comprehensive perspective on church-planting methodology, but neither did the founders (and successors) of the UPGM approach.

At least from a Western perspective, the UPGM has become the standard by which evangelistic mission effort is planned and measured. It may even be said that the UPGM has become an industry, spawning an array of spin-off initiatives like "mapping" and "adoption." In this sense, the UPGM has become an institution, representing a perspective which most assume is infallible.

Clearly, we owe a great debt to those who raised our attention to the reality of distinct peoples and the need to contextualize the gospel within these cultural traditions. At the time, mission endeavor focused on the generic "lost" and cultural sensitivity was often lacking. The UPGM founders were responding to the status quo in a necessary and timely manner.

Recently, while teaching pioneer church planting as a part of the Perspectives course, I mentioned the limitations of the UPGM to the incredulous surprise of the gathered students. Many had been thoroughly steeped in this approach to the point that they were quite knowledgeable of the UPGM lingo and methodology. More importantly, they assumed that a distinct people group focus was the *de facto* approach to church planting.

In order to stave off misinterpretation, I will reiterate that my concerns do not lay with the practice of contextualized church-planting methodology, which is clearly necessary and which I have employed.

Instead, my unease centers on the pervasive institutional assumption that

WHEN THE RELATIONAL component is missing, those trained in a UPGM perspective, with freshly-minted masters degrees in intercultural studies, often arrive on the field with a fairly well-shaped idea of how their ministry should unfold.

exclusive focus upon a people group is the way to proceed in church planting. This perspective has engendered a generation of mission activity which has embraced the theory and launched toward new horizons. There have been many laudable results, but unexpected ones as well.

UPGM champions would likely agree with the import of the above lessons; however, the pervasive wingspan of UPGM teaching communicates simplistic, universal impressions of the church-planting process. Likewise, the UPGM philosophy tends to emphasize the structural aspect of God's kingdom—that is, the multiplication of church-planting movements made up of the various parts of the kingdom.[1] However, there is usually little attention toward interrelationship and collective character.

When the relational component is missing, those trained in a UPGM perspective, with freshly-minted masters degrees in intercultural studies, often arrive on the field with a fairly well-shaped idea of how their ministry should unfold. One such couple exuded competence and confidence. Being exceptionally gifted in language ability, they made rapid progress in cultural acquisition among the Woda'abe (nomadic) Fulani of eastern Niger. They were thoroughly focused on this unreached people group, a small minority population in the area.

Believing they were called solely to the Woda'abe, they would not associate with those from any other group, and they would not fellowship with believers from other ethnicities. Some would commend these choices as appropriate targeting discipline; however, the UPGM approach can have collateral consequences—the most serious of which is ethnocentrism, a natural human tendency which the gospel seeks to correct.

In their daily life this missionary couple was widely misunderstood by the population at large (which was ninety-nine percent Islamic and multiethnic). Likewise, the local believers (often Muslim Background Believers) were dismayed at their rejection. Granted, this young couple made significant relationships among the Woda'abe community; however, in the process they alienated themselves from the wider community and the local believers, in particular.

Their response was essentially, "So what? We have been called to the Woda'abe." As I counseled them I sought to paint a picture of the eventual consequences of their choices—particularly with regard to the example they were setting. Should the Spirit of God bring about a movement among the Woda'abe, these new believers would follow the relationship pattern modeled by this couple—they would ignore other believers and stick to themselves.

Tragically, after twenty months, this missionary couple burned out and never returned to their ministry.

Learning Lessons about Church Planting and Kingdom Building

The above story points to two more lessons about pioneer church planting and kingdom building:

1. Best intentions do not always communicate what we intend (and sometimes the opposite). Ethnic co-identification and exclusivity are hallmarks of the UPGM approach, and we may think they display undivided consideration. Such attention naturally communicates this sentiment in an ethnically homogenous environment; however, in a mixed region, exclusivity can lead to uncertain results. Perceiving eventual impact leads to the second church-planting lesson.

2. Long-term vision must dictate short-term ministry choices. That which will grow a church the fastest may not provide the best foundation for a mature church in the next generation. Furthermore, UPGM theory, which necessitates a distinct church movement within a people group, pushes this sort of exclusivity—seemingly without taking into account that this may not be the type of church movement which the Spirit of God desires. In other words, this may or may not be the way the Lord wants it to unfold in a particular place. Again, I emphasize that context makes all the difference, and every context is unique.

The foundational theological structure of the UPGM teaches that "biblical unity" means a healthy diversity within the universal worldwide Church, which leads to the conclusion of a church for "every unchurched segment of mankind" (McGavran 1998, 308). A complementary teaching instills the importance of authentic cultural self-expression in church experience; that is, "Christian liberty" means that each people group should be free to pursue self-expression in worship.

These biblical conclusions join with the sociological observation mentioned above of "attraction." As Donald McGavran further explains, "It takes no great acumen to see that when marked differences of color, stature, income, cleanliness, and education are present, men understand the gospel better when expounded by their own kind of people" (1980, 227).

In other words, more people will follow Christ more quickly if they can join their own kind of people. This latter principle points to an abiding limitation of the UPGM, namely, the thread of expediency which accompanies the approach. In discussing the theological rationale of developing ethnically distinct congregations, Ralph Winter writes,

> In my opinion, this question about evangelistic strategy in the forming of separate congregations must be considered an area of Christian liberty, and is to be decided purely on the basis of whether or not it allows the gospel to be presented effectively to more people—that is, *whether it is evangelistically strategic.* (1998, 406; emphasis mine)

In other words, evangelistic expediency is one of the main criteria for decisions in pioneer church planting. Therefore, the progression of conclusions flow as such: since God intends that all cultures have unique worship self-expression, and people who are alike naturally flock together, then ethnically exclusive evangelistic efforts are the most strategic means toward a church movement. This stream of interpretation forms the basis of the UPGM approach, but it is also "strategy by assumption."

Visible Unity in the Church

Although these biblical and practical conclusions have been challenged from the beginning of the UPGM, this counter-balancing voice of character and relationship has not received equal time. Throughout the last thirty years there has been an abiding question as to "whether the best way to express the diversity of human cultures is to encourage a diversity of homogenous unit churches" (Lausanne Occasional Paper 1 1978).

However, in the popular stream of pioneer church-planting education, this caution is largely non-existent. Instead, the UPGM has promoted the singular theory of ethnically-specific church planting as the way to proceed. Note one of the central passages of Lausanne Occasional Paper 1, which was the product of The Pasadena Consultation on the homogenous unit principle:

> All of us are agreed that in many situations a homogenous unit (HU) church can be a legitimate and authentic church. Yet we are also agreed that it can never be

complete in itself. Indeed, if it remains in isolation, it cannot reflect the universality and diversity of the Body of Christ. Nor can it grow into maturity. Therefore, every HU church must take active steps to broaden its fellowship in order to demonstrate visibly the unity and the variety of Christ's Church. This will mean forging with other and different churches creative relationships which expresses the reality of Christian love, brotherhood, and interdependence. (1978)

As the above comments reveal, the development of a homogenous unit church movement is incomplete without engagement with the wider universal Church. Indeed, without an opportunity for interdependent diversity, its Christ-like character remains stunted because it is, intentionally, ethnocentric. Such concerns reflect the import of John 13:34-35: "A new command I give you: Love one another. As I have loved you, so you must love one another. By this all men will know that you are my disciples, if you love one another." This is "attraction" of a different sort, for it refers to what makes believers attractive. Note also what Jesus prayed prior to his crucifixion:

> I pray also for those who will believe…that all of them may be one, Father…so that the world may believe that you have sent me…May they be brought to complete unity *to let the world know* that you sent me and have loved them even as you have loved me. (John 17:20-23; emphasis mine)

These verses present much more than a theological oneness in the person of Christ; they tell of a visible unity. Believers loving one another intra-ethnically is noteworthy; however, when believers are in loving relationship with each other inter-ethnically, this is an exceptional testimony before the watching world. It is the visible witness our Lord desires. The world sees the transforming power of the gospel when those who are not naturally together are together in Christ. This demonstrates a kingdom character, where interrelationship witnesses to the presence of Christ. The church at Antioch exuded this sort of character—and it is there that they were first known as "Christians."

Modeling a Unified Church

Therefore, it is imperative that this form of unity be modeled, where contextually possible, and taught, even where it is not readily visible. From day one, discipleship teaching must demonstrate cross-cultural unity as normative in the Body of Christ. Such issues go beyond that which is "evangelistically strategic" to that which is "kingdom strategic."

Focusing on relationship and character right from the outset demonstrates a sense of long-term vision and impact. The lessons I learned in my first twelve years of church planting I sought to apply in the next twelve when my family moved to new contexts. In due course, I assumed responsibility for Serving In Mission (SIM) church planting in the east of Niger, and I encouraged two defining parameters for this region.

1. All missionaries were to be community-based, that is, involved with all peoples who inhabited a region (this is partially because only isolated villages were homogenous).

2. All church planting was to be church-based, that is, in partnership with the established national Church. (In this way, relational interdependence and kingdom character were a part of the discipleship process right from the start.)

Since the region was politically and religiously tense, there were no guarantees that expatriates would be able to remain alongside those in the national Church. This task was theirs first, then ours, as partners and co-laborers. In the process, it allowed us to model unity from the outset since ethnicities were thoroughly mixed in the area.

Conclusion

In my current role as an intercultural ministry coach, I visit churches and interact with pastors and lay people interested and passionate about mission. Often, I am thrust into a quandary as they share about "adopting" and "targeting" people groups, especially in the 10/40 Window. I am thrilled they are looking to the horizons in such ways; however, I am troubled by the spirit of vision management and efficiency. Usually these folks are up-to-date on the latest statistics.

Yet do they realize these people are real individuals, not just flip card profiles? I even wonder about the accuracy of the figures. If the stats I have seen about the peoples I know personally are not correct, then is this true of other areas?

Furthermore, in the realm of pioneer church-planting education, especially in lay forums, the UPGM approach is thoroughly dominant. All mission awareness programs (Perspectives, Global Focus, Global Outreach, DYI, etc.) promote the UPGM approach unquestionably. Likewise, the institutional nature of the movement reinforces this position.

Unfortunately, many of the initiated are "theoretically conversant," but not "reality tested," in the arena of pioneer church planting. Such wide propagation of UPGM teaching by those who have not had any experience in pioneer church planting is disconcerting. Occasional short terms and academic courses do not replace the reality of cross-cultural life and ministry. Yet their influence significantly impacts the mission planning, strategy, and policy decisions of countless churches.

Yes, the missiological changes which the UPGM brought were quite necessary. Contextualized attention toward hidden people groups was long overdue. It was time to challenge the status quo. However, in my opinion, the pendulum has swung past the balance point and the UPGM has become the new status quo. Through this article I have attempted to reveal some shaky assertions of the movement's philosophy. Likewise, my anecdotes are not designed to criticize as much as to point out the consequences of presumption.

There are church movements around the world which have evolved differently, many of which are a testimony to unity in diversity. UPGM promoters could introduce a greater balance of approach considering historical evidence of the movement of God's Spirit in a variety of methods. Global church planting involves the structural growth of the Body of Christ throughout the world;

however, kingdom building expands the concept of Christ-like character built upon a biblical interrelationship of the Body of Christ.

Endnote

1. The issue of denominations is an entirely different, but related, topic.

References

Lausanne Occasional Paper 1: "The Pasadena Consultation: The Homogenous Unit Principle."1978. Accessed November 19, 2008 from www.lausanne.org/pasadena-1977/lop1.html.

McGavran, Donald. 1980. *Understanding Church Growth.* Pasadena, Calif.: William Carey Library.

_____. 1998. "A Church in Every People: Plain Talk about a Difficult Subject." *Perspectives on the World Christian Movement.* Ed. Ralph Winter, 398-401. Pasadena, Calif.: William Carey Library.

Winter, Ralph. 1998. "The New Macedonia: A Revolutionary New Era in Mission Begins." *Perspectives on the World Christian Movement.* Ed. Ralph Winter, 404-407. Pasadena, Calif.: William Carey Library.

January 1986

It Takes Team Effort to Root Churches in Hard Soil

Johan Lukasse

Practical suggestions for teams working in difficult areas.

This way of church planting has stolen my heart. We began working with our first church-planting training team in 1972. In one year, a church was started. A second, smaller team followed up that effort and in two years there were fifty adults attending with three elders and two deacons. That church produced a second congregation two years later, a third one four years later, and still another church some time after that.

We have used this team-year approach because we have found it to be biblical, practical, and effective. Although we have made mistakes and the Lord still has much to teach us, we have been able to start fifteen churches in eight years.

In church planting, we need to consider not only the approach used, but also the steps involved, potential obstacles, and the ultimate goal.

A church-planting team is usually made up of career missionaries or short-term workers helping a missionary church planter for one or two years. In some cases, the team is a mix of career missionary couples who are nationals. Sometimes, the team lives as a community. At other times, families are spread over a specific area of a town and operate from a central place, such as an existing church building.

We use teams of young people (20 years of age and up) under the leadership of an experienced church-planting missionary. They are recruited through Christian magazines, conferences, Bible schools, and seminaries to give a year to this program.

A team is a combination of people with training (such as Bible school students) and those without. Members also vary in age, background, interests, education, and spiritual gifts. Together, team members take part in an initial two or three-week training period. Afterwards, they move into the target area where a house is rented. There, they live in a community lifestyle under the direction of a missionary couple. (It is very important that moral standards be high, so in some instances two houses might be rented—one for men and one for women.)

Once in the community, the church-planting team goes into action. First, *each team member joins at least one or two social or cultural groups*. As a result, they will be able easily to contact and penetrate that part of the population. This is a natural way of getting close to all levels of society and opens tremendous doors.

Second, *members begin to follow a program of different evangelistic approaches.* During this time, they build relationships and get to know people. Some also do additional research into the local situation to complement the initial work done prior to the selection of the target area. Then, each young person decides how he or she can best communicate the gospel to that particular segment of society in which they are working.

The results? There are as many different ways of sharing the gospel as there are team members. Some immediately begin inviting people to meetings, or start Bible studies and Sunday services. Others prefer to work through home Bible studies in different areas, at different levels, and bring the results together at a later stage. Still others adopt the cultural bridge-building method of communicating the gospel.

While the young people do outreach, they also get training in subjects such as church planting, church growth principles, and effective witness. Heavy emphasis is placed on evaluation and a lot of the learning is by doing.

Why do we do church planting this way? In the past, we had seen some team efforts that were just too swift—they passed through villages and towns and left again without consolidating the fruits they were given. So those of us at the Belgian Evangelical Mission spent much time in prayer and in studying the New Testament. As a result, we believe that the Lord has shown us this way of working.

Biblical Principles

Our first biblical principle is drawn from Matthew 18:20: "For where two or three are gathered together in my name, there am I in the midst of them." The key question here is: *how can Jesus Christ be in the midst of us?* He must be more than just living in our hearts—he must be detectable. He must be revealed as we are gathered together in his name.

Look at Jesus during his public ministry. He chose twelve disciples and lived with them day and night. He walked and talked and shared his life with them in all circumstances. And all the way through, he revealed his Father, for that was one of the main reasons he came to earth (John 1).

When Jesus left his disciples, he told them that they should love one another as he had loved them and that "by this shall all men know that ye are my disciples, if ye have love for one another." We must communicate this agape quality of love as he did. If we act in love, the world will sit up and take notice that we are disciples of Jesus Christ.

The second biblical principle is unity. In John 17:20-24, we read, "...that the world might believe that thou hast sent me." The world will believe that, if we are one just as Jesus Christ and the Father are one. As Jesus revealed his Father, so we should reveal Christ by the very way we act and interact with one another.

We also find this principle of love and unity in practice in Philippians 2:1-4 and 1:27. In Acts 4:13 we see that the disciples were recognized as those who "have been with Jesus." This demonstration of love and unity is only possible in a group. Christ can be in our midst if there are two or three or more of us. That is how he wants to reveal himself to this world, not just by our words, but by the very life he lives through us.

An example of this approach is Paul and his colleagues. Nowhere in the New Testament was he alone; Paul was always teamed up with other people like Silas, Timothy and Luke. In Acts 20:4-5, we find names of at least eight people who were traveling with him as a team. The only place where Paul was alone was in Athens and the Bible does not record a church there. The great church planter was part of a team.

Practical and Effective

Not only do we believe this particular team approach to be biblical, we have found it to be both practical and effective. The team sets an example. It is already a group of people who are more or less a church. When local people come to know Christ, they join this existing body, which is much easier than being the first converts in the area.

The new members follow the example of the team. They sing as the team sings and they read the Bible because they see the team members reading the Bible. They confess their sins because they hear other team members doing the same. And they reach out to their family because they see the team members reaching out to people and telling them about Jesus. To them, this is normal Christian life.

But this method is still only as strong as the team itself. The principle of the team multiplying itself always applies. It is at the same time the strongest and weakest point of this method.

One team, for example, quarreled endlessly about details. Some would say, "We must pray before we go out to do door-to-door work," and others would say, "No, we can pray when we come back because now is the right time to go door to door." Today in that place there is a tiny church, and do you know what they do all the time? They quarrel.

A strong team, however, means a strong beginning for the new church. A man used to come into one of our team houses just to find out if we were genuine. He visited morning, afternoon, and night for up to ten minutes at a time. One night, a team leader announced the start of the prayer meeting. This man was about to leave when another team member insisted, "No, you had better stay and see this because we walk in the light. You are welcome to stay."

When the prayer meeting was over, the man asked, "Some of you are praying for a 'contact.' What is a contact?" The leader replied, "A contact is someone who has been listening to the gospel. Maybe he has understood it, or maybe he has only partly understood it, but he has not given his life to the Lord Jesus Christ yet. Someone like that we call a contact." This man came to know the Lord a couple of weeks later. And when he came to the prayer meeting, the very first thing he prayed was, "Lord, give me a contact."

This man and other new believers join the first nucleus—the team brought in from outside the local area. After the year is up (or longer if necessary), the first nucleus of Christians leaves. Then, the local people who have come to know the Lord stay and continue under the church planter's leadership. From that moment on, they become a team.

A tremendous by-product of this particular team approach is that the young people receive valuable, practical training. Working on such a team also serves as a screening process. Some young people join the church-planting effort believing they are called to be missionaries. In the team, they are sorted out by the Lord and the other team members; they return home having seen they weren't called to the mission field and instead become active in local churches. On the other hand, the Lord very often uses this team approach to call people to further training or to the mission field.

Experience has shown that team efforts by career missionaries only have not been as successful as those by young people. One reason for this is the risk of the foreign image. As a result, some missions work with mixed teams—nationals and missionaries together. This combination makes it easier to produce local leadership.

How We Go about It

Like other approaches to church planting, the essence of this method is contacting people and challenging them with the gospel. But you not only want to bring them to Christ, but to gather them together out of the world so that they become the *ecclesia*. How do we go about this?

1. Look for people who are open. Rather than starting with the vision of converting the whole town, it is better to find people who are open and receptive. Lead them to Christ, train them, and gather them together. They will, when the Lord by his grace gives a local church, be the people who will present Christ to the difficult cases with whom the team might lose precious time.

For example, in one of our church-planting situations, there was a man who kept us occupied for hours with questions about evolution. Finally, we decided to stop discussing it with him. He was angry about it, but we were firm, so we lost contact with him. Four years later, when a local church was established there, some of the members came into contact with him again and reopened the discussion. He came to know the Lord after a long time, when the church was there and had time to do the work.

2. Form a nucleus. Paul not only brought people to Christ, he brought them together to learn principles of Christian living and what it means to be part of Christ's Church. Paul made not just converts, but disciples.

We have to demonstrate the new society in the midst of the old society. They have to taste the new wine and to demonstrate Christ's power and love to the world. Forming a nucleus is teaching people to live the Christian life. We do this by our own example, our blessings, our failures, and our victories.

3. Train them. Training is preparing a soldier for the battle. It is learning by exercising and repetition. It is following courses and putting them into practice.

Training also involves learning how to defend one's faith. In continental Europe, apologetics plays an important part in the training of new converts. These new Christians frequently have their faith attacked by family and relatives. If they want to win their loved ones to Christ, they will have to answer some tough questions.

4. Make the discipling process continuing. We must make disciples who soon learn for themselves how to make disciples. I had the privilege of starting a church through a home Bible study. I led this in the home of one of the Christians, teaching the word of God with enthusiasm, and calling them to recognize the authority of the word and to obey it. These members began bringing other people. After six months we had these new people raising the same questions as the first ones had done before.

In one instance, when a question came up, the Lord led me to ask those who had been with us longer: "Who knows the answer?" One or two started to answer, but I said, "Stop, don't answer now. I will finish by ten o'clock and then you can answer. Is that all right?" All agreed.

We had several questions like that in one evening. Then, when the Bible study stopped, I reminded them that several had to answer questions. And so the real thing only started when they began teaching one another. Disciples making disciples while I was disciple-making.

5. Making the disciples co-workers. The next step is to bring the disciples alongside the church planter. The Christians in Thessalonica not only became imitators of Paul and the Lord Jesus Christ, they became examples.

6. Make them leaders. This means stepping aside and giving them responsibility and authority. Occasionally, you have to come back to give them additional training or to help them with problems. But you must "throw them into the water," so they will have to exercise their gifts and training. Often, they will do much better than we ourselves have done.

Potential Pitfalls

Yet in any church-planting situation, there are potential pitfalls. Below are some of the most common ones.

1. A bad example. The poor example of a team reproduces itself in a poor church. Yet the same could happen if there was only one missionary couple whose family life was not as it should be. We can be examples in the way we act, teach, and expect new converts to react. We will always reap what we have sown.

2. False starts. Let me give you three examples of false starts in church planting that I have seen during the last ten years. In the first situation, there was an overemphasis on youth. The church ended up with lots of young people and no couples. If this is your emphasis, you could find yourself with a great number of young people who have no one to go to but you, the church planter. You will be overwhelmed by problems and questions. This church struggled for years until some of the young people married. Slowly, the church stabilized and the problems were solved.

In the second instance, a church attracted difficult social problem cases right from the start. We preach a gospel of love. People who are living on the margin of life realize that they are fully accepted in our circles and are attracted to us. But if a team starts with several of these kinds of people, it will carry that image. Other people hesitate to join this group.

It is much better to start with "normal" people and take care of the social cases later. Of course, the church has a responsibility toward the people who live on society's edge, but you must have a church before you can take care of them.

A third false start I have seen is when a church-planting effort collects "religion runners." In one town, several people joined the Jehovah's Witnesses when they began a group, but after a while these people left. When the Mormons came, the "religion runners" joined them, too, but also left the group after a while. Then we came along, and there they were. So then the whole population already "knew" we were another sect. One of the best ways to forestall this problem is to begin with a home Bible study rather than immediately starting with Sunday services.

3. The foreign image. This is often a problem for North Americans who are planting churches in continental Europe. Cultural sensitivity is very important.

4. False emphasis. By this I mean giving our doctrinal hobby horses too free a rein. I have seen men trying to start a church and on whatever subject they preached, they always ended with the return of Jesus Christ. It was the only thing in their Bible.

5. Weak continuation. Many evangelists and church planters know how to preach the gospel, but little more than that. The result is that this nucleus of new believers will remain very weak, since the church planter is an evangelist and not a teacher.

In one area, some of the local people confronted the church planter after two years. They told him, "It is better for you to leave because we have already heard whatever you have to tell us." We must be able to teach them the full counsel of God. If we are not able to do so, then we have to find people to help us.

6. Weak training. One great weakness is in training local leaders. Elders are of vital importance in church planting because they represent biblical authority, local insight, and knowledge. They are the people we must train and equip, continuing to do so even after the church planter has been gone for a long time.

7. Late appointment of local leaders. There must be a fine balance between how long to stay and when to leave. If the church planter leaves too soon, he leaves behind a weak baby who will struggle for a long time before starting to grow. But if the church planter stays too long and does not appoint local leaders quickly enough, he might become an obstacle himself. "Get out of the way!" is an important step in missionary work.

8. Lack of discipline. Especially at first, we tend to be slow in disciplining people. Why? Because the group is small and if we discipline one or two, we might have a few less. As a result, others might also leave. So what we are actually doing is placing quantity above quality.

This approach is totally wrong, because we then lose respect and the image of Christ in the area suffers. This will be terribly hard to overcome at a later stage. Rather, it is much better to follow the Lord Jesus who said to his disciples, "You do not want to leave too, do you?" and to receive Simon Peter's reply: "Lord, to whom shall I go? Thou hast the words of eternal life."

What Is Our Goal?

Even if we manage to follow these steps precisely, and avoid the most precarious obstacles, we are still faced with this question: *what kind of church do we want this particular group to be in fifteen or twenty years?*

Our goal and vision should be not only to start a church that reaches its own area and has a worldwide vision. We need to plant churches that will become the image of Christ. These churches will adore our great God, become the presence of the Kingdom of God, and demonstrate the quality of life that reveals God's purpose for his creation.

This is the highest goal. If we are going to reach a target, let's aim high. Let us pray that God will multiply this vision for planting churches that express Christ's likeness.

Issues for Women in Church Planting

Linda Wilson

Women continue to be the backbone of missionary endeavors.
Here are eight issues many of these women face.

You've been in church planting for twenty-one years and you're still alive (and smiling) to talk about it?" I chuckled inside. This is one informed mission's chairman, I thought. I not only survived, I'm living my missionary dream come true.

Even though we are not experts, my husband and I recently became church-planting coaches for about twenty-three missionary units. I am thrilled to be able to visit different fields and interact with women in ministry.

With higher missionary attrition, mission boards are realizing the importance of caring for their missionaries, including the women. In one study, inadequate pastoral care and supervision were responsible for eighty percent of all attrition (Taylor 1997). That's preventable.

Although we have much accountability in our mission, never has a female mission representative with church-planting experience visited us for our yearly debriefing. This is a need, especially considering women make up fifty-one percent of our missionary family, and approximately two-thirds of the global missionary force (Kraft and Crossman 1999). Our mission is striving to equip the equippers, both male and female.

We visit and debrief with church planters on site. Fields request workshop topics for missionary and national church planters. I compiled a list of major concerns women (and some men) have, and use it as a springboard for conversation. These issues can be discussed on a one-to-one basis or used as an interactive workshop when debriefing with missionaries.

1. Building Evangelistic Contacts

Women are the largest unreached people group in the world (Zoba 2000). Women have creatively built bridges through language exchange, crafts, homework clubs, children's clubs, community groups, exercise, visitations, drama, music, cooking, and Bible study. While some women have numerous ministries, others are still searching for ways to contribute. Talking about their gifts, life stage, and context stimulates fresh ideas.

As a young missionary mother, I combined my language-learning journey with my gifts. Initially, I used hospitality and invited my children's teachers over for dinner every year. Some long-lasting friendships developed. Still focusing on my children's school as my area of influence, I volunteered for class field trips and joined the parents' committee. As fluency developed, I was asked to substitute teach. Later, I was invited to join the committee that represented parents' educational concerns to the Ministry of Education.

When my daughter came home crying one day because her teacher taught that Protestants were a cult, I was in a position to propose changes to the mandated curriculum. When I brought it before the committee, the government official promised he would look into it. One year later, I received a letter stating that the course content had been changed. Many children, parents, teachers, and even bureaucrats were exposed to the gospel through the years.

2. Adjusting Identity and Roles

Connections and relationships are vital for women. Until we are comfortable with the language and customs of our new culture, the inability to communicate affects our sense of belonging. Acculturation can have disturbing effects on our sense of self and requires identity and role adjustments.

Many women who had careers in the U.S. are suddenly identified in relation to a family member. I became Gene's wife, Michelle's mom, or the pastor's wife. In Haiti, you are called "Madame Tom" or "Madame Pasteur" (Mrs. Pastor) instead of being called by your own name. One resentful newcomer to the Philippines wrote: "I'm not just Richard's wife and Jay's mom. I want them to know ME! I had my own identity and business before!" Additionally, some wives of field leaders feel this role sets them apart from their colleagues. Women wonder, "Am I a missionary or a missionary's wife? Where do I fit in? What good am I here?"

Single women struggle with identity/role issues as well. In many countries, singleness is not valued as much as marriage and motherhood. In some cultures, it's desirable to have a baby, even if it's out of wedlock. And a married but barren woman is not as esteemed as a single mother. With all of these adjustments, it's important to root our identity in Christ.

3. Dealing with Loneliness and/or Discouragement

Loneliness is especially acute in the beginning of a woman's missionary career. All our supports are stripped away, and we learn the painful but necessary lessons of trusting God alone. A young woman commented, "I think God cares more about working on me than he does saving the lost!" Sometimes, husbands don't realize how difficult loneliness is for their wives. Many women explain that because men are more task-oriented, they are at a loss as to how to help their wives cope with relational losses.

Journaling can be therapeutic and a vital means of support and growth. Journal writing can take on another twist as husbands and wives journal individually, then share their entries.

Church planters face discouragement when they don't see enough fruit for their labor. Much time is invested in someone, and then he or she moves away. We must believe we are not only building a local church, but also contributing to God's universal Church.

4. Counseling Believers

Many people need professional help, but for various reasons, they turn to the missionary for "free" help. The needs are so overwhelming that we could be full-time counselors. But not all of us have the appropriate training or emotional stamina. Ongoing training and resources are necessary. After a serious bout with burnout, I learned to limit whom I invest in and also the importance of caring for myself.

5. Training Leaders in the Church

Lack of trained leaders is a problem in U.S. churches, and is even more so in Third World countries because of poverty and illiteracy. Many nationals quit school because they have to work. Resources are few and expensive. National leaders are gifted and passionate about ministry, but have limited time to be trained or to train others. It may be inappropriate for men to train women; thus female trainers are needed.

Ingenious missionary women in Mexico teamed up with a national couple to reach and train children and women. The workers met weekly for prayer, Bible study, and planning. They started a kids' club where children and their mothers listened to Bible stories using a flannel graph. Then while the kids did crafts, memory verses and ate, the national worker led a Bible study for the mothers. The kids' club has added workers and sponsored several community outreach events.

6. Raising Children Cross-culturally

As parents, we learn about our host culture with our children. In fact, sometimes they teach us more than we teach them. Missionary children have been termed "third culture kids" (Blomberg and Brooks 2001; Pollock and Van Reken 1999) because they integrate the elements of both cultures into a third culture. When I asked my daughter which culture she identified with, she replied, "Neither. I'm a chameleon! I know how to be like either of the cultures depending upon whom I'm with."

Parents have major concerns with their children's education and spiritual training. We want to teach our children how to live in any culture without compromising their biblical values. But in church planting, how do you accommodate Sunday school classes for the few children of varied ages when there's also a lack of trained teachers? We had to find appropriate resources to enrich their instruction at home. We also joined with another family to carpool across town so our teenagers could attend a quality youth group in their language.

7. Coping with Financial Disparity and Expectations of Nationals

In many countries, the average person earns a few dollars a day; therefore, people are looking for ways to earn money. Missionaries admit it's hard to know how to help or how much to give. There's also a tension between the desire to meet needs and the fear of creating dependency. We met nationals who became believers because missionaries hired them for services such as painting, cleaning, and lawn care and developed relationships with them. Other missionaries bought shoes and books for local children so they could attend school. A solution some church planters shared was to budget a monthly amount toward the needs.

8. Developing Boundaries

Well-defined lines between home and "work" do not exist in church planting unless they are carved out, which is not easy. We tend to take on too many responsibilities and work long, irregular hours. Learning to establish clear, healthy boundaries is essential to a balanced lifestyle. For us, that meant getting the church office and phone out of our home. In addition, we focused on leadership development.

Certainly other issues such as female leadership roles, hospitality demands, marital stress, team building, and health concerns can be discussed. Women continue to be the backbone of missionary endeavors. God cares about these servants. We need to provide them with resources, ongoing training, encouragement, appreciation, and prayer.

References

Blomberg, Janet and David F. Brooks, eds. 2001. *Fitted Pieces: A Guide for Parents Educating Children Overseas.* St. Clair Shores, Mich.: Share Education Services.

Kraft, Marguerite and Meg Crossman. 1999. "Women in Mission." *Mission Frontiers.* August, 13-17.

Pollock, David and Ruth Van Reken. 1999. *The Third Culture Kid Experience.* Yarmouth, Maine: Intercultural Press, Inc.

Taylor, William D., ed. 1997. *Too Valuable to Lose: Exploring the Causes and Cures of Missionary Attrition.* Pasadena, Calif.: William Carey Library.

Zoba, Wendy Murray. 2000. "Trends in Missions: A Woman's Place." *Christianity Today.* August, 40-48.

SECTION 4

Church-planting Strategy
(how to do it)

As workers in God's force, we want to excel—to be the best we can be and also to see results that are pleasing to God. Church planters, in particular, face a daunting task as they seek to balance the two. Armed with solid, biblical, proven strategy, we do the best we can and leave the results to God. But what exactly can we do to ensure we are honoring both God and those in the culture where he has placed us? Whether in evangelism, discipleship, teaching, meeting felt needs, addressing interpersonal issues, meeting financial needs, etc., the authors in this section encourage us toward extraordinary church-planting strategy.

Gary Corwin calls us to take a look at how God has worked historically and to redouble our efforts to see successful practices applied today. **Derek Seipp** lays out the integration and interrelatedness of discipleship and church planting. **Dietrich Schindler** calls us to a higher standard—moving from good church planters to becoming great in nature.

Charles Troutman shares a story about what true church growth requires. **Gailyn Van Rheenen** then takes us through the process of establishing church-planting movements, from beginning to end. **Tom Steffen** discusses phase-out, and how we know when we have been on the field too long.

David Diaso speaks to mission leaders on how to help those on the field find success. **Ken Baker** then addresses missionaries working in areas where power encounter is a major issue. **Dwight McGuire** explains how the power of anomalies can become a gateway to spreading the gospel through media.

Dick Scoggins offers a comprehensive guide for church planters, particularly those in Muslim contexts. **Scott Breslin** concludes by providing a powerful tool to help church-planting teams get a snapshot of their progress and move toward building off their strengths.

April 2005

Church Planting 101

Gary Corwin

*We would do well to recognize essential biblical patterns that
God has blessed through the centuries and redouble our efforts
to see them universally applied among all the unreached peoples
of the earth.*

There are few phrases more frequently spoken in church and mission circles than "church planting." There also are few subjects around which ministry mavens work harder to be distinctive. Some tout valuable methods that are of a contextually limited scope, while others like David Garrison's *Church Planting Movements* (2004) seem to capture the essential elements of transcultural movements.

One of the really interesting things about the new methods, and even of very helpful research-based analyses like Garrison's, is how "back to the future" so much of it is. Roughly a century ago people like Henry Venn, Rufus Anderson, and John Nevius became the modern apostles of "indigenous principles" of church planting, perhaps better known today as the "three-self principles."

In spite of many significant twentieth-century successes for these principles (places like Korea and Ethiopia come quickly to mind), this idea that new churches ought to be established that are self-governing, self-supporting, and self-propagating has not received good press in recent years. There are several reasons why this is so.

The principles have suffered in the minds of at least some because of their negative association with the Chinese adaptation of the term for their government-approved brand of Christianity—the "Three-Self Patriotic Movement." The principles have also commonly been accused of promoting a self-focus at the expense of a Christ-focus. (Unfairly, I think, because the real converse to self-initiative was foreign-initiative.)

On the other hand, the principles have been criticized for not going far enough, most notably for neglecting self-theologizing. While a reasonable concern, it is also fair to say that many proponents thought theologizing would be an aspect of self-governing and self-propagating.

Perhaps more telling has been the criticism received because of widespread misapplication of the principles themselves. They were often applied too tightly, particularly in the area of finance. Not only were local churches expected to be "self-supporting," but they were often left to fend for themselves, even in the areas of broad-based and strategic ministry, mercy, and training opportunities.

The principles were thus made to appear contrary to the biblical teaching on interdependence in the Body of Christ, and simply an excuse for rich, Western

Christians to withhold essential and appropriate assistance to their less fortunate brothers and sisters. While the best church-planting endeavors managed to avoid this pitfall, many others did not. In any case, the "indigenous principles" are largely out of favor today as a result.

One of the things I like most about work like Garrison's is that it uses well-documented research to point us back to what God has used to accomplish his purposes in earlier days, and in a wide variety of contexts. Methods that were true in the first century, and were true during the heyday of the "indigenous principles," and are still true today.

While the following list is by no means exhaustive, key principles like the following are ones that no church planter should miss.

1. All ethno-linguistic peoples need churches that feel like home to them.
2. The same is true for people divided by all kinds of barriers, at least to the extent that a missiological breakthrough among them requires it.
3. There should be a linkage as much as possible of all local congregations in a national fellowship. People need connectedness to God's people beyond their local context.
4. There should be an inculcation of an outreach mentality from the very beginning. "As the Father has sent me … I send you" (John 20:21).
5. There should be indigenous leadership of each local church from the beginning. It is, after all, Jesus' church first, and the local people's church second. In most local congregations, that should consist of a plurality of leaders.
6. House churches or other easily reproducible meeting places should be the rule rather than the exception.
7. There should be a high commitment to financial self-sustainability and to the reproducibility of congregations. Foreign funds should not be used in dependency-creating ways, but should be used creatively for kingdom extension, mercy, and to strengthen the churches.
8. There should be cooperation with other missions and churches to the extent that the above principles are not compromised. That which can be done better together should not be done alone.

As intimated above, these principles are neither new nor radical, though they were largely both in the early Church. After two millennia of practice, however, they are time tested. The question that remains is whether Great Commission Christians (particularly those of the West) will more consistently and vigorously pursue them, or continue to scurry along down diversionary rabbit trails.

Whether it is the idea that a formally-trained, paid clergy is an essential prerequisite for "real" church or the seemingly endless search for newer and better church-planting models, the opportunities to get sidetracked are legion. The better option is to recognize essential biblical patterns that God has blessed through the centuries, and to redouble our efforts to see them universally applied among all the unreached peoples of the earth.

Which Should Come First—
Discipleship or Church Planting?

Derek Seipp

Discipleship and church planting must exist as a part of a goal-oriented process that includes new disciples and new churches.

The classic debate is an impassioned one with the goal of igniting the hearts of devout church planters, evangelists, and teachers. The question goes something like this: *what should we focus on: discipleship or church planting?* Given that there has been no definitive answer on this topic, I propose another alternative altogether: the question itself is intrinsically flawed and, in fact, sets up a duality: A vs. B. Meanwhile, A and B were both commanded by God: "Go and make disciples" and "Build my Church."

Looking at the state of church-planting movements (CPMs) around the world, we see examples of how thousands have come to Christ. Indeed, there are many more believers than there have ever been as a result of CPMs, and these believers know they are saved by grace and that Jesus is the only answer for their sin. These believers are very active in sharing their testimony, evangelizing, and in the ministries of the church (although these ministries may be much less developed overall).

However, the overall theological depth of the believers is far less than optimal, and there are issues of true repentance and holy living. Compare this to some of the more traditional churches in these countries, where there is a greater depth of knowledge and a more stable platform from which teaching, baptism, and communion are performed. The teaching is generally much greater in its depth and more applicable to life in these traditional churches.

Believers in these churches, however, are much less likely to share their faith (as proved by evangelism rates) than those in the church-planting movements. And although the ministries of the church are much more developed, there is generally a significantly lower percentage of individuals involved in the implementation of those ministries.

Having been teaching new church leaders for seven years, I believe that both models are significantly flawed. There are two issues that must be addressed. The first is a definition of terms. *What is discipleship? What is church planting?* The second is the primacy of either one.

True discipleship. True discipleship, I propose, is much more "active" than people traditionally think it is. Discipleship, in fact, encompasses three aspects—knowledge, skill, and relationship. If emphasis is placed on knowledge alone, we are only covering one-third of the requirement of complete discipleship. Sadly, most discipleship programs are based on knowledge-based curricula because it is the easiest to bring people through and measure results.

Discipleship should have a goal of producing leaders in ministry. Certainly not everyone is going to get there; however, if you leave it out as a goal, hoping for new leaders will not give you consistent results. Most churches stop discipleship at a certain knowledge-based level. I propose that discipleship ends when a leader is produced. Eighty percent of individuals may find their comfort place along the way and cut their own discipleship short. However, unless we develop systematic methods that produce new leaders, they will never emerge—and neither will a new church. At the same time, if we never plan for a new church, it will never happen.

True church planting. While critics of CPMs say this view of church planting is too simple, critics of the traditional church say it is too complex. It is entirely possible that both are correct. Just as people have DNA which guides

BOTH DISCIPLESHIP and church planting are of vital importance; to have one without the other skews the results. Both must exist as a part of a goal-oriented process that includes new disciples and new churches.

their development, discipleship must have systematic DNA that leads a convert to be maturely participating in ministry. Additionally, perhaps churches must be planted more simply, but with DNA (systems, etc.) that will eventually guide this immature group into being a mature church. Although our goal should be mature churches, if we strive to plant a fully-mature church, we may never get there. The question then becomes: *how do we create those systems?*

Both discipleship and church planting are of vital importance; to have one without the other skews the results. Both must exist as a part of a goal-oriented process that includes new disciples and new churches. If either one of these is lacking, one must look at one's process to see where the deficiency lies. This, then, becomes the measurement of effectiveness. God's purpose calls us to lay down our assumptions and press on to find better methods. Ultimately, God is in the business of filling the earth with his glory, as the waters cover the sea. Discipleship and church planting together are the only way to get there.

July 2008

Good-to-Great Church Planting: The Road Less Travelled

Dietrich Schindler

Exploring the regions beyond successful church planting in a Western culture and explaining how it can rise to become great in nature.

The business world awakened to a new benchmark one morning when Jim Collins published his provocative findings in the book entitled *Good to Great: Why Some Companies Make the Leap...and Others Don't.* Supported by a large research team, Collins identified companies that made the jump from good results to great results—and sustained those results for fifteen years or more. Good companies have been lulled into doing business as usual, while great companies have excelled in the areas of personnel appropriation, reality checks, "transcending the curse of competence," cultural discipline, and technology acceleration (Collins 2001, 13). The elaboration of these disciplines riveted the attention of many, and made the book into a long-standing bestseller.

What surprised Collins was not the enthusiastic reception his work received from the business community, but the reaction from members of the non-profit sector. One-third of his readers resided in social occupations, and they were most eager to apply his principles to their settings. Collins obliged the hunger of the non-profit community for greater clarity by writing a supplemental monograph on how good-to-great principles could be carried over to the social sector.

The imagery of "good-to-great" applies not only to businesses and to the social sector, but also to church planting. Stellar church-planting churches bear down on specific disciplines that infuse their ministries with remarkable movement-based energy, vision, and effectiveness. The purpose of this article is to explore the regions beyond successful church planting in a Western culture and to explain how it can rise to become great in nature. This article is written for church planters and church-planting churches.

In the past twenty years as a church planter in Germany, I have come to refer to six disciplines of good-to-great church planting as "G6." By that I mean that great church-planting ministries seem to have six great qualities that set them apart from merely good church-planting ministries: timed release, generational distance, discipleship depth, intentional mindset, external focus, and reproducible models. I will explain them in the order listed. These six elements were developed after studying church planting in both the established Protestant Church and the various larger Free Churches in Germany.

The chart below succinctly illustrates the major differences between good and great church planting. Individual elements will be addressed, explained, and illustrated in the rest of this article.

Good-to-Great Church Planting

Good Church Planting	Great Church Planting
• Long recovery time • Direct involvement • Emphasis on leadership • Haphazard and situational • Centripetal force • Emphasis on giftedness	• Time released • Generational distance • Discipleship depth • Intentional mindset • External focus • Reproducible models

1. Timed Release

For colds, the flu, headaches, and insomnia, pharmaceutical companies have given us the ubiquitous tiny-time capsules. These tiny-time capsules are controlled-release systems engineered to provide ongoing medical treatment with one kind of capsule beginning to work when another has exhausted its capacity. Great church planting incorporates the concept of timed release. Timed release is the discipline of setting the date of the next church plant shortly after the current church has been launched.

My wife and I, along with two other adults, planted a German Evangelical Free church in the city of Kaiserslautern in March 1999. Four years later, with sixty members and one hundred adults in worship services, we launched our first daughter church in the nearby city of Ramstein. The mother church was not big, but it was healthy.

Too often, I have observed a mother church, after having planted a daughter, go into what seemed like an unusually long recovery period. In our European context it might take a decade or more before a church summons enough resolve and resources to begin another daughter church. Such is the fate of church starts that fail to begin with the end (the genesis of a new church) in mind.

Church-planting churches will hardly impact their society with the power of the gospel in increments of ten or twenty years. The discipline of timed release on the other hand puts before us the goal of launching new churches in shorter periods of time, consisting, at the maximum, of five years. Every five years, high-impact churches will see to it that a new church is birthed from their midst. To use another analogy, every five years these churches set their clocks to run down to the date of their next launch.

2. Generational Distance

Whereas timed release is the discipline of chain reaction church planting, generational distance is where multiplication begins to set in. My wife's grandparents were married for more than seventy-five years when they died. Grandpa was 105 and Grandma was 97. They left behind over 150 progeny. In their lifetime, they saw themselves forwarded into five generations! Imagine holding a fifth-generation baby in your arms, knowing you and your spouse were the first cause.

How effective a mother church is in forwarding itself via ensuing church starts reflects the issue of generational distance. Thus, great churches focus not so much on the churches they have spawned, as on the *number of generations* they have spawned. Great church planting counts the generations, not just the number of children it has fostered.

This is the stuff of multiplication. For multiplication to occur, the first cause of new life must free itself from direct involvement. Great-grandparents do not give birth directly, but indirectly, to their great-grandchildren. Direct involvement is the vocabulary of addition; one church starting another church via direct influence. Multiplication's quality, however, lies in its indirection: one church setting its offspring free to procreate churches. Generational distance is an emphasis that has rarely occurred in our European setting; however, it is a key ingredient needed for multiplication to take place.

3. Discipleship Depth

Why is it that the vast majority of churches never experience such a level of church-planting growth? The answer lies in the third dimension: discipleship depth. This takes seriously Jesus' charge for his followers to make other life-long learners. Dallas Willard's paraphrase of Matthew 28:18-20 states it best:

> I have been given say over everything on heaven and earth. So go make apprentices to me among people of every kind. Submerge them in the reality of the Trinitarian God. And lead them into doing everything I have told you to do. Now look! I am with you every minute, until the job is completely done!

The quality of depth in good-to-great church-planting churches is directly linked to how well they make disciples who in turn make disciples. The constant need for new leadership is the challenge of church multiplication. But good leadership begins with good discipleship. A proven disciple is the best foundation for an influential leader. In short, making disciples that make disciples becomes the launching pad for churches planting churches.

To get to the place where discipleship is intentional, reproducing, evangelistic, and leaning into leadership development, we need more than gifted leaders. We will value and implement healthy systems of discipleship training that are better than the people using them. A healthy system of reproduction does good things to all involved. It instills Christ-likeness into people in a manner in which they have not done for themselves.

Great church-planting churches witness life change and healthy growth in their smallest life units: small groups or triads. Churches reproduce rapidly externally because they have been systematically reproducing internally. As is with the church organism, its various disciple-making members will live with timed-release dates. Enfolding non-Christians as well as believers, seeing both make strides in coming to or maturing in Christ, is assumed and experienced in such systems.

Parallel to our small group Bible studies, we have fostered triad discipleship groups in our fellowship in Kaiserslautern. Last year, a man in his early 30s by the name of Falk gave his life to Jesus. I promptly invited him to join two others along with myself in a mini group. The group has since divided and now Falk and I are beginning our next group with a young man who is seeking. The three of us are reading three chapters in the Bible daily, meeting together weekly to share and pray with one another. Our weekly checkups regularly deal with topics pertaining to family, temptation, finances, anger, and sharing our faith. I have seen so much change in Falk's life as a result of high biblical intake and regular sharing of how we are doing in our daily walk with Christ.

4. Intentional Mindset

The will to want church growth is the engine that drives it. This is the succinct conclusion of C. Peter Wagner (Wagner 1984). The same applies to good-to-great church planting. It must be intentionally sought after for it to occur. No person has ever drifted into becoming a concert pianist; in the same way, no church-planting movement emerges from nonchalance.

Inspiring vision and deeply felt need are the propellant fuels of purposeful action. God inspired the patriarchs by transmitting wide-eyed pictures to them of what was to come: teeming masses of people as countless as the stars of the heavens or the sand granules on the seashore. A truly inspiring vision sees the future with the grandeur of God and draws the onlooker into it as metal is attracted to a magnet.

But even the most compelling vision loses its drawing power with time. The builders of the wall around Jerusalem were obviously inspired by Nehemiah's vision. They set to work immediately. Yet this vision did not prevent them from stopping what they were doing. In their case, the vision lost its luster after twenty-six days, and they subsequently stopped doing the work.

Vision is like a campfire: it cools off with time, and thus needs periodic stoking, preferably monthly, for people to remain committed to it. Vision, by itself, even if periodically "stoked," is insufficient to propel most people toward action. Inspiration needs the additive of deeply felt need. Need propels us to act. Spiritual and societal movers and shakers such as Martin Luther King Jr., William Wilberforce, Madame Curie, or Mother Theresa bear this out.

My father died at the age of 58. It was brought on by a heart attack that was preceded by kidney failure. Knowing this, my doctor urged me to have my kidneys checked annually. I nodded in assent—and did nothing; that is, until one morning when I noticed symptoms that could be indicators of kidney problems. Within an hour and a half I was sitting in the office of a specialist. What brought about the change in behavior was not the vision; it was a deeply felt personal need.

A great church-planting multiplication movement shifts into gear by feeling the brokenness, hurt, and pain of those not being reached by conventional churches. Jesus was angered and smitten by the hardness of heart of some of his hearers (Mark 2:5); he was in psychosomatic pain over the lostness of the lost (Matt. 9:36). It was this deeply felt sorrow over that state of the heart of the lost that propelled him and his followers to move into the harvest.

It has been twenty-eight years; however, I still remember the first sentence spoken by my first homiletics professor in my first hour of class. Quietly yet firmly, Dr. Holmes said, "Most of you will not become great preachers...because you do not plan on becoming great preachers." Intentionality is the mother of quality. Although there is no guarantee of a qualitative spiritual movement, such a movement is not the by-product of chance, but of intentionality.

Early on in the church plant in Kaiserslautern I secured a colorful bag of plastic locomotives from a toy store. As people became members of the church, each was given a locomotive to place on his or her desk at home. The locomotive was a word picture. We told our people that we were praying and working toward establishing new main train stations, or Hauptbahnhöfe, which were new churches. We put church planting in our literature, talked of it often, did it, and are intent on continuing to do it. This is intentionality at work.

5. External Focus

Where we spend our time underlies our values. Thus, our behavior will always serve to surface our true beliefs. Behavior is belief. We may profess the importance of seeking the lost, but where we spend our time decrees what we truly deem important. The men and women behind great church-planting ministries spend much time with those they are called to reach. As they do this, they behave as Jesus did. He was internally motivated while being externally oriented.

For many people in ministry, time spent with the already-reached is where they devote their energies. The study desk can become a convenient barrier to time spent with the lost. We must overcome this barrier. When we look at where Jesus spent his weekdays, we see him in the harvest, crisscrossing Galilee with half-baked, seeking followers.

The older a ministry gets, the stronger the gravitational pull is exerted toward the inside people. Gravity is the problem in wanting to get from Frankfurt to Chicago. To get from the barn to the harvest, we will need to be externally-oriented and pull away from the centripetal force of the church.

In the first two years of our church plant in Kaiserslautern I intentionally visited over four hundred businesses. I purposefully asked to speak with the boss, stating that I was the new pastor of a new church in town and as such wanted to meet the "neighbors." Significant and memorable conversations, some ending in prayer, resulted from those visits. I certainly had enough to do without seeking out the business community; however, I realized that I needed regular contact with non-Christians—and vice-versa.

Should we intentionally want to see a church-planting multiplication movement occur, we will emphasize the size of each individual's OIKOS. Tom Wolf and Ralph Neighbour have illuminated the concept of OIKOS as it relates to evangelism (Neighbour 1990, 82). The OIKOS is our relational network. To discover our evangelistic OIKOS, note the names of every non-Christian person with whom you spend an hour or more in an average week. These people make up our natural bridges into the gospel.

The more such relationships we have, the greater the inroads that God has into their lives through us. The composite OIKOS of church-planting teams makes up the potential church. Neighbour summarizes the problem of church-planting dysfunction when he states, "Less than one percent of the salaried pillars of the church were…investing one hour a week developing personal relationships with the huge mass of totally unchurched" (1990, 82). Is Neighbour perhaps telling us that being off the job is really being on the job?

Jesus taught us to be externally-oriented, the focus upon which a good-to-great church-planting movement thrives. The future of every visible ministry is in the harvest (Matt. 9:35-38) from which will come tomorrow's leaders. The future of the Church consists of people who today are not yet believers. The external mindset is the missional mindset.

6. Reproducible Models

Every great movement needs healthy systems of reproduction that are better than the people using them. Such systems are not only practical, easy to use, and reproductive, but exert benevolent power upon their users. Benevolent power is the power to change into Christ-likeness and the power to reach outsiders.

In the church we planted eight years ago in Kaiserslautern (pop. 100,000), we have been experimenting with a hybrid form of triads made popular by Neil Cole. The model is as simple as it is reproducible.

Initially, three men or women, all Christ-followers, band together to form a triad, or a mini-group. At the first meeting an "expiration date" of six months is given to the group. Each member covenants with each other to exercise what Cole calls "spiritual breathing." In our context, we each inhale (read) three chapters of God's word daily, all reading the same texts. When we come together once a week, we share how God has been speaking to us, and then we exhale (confess) how we have lived during the previous week.

Much discipleship falls short of life change because it tells people how they ought to live. Only when we honestly tell one another how we actually live does deep life change occur. Thus, we ask questions related to temptation, finances, family, anger, and so on. Over the next several months we add a fourth member to the group.

At the end of the six months each group meets for a meal to celebrate God's goodness and to signal the division of the group into two groups of two. Each dyad then invites a non-Christian from their OIKOS to join their mini-group for an initial two-week period. In this way, we give the seeker enough time to get wooed by the grace of God as well as give a convenient and face-saving exit, should he or she desire to discontinue. The groups are intent upon seeing non-Christians come to faith in Christ and continue on in life transformation in the mini-groups. These are again time-released to divide after six months.

The beauty of this reproducible system of disciple-making is that it is leaderless. It is not dependent upon giftedness to make it work. And it not only sees the lives of believers grow deep; it is harvest-oriented, seeing people come into the Kingdom of God by virtue of its essence.

It takes effort and a good reproducible model to make disciples. John Wesley discovered this in his reproducible system which he labeled the "class meeting." According to D. Michael Henderson, "They met weekly to give an account of their personal spiritual growth, according to the rules and following the procedures which Wesley had carefully crafted" (1997, 11). Life change occurs where there is nearness, openness, and accountability. It is the stuff out of which movements of God stem and lead to healthy multiplication.

Conclusion

Although the Western world has seen a new impetus to plant churches, many efforts have and will continue to be good at best. As in the business world, so too in the world of church planting, new benchmarks or disciplines are needed to travel from good to great. It will take the power of God and the steady determination of purposeful men and women to see great church-planting movements birthed. As Robert Frost indicates, not many travel such roads, for only a rare few are willing to go the way less travelled.

Two roads diverged in a wood, and I—
I took the one less travelled by,
And that has made all the difference.

The power of God and the power of choice will make all the difference in the impact we have in planting churches. The difference marks our determination to rise above the good to get to the great. We will determine to be intentional, external, and reproducible in our drive to see G6 churches planted.

Missionary statesman Roland Allen put it succinctly, "The great things of God are beyond our control" (1997, 13)—beyond our control, but not beyond our faith or our influence as we partner with the Spirit of God in alignment with his word. Great church planting takes the road less travelled—and that will make all the difference in the destiny of many people.

References

Allen, Roland. 1997. *The Spontaneous Expansion of the Church*. Eugene, Ore.: Wipf and Stock Publishers.

Cole, Neil. 1999. *Cultivating a Life for God*. Carol Stream, Ill.: ChurchSmart Resources.

Collins, Jim. 2001. *Good to Great: Why Some Companies Make the Leap… and Others Don't*. New York: HarperCollins.

_____. 2005. *Good to Great and the Social Sectors: Why Business Thinking Is Not the Answer*. Boulder, Colo.: Jim Collins.

Henderson, D. Michael. 1997. *John Wesley's Class Meetings: A Model for Making Disciples*. Nappanee, Ind.: Evangel Publishing House.

Neighbour, Ralph W. Jr. 1990. *Where Do We Go from Here? A Guidebook for Cell Group Churches*. Houston, Tex.: Touch Publications.

Schindler, Dietrich Gerhard. 2006. "Creating and Sustaining a Church Planting Multiplication Movement in Germany." Unpublished DMin Dissertation, Fuller Theological Seminary.

Wagner, C. Peter. 1984. *Leading Your Church to Growth*. Glendale, Calif.: G/L Regal Books.

A Fallacy in Church Planting: A Fable

Charles Troutman

It takes more than evangelism and discipleship to plant self-supporting churches. Growth requires literacy, health, and economic services.

O nce upon a time an experienced missionary established two strong churches in a capital city. Each church called a national pastor and maintained several preaching points under lay leadership. It was slow going at first, but some excellent young men were trained, although the problem of their support was never satisfactorily resolved. Five terms of service had produced spiritual leaders, but the believers were still so poor and employment so erratic that mission funds had to make up annual deficits. The city itself was prospering, but the concept of Christian stewardship was slow in taking hold.

The missionary had a pioneer's heart and with nine years to go before retirement, felt that a younger man could handle the support matters better while he moved on to open new areas. His special burden was for the coastal jungle region of his adopted country, recently opened for settlement. The area had no medical services, only a few schools, no churches, and just one impossible road.

Although it was potentially the richest part of the nation, the government had not yet begun to plan for roads, clinics, schools, or police. In spite of this, the area held out to its country's poor people the possibility of eventually owning their own land. This primitive and unhealthy sector contained a growing population for whom Christ died. The missionary couple received permission from their board to spend their final two terms in this coastal region in church planting.

From the beginning, the couple found an unusual response to the gospel: "More than we had prayed for," they wrote home. Converts, in the enthusiasm of their new faith, roamed the countryside telling of their own experiences of Christ and explaining the gospel as best they could. Interest was high.

In the course of time, however, these new believers began to understand their responsibilities for their Christian families, the proper use of their few possessions and their land, the needs of their churches, and especially the education of their children. This meant less time for freelance witnessing, Nevertheless, the good news continued to spread. Self-propagation was never a problem.

Neither was self-government. The people had learned to work together for sheer survival. And the idea of running their own congregations was very attractive to those who had been put down and shoved to the margins of society. They did an excellent job, although their ideas of organization were so informal that the missionary often longed to bring his kind of order into their church life.

But, even when he was unable to visit a place for months, the meetings, teaching, and study continued. In their own way, the elders were fully responsible for their own work.

Self-support for a fully-established church was another matter. The people were so desperately poor that, as one government official observed, "There is not enough loose change on the whole coast to pay one of your pastors for a month." The missionary took this as a challenge, for "with God, nothing is impossible."

His report upon retirement nine years later showed fourteen organized congregations and over three times as many regular preaching points. Only two buildings could qualify as church structures, yet every group was growing under its own lay pastors. The board rightly acknowledged this couple's work and made good use of their story to show that God's blessing rests on those

TWENTY YEARS PASSED and these replacements, now veteran missionaries themselves, reported forty-eight organized congregations and an unknown number of preaching points.

who follow the New Testament pattern of church planting and do not get sidetracked by secondary activities. A younger couple was assigned to this coastal area to direct the final steps into a truly indigenous church.

Twenty years passed and these replacements, now veteran missionaries themselves, reported forty-eight organized congregations and an unknown number of preaching points. Many churches had a Sunday attendance of two hundred.

Some North American churches had been persuaded to help erect suitable buildings and they responded generously with donations and work teams. There were now twenty-one buildings, but interestingly enough, none large enough to hold its congregation. Laymen still pastored the churches, but their size made it increasingly difficult for such part-time activity.

Theological Education by Extension (TEE) had done wonders to improve the effectiveness of these men. The board appointed a national pastor to help the missionary, but the day of fully supported local pastors was still as far off as ever. As it did two decades before, the mission board used this area as a remarkable illustration of church planting and church growth to show that God's work done in God's way always has his blessing.

North American churches seemed glad to support such a successful and biblical work. In fact, a new missionary couple was being sent to help in this showcase of God's grace.

This couple was impressed that after only twenty-nine years the churches were so alive and the believers so spiritually mature. They were effective witnesses and good teachers of the basics of the faith. But as to the stated purpose of the missionary society—to plant indigenous churches—the effort was a miserable, though unrecognized, failure.

Not a single church existed without aid from North America. They were still dependent upon the board's ability to supply what missionaries and funds it could. There was this curious fact that the greater the success of the missionaries, the more money and personnel the board had to pour into the region. Indigenization seemed to be going backwards.

It was the U.S. mission board that first noticed this contradiction. The field workers were so absorbed and busy with their growing work that they resented

THE MISSIONARIES and their board

assumed that the North American pattern of church

organization was the only one available.

this questioning of an obvious spiritual success. How could North Americans, most of whom had never visited this part of the field, know what was going on?

The board finally asked for an evaluation survey, but nothing surfaced to criticize. It did, however, take action. It established a target for the churches of fifty percent self-support in six years and appointed another couple to concentrate on a stewardship program. The new man had majored in Bible and philosophy in college and in missions in seminary. His wife had an elementary teacher certificate. There was every reason to expect the churches to reach this goal.

Yet when the target date passed, although church growth had continued, the lay pastors had improved their work and more congregations had been organized, the financial picture had only improved slightly. The board had to face its dilemma: How long could it afford to support a growing success?

Unfortunately, the above is not a fable! Three things went wrong:

1. The missionaries and their board assumed that the North American pattern of church organization—pastor, building, and program—was the only one available. There are other models. What they did not see was that the social and economic conditions of this particular area did not provide for this type of self-support.

This meant that stewardship was thought of solely in terms of motivation. If the believers could only be taught to give liberally, there would be no support problem. Holding to this unachievable goal, the lay pastors were only stepping stones, temporary expedients to be eventually replaced by full-time pastors.

As a result, these laymen were never fully confident or secure in their leadership, nor did they ever take the missionary's ideal too seriously. Instead, they turned their efforts to what they could do better: initial evangelism. National leaders often used this method of getting around missionary miscalculations.

2. The missionaries did not see how the social system in which the believers were trapped made them unable to become self-supporting. There were no health services available in the area, so disease and malnutrition often left whole families too weak to get to church services; it was not because they had backslidden. When the crops had a good year, they had no way to get them to market; the people were not lazy.

Not seeing the intimate connection between these social problems and the self-support problem, the missionaries considered the believers to be unspiritual and lacking interest. Yet the mission continued to send more couples into this area, and to other fields, to plant churches.

3. The missionaries misread the absence of specific social and economic instructions in the New Testament to mean that they have no part in church planting. Actually, the social and economic structures of the first-century Mediterranean world were such that they favored the establishment of nondependent churches. Paul was able to concentrate on evangelism, teaching, and leadership training.

Thus, in the power of the Holy Spirit, a new congregation could become self-propagating, had the educated leadership to become self-governing, and lived in an economic situation in which it could become self-supporting. The missionaries in this particular coastal area had several strikes against them and did not know it.

If church planting is the goal of missionary endeavor, as it should be, then why are evangelism, teaching, organizing, and leadership training not always enough? These activities are sufficient in most home missions. The confusion lies partly in the past two centuries of the modem missionary movement.

Evangelicals have always been rightly suspicious of mission boards that concentrate on education, medical, social, or economic ministries to the exclusion of or downgrading of evangelism and spiritual development. Yet in most fields, there exists one or more of the following conditions, which if not attended to, will inhibit the development of nondependent children.

• Where public education is absent, church planting must include education to enable members to read scripture.

• Where sickness and malnutrition sap energies beyond the struggle for mere existence, church planting must include public health and nutritional services.

• Where there is just enough food to survive, church planting must include agriculture and related sciences.

• Where there are inadequate means to get products to market, church planting must include road promotion and perhaps even road building.

• Where individual initiative is not enough, church planting must include organizing agricultural cooperatives and credit unions.

• Where there are artistic or technical abilities, church planting must include the development of these talents and, where necessary, the distribution of products.

• Where small businesses are possible and needed, church planting must include training in business practices and perhaps even financial help.

The list could go on, depending upon local conditions. In other words, in order to fulfill the church-planting purpose of most missionary societies, a church planter must have to engage in more than evangelism and leadership training.

Is it too hard to say that it is criminal to go on establishing organized churches that are condemned in advance to be indefinitely dependent upon foreign money and personnel, simply because we neglect those factors in their society that make self-support possible?

January 2000

Learning...Growing...
Collaborating...Phasing Out

Gailyn Van Rheenen

The process of establishing church-planting movements from a missionary's initial entry onto the field to the passing of the baton of leadership to the national church.

Many "trained" missionaries begin their work in a cross-cultural context without a clear understanding of the missionary task. From a personal perspective this statement was partially descriptive of our mission team. We were well prepared to learn new languages and cultures. We had basic preparation to lead unbelievers into a saving relationship with Jesus Christ. We effectively struggled with contextualizing the gospel in a new and different culture. Our team, however, consumed hundreds of hours trying to determine what to do next. And because we did not adequately understand the process of missions, we made many mistakes along the way.

This article attempts to outline the broad process of establishing church-planting movements from the missionaries' initial entry onto the field to the passing of the baton of leadership to the national church. It was written for two major reasons.

First, to enable missionaries to visualize the broad process of missions and the roles and skills required of missionaries during each stage of planting and developing a new mission movement. Second, to challenge those who equip missionaries to focus not only on the initial stages of church planting—the "learning" and "growth" periods—but also on the final stages of church planting—the "collaborative" and "phase-out" periods. Traditionally, the study of church planting has focused more on church initiation than on church maturation.

The Learning Period

Approximately the first two years on the mission field are appropriately called the *learning period* or the *adaptation stage*. Missionaries are learning to live in new contexts and adapt to them. During this period, four interrelated types of learning take place. Missionaries learn (1) to speak a new language, (2) to understand the culture of the people among whom they are working, (3) to form personal relationships within the culture, and (4) to develop models of ministry appropriate to the context.

Two extremes are common during this stage. On the one hand, some missionaries assume that they should not begin communicating the gospel until the learning stage is completed—until language and culture learning are accomplished. Christianity, however, is the core of identity. Missionaries cannot easily lay aside their identity even during the early stages of missionary work. They should learn languages and cultures as Christians and thus express and live out these distinct Christian perspectives.

Christian proclamation must be incorporated rather than marginalized during the learning of language and culture. When effective language and culture learning takes place, the first converts are frequently made and a church established, even during this preliminary learning stage. Missionaries must, however, understand their communication limitations and work within them. They should teach using broad, general concepts and use indigenous illustrations only with the greatest of care.

On the opposite extreme, some missionaries naively bypass the learning stage. They conceive that "people are people all over the world and the gospel can be presented in the same way in all contexts." They, therefore, desire to be teachers without learning first. Without active language and culture learning during the first months on the field, the missionaries' effectiveness in all other stages is reduced, and the resulting movement is typically anemic.

As stated earlier, effective missionaries should be identificationalists, but the

ALTHOUGH MANY PEOPLE know the trade language, we found that for communicating the message of Christ, the trade language would not substitute for the heart language.

nature of their identification varies from stage to stage as the Christian movement matures. In this early adaption phase, missionary identification is broadly focused and may be defined as learning the general patterns of a new recipient culture. The major role of missionaries during this stage is that of a learner.

During this stage of missionary life, our team first learned the Kiswahili trade language and then the Kipsigis vernacular. Although many people know the trade language, we found that for communicating the message of Christ, the trade language could not substitute for the language of the heart. As we learned the Kipsigis language, we also learned Kipsigis culture. It became evident that to learn the language was also to learn the culture. Language categories form the cognitive domains expressing the building blocks of the cultural worldview.

Four months after our arrival in Kipsigis, the first six people came to Christ. We found that language/culture learning and ministry could not be segmented: as we learned, we also expressed who we were and taught the message of reconciliation to God in Christ in our own very elementary way.

During this stage, I personally was pulled in two different directions: not only was I working with those of the Kipsigis tribe, but I also found hundreds of workers on the area tea estates who were receptive to the gospel. Within a year, I baptized 150 people in these estates. But we soon found that the workers were all visitors, living out of their tribal area and that establishing a permanent movement where all the people are visitors is very difficult.

Although a large number were converted, without the support of the home community many reverted to their old ways. We came to realize that stable churches are established when people are converted where they "live" rather than where they "stay," a linguistic differentiation made by local people in both the Kiswahili and Kipsigis languages. Thus, our model of ministry radically shifted to preach where people "live" (i.e., their home area) rather than where people "stay" (i.e., their work place).

The Growth Period

Effective missionaries, having learned language and culture and shared their faith, begin the *growth period* with a vision of how God will use them to mobilize a movement in the area in which they are working. They realize that their task is not merely to plant a church, but to initiate a movement of God. They have developed the cultural and linguistic understandings to think missiologically about their cultural context.

Developing a strong movement of God in a new city or ethnic area requires three essential, interrelated tasks. First, initial evangelism leads to new churches. Second, Christians are nurtured to maturity within these churches. Third, leaders are trained to evangelize and plant other churches, pastor and shepherd the community of believers, and train still other leaders.

Effective missionaries successfully develop models for accomplishing each of these central missionary tasks. While other mission endeavors may amplify these three central tasks, without them a strong movement of God cannot come into being. *In receptive areas of the world, accomplishing these three tasks will require a minimum of eight to ten years of focused ministry during the growth period to enable mature local churches with trained leadership to come into existence.*

Care must be taken that these three tasks not be performed artificially by inducing people to come to Christ because of finance or favor. Western missionaries come from very wealthy countries. Without realizing it, they frequently magnetize the leeches and con men of the culture and then attempt to build a church around them.

Effective learning during the first stage equips effective missionaries to deal with the many dilemmas concerning the disparity of wealth in the world and the resulting expectations of the poor. God's Church, moreover, must reflect the compassion of God for the poor and disenfranchised. God's people are called to preach good news to the poor, freedom for prisoners, recovery of sight for the blind, and release for the oppressed (Luke 4:18-19).

These ministries, however, occur within the context of genuine Christian conversion: Unbelievers must "open their eyes and turn...from darkness to light, and from the power of Satan to God, so that they may receive forgiveness of sins" (Acts 26:18).

Perhaps the greatest challenge during this stage is developing an effective paradigm of church planting which is both biblically integrated yet reproductive. For example, one missionary team may plant a single church in a city or ethnic unit while another employs a multi-church orientation to plant numerous viable churches within the same culture. One team may smother national leaders by micromanaging church affairs; another may work with maturing leaders to develop models of mobilizing national leadership. (The models or paradigms used in church planting and development make the difference.)

Church-planting teams in receptive areas should develop a full-city, multi-city, or full-tribe perspective rather than expecting to plant only one local church. Their model should be that of Paul, who planted and nurtured, but expected Apollos to water (Rom. 15:17-20; 1 Cor. 3:6, 10).

When a team focuses on establishing one church, a missionary enclave is almost always created, and the presence of many trained foreign leaders tends

CHURCH-PLANTING TEAMS in receptive areas should develop a full-city, multi-city, or full-tribe perspective rather than expecting to plant only one local church.

to smother development of national church leaders. Frequently only an anemic church, transplanted from the sending culture, is established. This church can only learn to grow and develop naturally when it learns to live within the social and economic realities of its own culture after the missionaries leave.

The nature of identification during the growth period becomes more focused: missionaries identify with (1) the broken sinfulness of unbelievers in order to lead them to Christ, (2) the struggles of new Christians to nurture them to grow to maturity, and (3) the equipping needs of developing leaders to empower them in ministry. In this stage, the missionary is more than just a learner; he or she is an evangelist and church planter, a nurturer of new Christians, and a trainer of developing leaders.

Our team working among the Kipsigis of Kenya developed a new paradigm of church maturation during the growth period appropriate for the context in which we were working. We sought to mature churches through four distinct stages. The first converts were brought to Christ through evangelism during the Initial Church Stage, a time lasting from five to ten weeks.

During this stage, church planters served primarily as evangelists who proclaimed the foundational message of the gospel. The objective of this stage was to gain enough converts to form a vibrant group; the joy was seeing a congregation born through public and private proclamation of the gospel.

The second stage of church maturation, called the Developing Church Stage, sought to form a sustaining fellowship from those converted during the initial stage. Initial Christians were nurtured to become reproducing, cohesive bodies through teaching and modeling of evangelism and church life. Church planters served throughout this stage as church maturers, nurturing members of the body to serve the function that God had given them within the body.

As mentors of new Christians, the missionaries spent one or two days each week visiting from house to house and holding evangelistic and nurturing meetings throughout the village.

The objective of this stage was to mold initial Christians into a body; the joy was seeing new Christians grow into a cohesive body able to stand on their own. This stage took from six to fifteen months, depending on how quickly the churched matured as a body. Interestingly, churches which rapidly became spiritually and numerically strong tended to become the most mature of the churches in their respective areas.

The third period of church maturation, the Independent Church Stage, began when founding church planters were able to allow local leaders to assume all major leadership roles. Frequently, a rite of separation—a time of commissioning, of laying on of hands to commend the new church to the Lord—signaled entry into this stage. The church had developed enough leadership to function as a cohesive body without the continual presence of the initial church-planting missionary.

While the focus during the Developing Church Stage was on congregational training, the emphasis during the Independent Church Stage was on leadership training. During the previous stage, leaders rose naturally to the surface as all members were taught the basics of the gospel and nurtured to become participants in cohesive fellowships. In this stage, special training was given to leaders to develop theological understandings and skills for practical ministry.

Thus, effective church planters among independent churches grew to be catalysts training congregational leaders. The objective was to train leaders to the point that local Christians were able to "build themselves up in love" (Eph. 4:16); the joy was seeing congregational leaders develop.

The Mature Church Stage was the final period of church maturation. At the beginning of this stage and after intense leadership training during the Independent Church Stage, church leaders were selected and ordained. Elders were selected to pastor the flock; deacons were selected to serve in various ministries. Evangelists were set aside to lead the congregation in proclaiming God's redemptive message both in the local village and in adjoining areas; Sunday school teachers and other ministry leaders were also selected.

As the founding church planters looked at the church, they saw how God had worked to bring this body to maturity. Because trained leaders had been ordained, founding church planters assumed the role of occasional guests, who came periodically to exhort and strengthen the body. They were, however, no longer needed for its continuation. Church planters, resisting the temptation to maintain control over the mature church, had to allow the church to continue on its own.

Many missionaries consider their task complete when a number of churches have been planted and leaders have been trained to minister within their local congregations. But communities of faith frequently erode if they are left as autonomous bodies without continued nurturing.

The work of church planting and development is not completed when local churches come into existence. These local churches need nurturing, equipping structures which tie them together as a movement and which empower ministers and elders as spiritual leaders to pastor their congregations and continue the process of local evangelism and church planting. This need for structures of continuity leads to the third period of church development.

The Collaborative Period

When a Christian movement is established without inducements of finance or favor but through heartfelt response to the proclamation of the Kingdom of God, authentic national leaders mature in Christ to stand with church-planting missionaries as leaders of God's movement. With the maturing of devout, responsible leaders, the movement enters the third stage—the *collaborative period*—of church planting and development.

Understanding the missionary-national leader relationship is essential to perceiving the need for this phase of church planting. Frequently, national leaders become disillusioned because of missionary paternalism, inappropriate or misunderstood strategy models, missionary turnover, and inadequate equipping of national leaders to assume traditional missionary tasks.

Heightened tension leads national leaders to challenge, sometimes covertly, sometimes overtly, missionary roles and methodologies. Alex Araujo of Brazil graphically characterizes this relationship as *pororoca*, a loud popping noise heard when the massive waters of the Amazon meet the rising tide of the Atlantic Ocean. Like the violent collision of two gigantic bodies of water, missionaries and developing national leaders clash, creating havoc for anyone caught in the maelstrom.

Such a clash between missionaries and national leaders can frequently be avoided if national Christians are nurtured to become evangelists and elders and collaboratively incorporated as leaders and decision-makers in the developing Christian movement. A process of leadership maturation is thus understood and employed from the inception of the missionary movement.

Araujo illustrates the merging of two leadership streams into one by describing two large rivers which flow into the Amazon River to become one near Manaus, Brazil. The Negro River appears dark and clear, like Coca-Cola seen through a glass. The Solimoes River, however, is full of sediment and appears grayish white. For miles downstream they appear as two rivers sharing the same river bed—dark on one side, grayish white on the other—but gradually the waters intermingle to become one mighty river. Likewise, national and missionary streams of leadership must flow together and intermingle to become one.

Collaboration implies the developing maturity of both the missionaries and national leaders, each with changing roles. *Missionaries who were culture and language learners in the Learning Stage become teachers, evangelists, and church planters in the Growth Stage and equippers, encouragers, and advisors in the Collaborative Stage.* National leaders who were converts during the Learning and Growth Stages become co-laborers and fellow resource people, full participants in a collaborative process.

In the Collaborative Period national leaders come to own their movement and make decisions for its continuity. All too frequently, paternalistic missionaries thwart national initiatives, believing the nationals are out of line, usurping authority, or acting naively. Effective missionaries, however, serve as encouragers and advisors, co-facilitators in decision-making processes. National leaders and missionaries thus work together to lay the foundations for eventual missionary phase-out and for the movement's continuity.

Cooperatively developing structures of continuity for the future is the major focus of the Collaborative Stage. Monte Cox, in an insightful PhD dissertation, says that "organization ambiguities" of certain anti-institutional movements like Churches of Christ have "dampened morale and perhaps stunted the growth of the church" in rural church plantings in Kenya. When churches reach what is here called the Collaborative Stage, they begin to ask structural questions: *What are the structures of governance, expansion, finance, and theological education? Or, in Kalenjin parlance, how can churches show* kipagenge *(unity) and cooperate for the sake of* ribset *(member care),* amdaet *(evangelism),* tesetab tai *(development), and* somanet *(education)?*

Strong movements develop structures of continuity on both the congregational and associational levels. On the congregational level the community of faith, guided by the word of God, must determine how local churches are organized and how these local congregations relate to one another. The community must also agree on the nature and roles of elders, deacons, evangelists, and other local church leaders and implement guidelines for their selection.

In addition, the local church must develop methods and structures for nurturing and equipping children, young people, and congregational leaders. These decisions, having begun with guidance from the church-planting missionaries during the Growth Period, become a collaborative effort during this stage of church development.

On the associational level mature leaders and missionaries collaborate in developing teaching, equipping, and encouraging structures above the level of the local church. Local congregations should bond together, as did the early churches in Jerusalem, so that they help each other.

Vocational, paravocational, and full-time national evangelists must form teams to complete the evangelization of their area and spread the gospel into adjoining and distant areas. Training schools on the association level—almost always, out of necessity—provide forums for creative reflection and equipping of leaders and youth for local congregations.

The need for such structures of continuity is frequently questioned in anti-institutional movements like Churches of Christ. Such movements espouse a sort of indigeneity which negates any sort of partnership even when a movement has developed roots and stability.

Our team working among the Kipsigis people of Kenya competently ministered during the Learning and Growth Periods but lacked understandings to go on to the Collaborative Stage. Developing leaders asked, "Does the Church of Christ in America only have local churches? Who equips and encourages these churches?" Others said, "We thank you missionaries for starting these churches and for teaching us to become evangelists and church planters. But should you not now equip us as leaders?"

Our team, however, holding firmly to an indigenous philosophy of missions, failed to see the validity of these questions and did not plan with the national Church for their future. The result was a movement that grew from the mid-1970s until the late 1980s. In the late 1980s, however, the inevitable clash between non-collaborating missionaries and maturing national leaders occurred.

National leaders met without missionaries to form a hierarchy to make plans for local churches. Like the clashing of two mighty bodies of water, *pororoca* occurred. Missionaries and many national leaders upheld the autonomy of the local church and refused to accept the authority of the proposed centralized leaders. Others, many of whom had personal agendas, attempted unsuccessfully to provide structure for the developing movement. Churches polarized. This tension and ambivalence caused the movement in Kipsigis to stagnate for a time.

During the 1990s, several factors worked together to reverse discouragement, to help the young movement stabilize, and to develop structures of continuity for the equipping of local churches.

First, a second-generation team of American missionaries worked in Kipsigis for approximately ten years encouraging existing churches and training leaders in congregationally-based courses. Second, churches from all areas of Kipsigis met together in 1990 to pray and forgive each other and acknowledge the unity of the Body of Christ. God worked powerfully to heal old wounds and unite the Body of Christ in love. Third, older missionaries returned to encourage national leaders and younger missionaries. At first they primarily taught textual courses to groups of national leaders in local churches throughout Kipsigis but eventually began to collaborate with national leaders to institute nationally led structures of continuity.

As a result, churches began to appoint elders over clusters of churches (rather than over individual churches), and Siriat Bible School was initiated to train leaders and youths of area churches. The school's schedule is unique but fitting for its rural environment. Leaders, selected and supported by their churches, study two one-week classes. They then return home to do required practicum as they care for their farms and continue their jobs. After five or six weeks they return to the school for the next two one-week classes. This cycle is continued for two years (twenty-four classes), then they graduate.

The school has been nationally run from its inception. A committee of national leaders from all areas of Kipsigis provides direction, and a full-time principal facilitates school activities. Structures of continuity are thus developing at a later period in Kipsigis on both the congregational and associational levels.

Two extremes are possible in regard to the Collaborative Stage. At one extreme, missionaries phase out before leaders mature and structures of continuity develop. Christians generally become discouraged in this situation because they are not ready for the missionaries' departure. Some Christians may, consequently, revert to the world, others affiliate with different Christian religious groups, and still others maintain their heritage and learn to survive without missionary support.

This premature phase-out ignores the need for collaboration. At the other extreme, missionaries naively jump past the Growth Stage by creating training institutions without adequately nurturing developing churches and equipping national leaders. These schools almost always reflect the worldview presuppositions and economics of the sending culture. Missionaries in this scenario generally assume that Bible knowledge alone enables national leaders to effectively minister in their own culture. They presuppose that cognitive information without contextualization and application is adequate for ministry preparation.

Both early phase-out and premature development of institutions imply inadequate understandings about the progressive development of Christian leaders. Just as children pass through several stages of development before they become adults, new leaders require growth through natural stages to become mature. When structures of continuity have been mutually developed by missionaries and national leaders, the stage is set for missionary phase-out.

The Phase-out Period

At the conclusion of his theological treatise to the Romans, Paul describes how he had fully preached the gospel from Jerusalem to Illyricum, laying new foundations wherever he ministered (Rom. 15:19-20). In this process, it was his custom to appoint elders, and through prayer and fasting, "commit them to the Lord" (Acts 14:23). His words to the Romans demonstrate the heart and motivation of phase-out: "But now, since my work in these places no longer needs my presence ....Let us go somewhere else....so I can preach there also" (Rom. 15:23). His goal was to visit Rome so that they might send him to new fields in Spain (Rom. 15:24).

Phase-out is thus the farewell period when missionaries overtly and intentionally pass the baton of leadership to national leaders as they transition to other mission contexts.

The major missionary roles during this stage are those of encourager and advisor of national leaders on both the congregational and associational levels. As encouragers, missionaries affirm nationals' abilities to carry the mission of God in responsible, reproducing ways. Elders and evangelists in local churches are affirmed as God's ordained servants. Equippers on the associational level are confirmed as leaders with godly dedication and experience.

As advisors, missionaries suggest models of teaching, ministry, and administration to the relatively new Christian movement and its leadership. A good rule of thumb is to make five affirmations to every one suggestion. In other words, the role of encourager should surpass that of advisor.

A significant danger during this period is inadvertent paternalism. Without realizing it, missionaries are tempted to control the structures that have been developed collaboratively with national leaders. They plan for disengagement with one hand while developing structures of control through money and placement of personnel with the other. Like parents of young adults, they know that they should not dominate but have difficulty letting go.

"Ownership," Cox writes, "should be the main criterion by which missionaries and nationals determine the timing of disengagement." This ownership is a process. During the Growth Stage, Christian leaders assume leadership roles in their home churches and learn how to plant and develop other churches. During the Collaborative Stage, missionaries and national leaders envision and plan together to develop the structures of continuity appropriate to the church in their context and are equipped and empowered to lead those structures.

It has been a joy to see the Church of Christ in Kipsigis grow during the past few years without missionary involvement. Recently, while visiting Kipsigis, I journeyed by public service vehicle and foot to an area where I had ministered many years before. During the time that I was a missionary in this area, the Church was weak. I had worked with national evangelists to start one church that, in turn, established a second.

Now, twelve years later, there are ten much larger churches in this particular area. A crowd of 489 gathered for the Sunday morning service, and 120 vocational preachers ministering in these churches attended the Sunday afternoon evangelists' meeting. I stood amazed at their mature faith in God, in-depth knowledge of the Bible, and incisive plans for ministry. I could only say, "Praise God. May he use the Kipsigis churches as mission-sending and mission-mobilizing churches!"

Conclusion

Each stage of church planting and development is important to the eventual maturity of a mission movement, and the result is predictable when any stage is neglected.

Bypassing the Learning Stage almost always results in anemic movements. This most strikingly occurs when campaigners from the West seek to plant a church in another part of the world without the presence of long-term missionaries and then hire missionaries to conduct follow up. Typically, these missionaries are given neither the time nor training to become cultural learners.

In fact, because the initial converts were taught in English, it is frequently believed that one can be effective in this context without language and culture learning. The eventual maturity of the mission movement frequently depends on the depth of missionary learning during the initial stage.

The Growth Period is frequently short-circuited when training institutions are established early in the work before contextualized models of church growth and reproduction are developed. The assumption is made that leaders are best trained in a formal school setting rather than by learning ministry in context—by going with mature evangelists and learning from them how to plant churches and nurture new Christians in these churches to maturity.

Thus, prospective leaders are taught information in an academic environment without adequate learning by the doing of ministry. If training institutions are developed too early in a mission movement, they are not only overseen and supported by missionaries rather than by national leaders who have progressed through a system of maturation, but are also geared more toward the dispensing of information than the training for ministry.

Negation of the Collaborative Stage is a common failing. Like our team among the Kipsigis of Kenya, missionaries naively believe that their task is complete when many churches have been planted and leaders trained to minister within local congregations. Without continued nurturing, however, communities of faith erode when left as autonomous bodies. Structures of continuity are needed to equip leaders and to serve as places for reflection and strategy development.

Finally, without phase-out, a movement tends to exist with missionaries at the pinnacle of power. Rather than equipping national leaders to assume missionary roles, missionaries remain lords in their created fiefdoms. In a number of mission works around the world—built on the missionaries' personality, power, and presence—there is no intention of missionary phase-out. Displacing missionaries from their pinnacles of power, if possible, would require catastrophic action by national leaders.

I, therefore, suggest that to be effective, all works initiated through cross-cultural missionary work must intentionally progress through stages emphasizing learning, growth, collaboration, and phase-out. Missionaries' roles change as movements develop. The intention is to phase out the missionary presence as mature nationals assume leadership roles.

July 1991

Phasing Out Your Work:
Make It a Plan, Not a Crisis

Tom Steffen

Church planters who leave prematurely may harm the church, but they can also harm it by staying too long. The balance lies in focusing on three things.

My former mission agency began church planting in the Philippines in 1951 and now works among nineteen tribal societies there. After forty years, only one tribal work has been completely phased out because their objectives were met. Why? Because neither the mission nor the church planters started with a clear definition of and plan for phase-out.

Without such a definition and plan, the church planters had no way to identify their role changes, much less work through them. Furthermore, the mission did not include phase-out in its selection and training of missionaries. Consequently, most of its church planters stayed on as evangelists and teachers, rather than becoming partners; they emphasized phase-in, not phase-out. The mission waited almost two decades before a church was completed according to its objectives. We desperately needed a definition of phase-out.

Of course, church planters who leave prematurely may harm the church. But they can also harm it by staying too long. We can maintain the balance between these extremes by (1) surveying various perspectives of phase-out, (2) isolating its components, and (3) defining phase-out.

Our Phase-out Roots

The debate over when church planters should leave is not new. Rufus Anderson and Henry Venn, both late nineteenth-century missionaries, were the first to expound the three-self formula: self-government, self-support, and self-propagation. They said missionaries had to follow this formula to develop churches capable of standing on their own. While not everyone agreed with them, their formula stimulated phase-out thinking.

John Nevius (1829-1893) built on the three-self formula in Korea (1958). Roland Allen (1868-1947) concluded that the formula was not only practical, but biblical (1962). Much later, Alan Tippett added self-image, self-functioning, and self-giving to the formula (1969).

William Read, Victor Monterroso, and Harmon Johnson advocated reaching autonomy by having missionaries change their roles over time from apostolate, to administrator, to partner, to servant, to consultant (1969). C. Peter

Wagner argued that no mission should be content to go out of business after a church is established. Rather, missionary work should move through four phases: (1) going to non-Christians, (2) church development, (3) becoming a consultant, and (4) launching another mission (1971).

Harold Fuller saw mission-church relationships advancing through four stages: (1) pioneer, (2) parent, (3) partner, and (4) participant (1980). While these writers may not totally agree with Anderson, Venn, and Allen, they nevertheless are not content to control a new church or remain in a maintenance role.

Current Thinking

A mission executive recently said his leaders continue to struggle with responsible phase-out. While they often talk about turning things over to the local Christians, much of their work continues as it has for twenty to fifty years. This executive, however, wants to empower local believers to take control within a much shorter time.

Another mission leader laments his organization's failure to focus on a church-planting exit strategy as opposed to an entry strategy. He recognizes there is no way the Church will keep pace with burgeoning world population if church planters are reluctant to release power to those whom they have come to reach. Like the first executive, he seeks to change the worldwide dependency patterns being instituted by his organization's people.

The time has come for a new look at our inherited departure strategies. We must correct and modify them if local Christians are to receive and reproduce a church-planting model that empowers others. It's time we move beyond the cliché, "Our goal is to work ourselves out of a job," and start to make it happen.

The New Testament

Acts gives a number of reasons why Paul and his team left cities in which they ministered. Sometimes, they left for their own safety (e.g., Pisidian Antioch, 13:50; Iconium, 14:6; Lystra, 14:19; Thessalonica, 17:10; and perhaps Ephesus, 20:1). But more importantly for our purposes, they also departed because of their desire and plan to reach as many places as possible with the gospel. After staying awhile in new places, they returned to previously visited areas to strengthen the believers and appoint elders (Acts 9:32; 14:21, 22; 15:36, 41). In some cases, Paul sent his team members to do this. When visits were delayed or inconvenient, he wrote letters of instruction and encouragement to the new churches.

Paul and his team also left places of ministry when they had completed their work for a particular visit (i.e., evangelism, discipleship, or both). Paul or one of his team members left Antioch (13:1-3; 18:23), Athens (18:1), Corinth (18:18), and Ephesus (18:21; 19:21) because their objectives had been met.

So departure occurred for a number of reasons: satanic hindrances, completed objectives, and designation of local leaders. As we plan our own phase-out strategies, we should take into account not only planned but also un-planned withdrawals due to political and economic necessities.

Key Components

To define phase-out accurately, a church planter should isolate all related components of the ministry, including:

1. A definition of a local church
2. The number of churches to be planted in a given area
3. The cycle of a local church
4. The roles of team members, local believers, and God
5. Theological training
6. When to begin phase-out
7. Ways of maintaining relationships after phase-out

We begin with a *definition of a local church*. How you define a local church determines what product you look for. What takes place in worship, instruction, sociality, evangelism—and the written and taped curricula to support these activities—determine when phase-out begins.

For me, a local church consists of a group of people who trust Christ as their Savior and organize their lives according to indigenous biblical principles. Their purpose is to glorify God through worship, instruction, sociality, and evangelism, which leads to new churches. They try by the power of the Holy Spirit to reproduce themselves in unreached areas locally and at a distance.

Another component is the *total number of churches required for the entire society to hear the gospel*. Several factors determine this number, one being demographic studies. These studies should indicate:

1. The route Christianity will most likely spread
2. The number of strategic church plantings required to put churches in the entire society
3. The number of church leaders required on the local and itinerant levels
4. Whether an association of churches is necessary, along with its size
5. The ties the society has to other societies

Discovering what constitutes a significant group within the target society will tell us how many churches we ought to project for the future. This requires cultural analysis. Add to this the demographic studies and your definition of a local church, and you get the broad parameters for a church-planting strategy that leads to phase-out.

Cycles of vitality, lukewarmness, and sterility in the local church are important for church planters to notice. Like all institutions, churches go through stages. First-generation believers often pay a high price for following Christ, but their strong commitment makes risk-taking possible.

But passivism tends to set in when second-generation believers join the church. They don't face the same burning issues their parents did, nor are the lines of difference between believers and unbelievers so clearly defined. While their parents often experienced a sudden, dramatic conversion, second-generation Christians tend to be more gradual and less emotional in their conversions. Structure often replaces spontaneity.

Third-generation Christians often face theological and ethical breakdowns. Nominalism tends to set in while they seek their cultural roots.

Church planters must not confuse generational issues when they define phase-out (i.e., by placing second-generation expectations on first-generation believers or vice-versa). Church planters must be adept at recognizing church cycles, and define their phase-outs accordingly.

The fourth component of phase-out calls for church planters to isolate the *different roles played by team members, local believers, and God.* As church planters move through evangelism, discipleship, church development, church organization, and church reproduction, their roles change as local believers do the same things, imitating the models set by the expatriates. The missionaries' roles include learner, evangelist, teacher, resident advisor, itinerant advisor, and absent advisor.

When the newly-established church reproduces another church close to home ("Jerusalem"), or cross-culturally ("Judea, Samaria, ends of the earth"), phase-out should be under way. Local Christians demonstrate their abilities in evangelism, teaching, meeting felt needs, administering church ordinances, implementing church discipline, and developing leaders for both local and itinerant ministries.

Their role changes include accompanying, participating, leading, and training. In all these activities, both expatriates and local believers must recognize God's sovereign hand on themselves and those whom they are reaching.

The fifth phase-out component is *theological training.* To be successful, it should provide a solid foundation for the gospel, be comprehensive (Acts 20:27), focus on the material as well as the spiritual world, and address cultural themes, cults, and political ideologies.

Theological training must move from the simple to the complex, from the known to the unknown, and be presented through viable cultural means. From the perspective of phase-out, it should include everyone from the start, emphasize church-planting evangelism rather than simply individual evangelism, be owned by the churches, and be reproducible. The aim is to train theologically-oriented church leaders who will model to their flocks the importance of starting new churches.

Sixth, church planters must decide *when to begin their phase-outs.* They start by setting a realistic timetable for the new church to reach its goals. This is critical, because it gives the team a specific goal.

Of course, one must be flexible. We set an eight-year goal, knowing that health, subversive elements, or stony hearts could change our projection. The timetable, like the strategy statement, must regularly be updated to allow for new developments and understandings. Phase-out begins when the stated objectives are met, not when the prescribed time arrives.

The seventh and final component is *determining how church planters can maintain good relationships after the phase-out*. They work themselves out of a job, but not out of a relationship. Continued fellowship includes prayer, visits, letters of challenge and encouragement, sending other people to visit, and financial assistance.

Defining Phase-out

First, let me say what I do not mean by phase-out. I do not mean abruptly abandoning maturing believers, even when they reach a certain level of maturity and Bible knowledge. Or when they appoint their own leaders. Or when things seem to be going well, with problems at a minimum.

Phase-out-oriented church planters build in their absences over time, so they can have interaction with the church throughout. They plan their disengagement. They start with short absences and move toward longer and longer ones, until they completely withdraw physically, but not relationally.

Church planters begin phase-out by stepping back from active leadership. By this time, the believers are doing evangelism, discipleship, leadership development, and organization, as well as starting new churches. The seven components surrounding phase-out begin to converge. It is now time for the church planters to distance themselves from the believers.

Of course, any phase-out strategy has to start long before the church planters land on the field. Closure must be designed before their ministry starts, because a planned exit affects all the steps in church planting: pre-evangelism, evangelism, and post-evangelism. Such planning gives team members the whole picture, direction, and a checklist toward closure. Just as a blueprint illustrates to construction workers the finished building and the steps to get there, so a planned phase-out strategy helps a church-planting team. Without such a pre-field plan, phase-out will be continually delayed, or, in all too many cases, never achieved at all.

Phase-out church planting must be integral to the entire mission. It's a comprehensive organizational approach that starts with the end product and works back to those who are responsible for producing it. It affects everything: how candidates are selected and trained, how they plan, form teams, handle social programs, evangelize, and develop leaders and curricula. When a mission agency works with such a definition of phase-out, it is not likely to wait forty years to achieve its first phase-out from a new church.

Conclusion

Phase-out is not pullout; it is the planned absences of church planters over time, so that believers can develop their own spiritual roots and grow strong, as responsibility for the church shifts to them from the church planters.

Phase-out begins with a closure strategy for the overall field and for each local church within that society. The strategy includes:

1. The definition of a local church
2. The number of churches required to finish the task in that area
3. The cycles of a local church
4. The different roles of the church-planting team, the churches, and God
5. Theological training
6. The timing of the phase-out
7. Maintaining relations after phase-out.

Such a closure strategy, crafted over time and seasoned with prayer, determines to a great extent whether the team will accomplish its goal in a realistic time. Such an effective strategy will also produce believers whose reliance remains on the Holy Spirit, not on the team. If we are to move beyond phase-in to phase-out, our agencies must be permeated from top to bottom with this kind of thinking and action.

References
Allen, Roland. 1962. *Missionary Methods: St. Paul's or Ours?* Grand Rapids, Mich.: William B. Eerdmans Publishing Co.

Fuller, Harold. 1980. *Mission-Church Dynamics: How to Change Bicultural Tensions into Dynamic Missionary Outreach.* Pasadena, Calif.: William Carey Library.

Nevius, John. 1958. *Planting and Development of Missionary Churches.* Philadelphia: Presbyterian and Reformed.

Read, William, Victor Monterroso, and Harmon Johnson. 1969. *Latin American Church Growth.* Grand Rapids, Mich.: William B. Eerdmans Publishing Co.

Tippett, Alan. 1969. *Verdict Theology in Missionary Theory.* Lincoln, Ill.: Lincoln Christian College Press.

Wagner, C. Peter. 1971. *Frontiers in Missionary Strategy.* Chicago: Moody Press.

January 2010

Preventing Discouragement and Keeping Church Planters Productive on the Field

David A. Diaso

Guidance for mission agencies and team leaders looking to help their church planters succeed in their tasks.

All church-planting organizations long to see God do great and powerful things through their efforts, acknowledging that the source of all missions comes from the heart of God for the world, and that it is only through his power that the best of human efforts can be effective. Most also acknowledge that a large portion of an organization's responsibility is to cooperate with the Holy Spirit by assisting workers to be effective and deeply satisfied at the end of the day.

Why, then, with such worthy goals, do church planters regularly quit in defeat or retreat to places of discouragement and permanent paralysis? Past and current studies demonstrate a strong correlation between cross-cultural church planters' satisfaction, sustainability, and the undergirding they receive from their sending agencies. How can mission agencies equip missionaries to thrive?

In the northern Indian state of Punjab, I recently observed a rapidly reproducing church-planting movement. The high excitement in evidence came not only from seeing entire villages come to Christ, but also from the quality training and coaching of the church planters.

Regional and strategic leaders come together once a month for training, prayer, testimony, and encouragement. The church planters are not only motivated, they are confident because of the intentional training in evangelism strategies, discipleship, church formation, and leadership training they receive. Assessment and accountability are present at each stage of the church-planting process. The church planters obviously know their task; they receive ongoing, on-the-job training in effective church-planting and discipleship strategies. Unfortunately, this is the exception rather than the rule.

I was a church planter in Mexico City for ten years. My family remembers the time fondly, yet we were often frustrated. Our team struggled to form shared goals, and when we began a partnership with the Mexican national Church, we realized that we lacked a cohesive plan for our work. What would a healthy, biblical church plant look like? How would we know when or if it was successful? How would training for reproduction occur?

Yearning for answers, I ended up on the doorstep of Dr. Thomas Graham in Colorado Springs, Colorado. Tom, recognized as a wise professor, an experienced consultant to mission agencies, and the "father" of church-planting assessment centers, helped me to voice my confusion, begin to ask the right questions, and transfer those queries into a survey and study that might assist others to find answers for the dilemma of church-planting equipping and supervision.

What the Church Planters Revealed

The mission agency and team leader/supervisors play key roles in church planters' well-being and effectiveness. They must assume responsibility for creating church planters' job descriptions, developing shared criteria for success, providing training, and offering tangible support and encouragement to those who focus their energies on establishing churches.

At some level, organizational leaders acknowledge that mandate, but often don't know how to proceed, so the intentional work of providing clear descriptions needed to achieve success is left undone. My study[1] confirmed research results from the mission community (2006, 110), and correlated interestingly with comparable findings from the world of business and development and management. The responses to a survey I conducted demonstrated that church planters are more likely to be motivated to continue if the following are in place:

- a clear definition of the criteria for success;
- a clear description of tasks required to plant a church;
- training, coaching, and mentoring in tangible church-planting principles; and
- consistent encouragement and feedback from the mission agency and team leader/supervisor.

Let's consider implications of the four components.

Success: A Clear Definition

Clearly-defined criteria for measuring success need to be in place in order for the agency and its church planters to know when a job has been done well. A clearly-defined job description is also necessary so that the missionary knows what tasks are to be performed. What are the organization and its missionaries seeking to accomplish? If they do not know, how will they accomplish it? As David Garrison says, the first of the seven deadly sins for church-planting movements is blurred vision (2004, 239-240). If church planters don't have a clear vision for how a church-planting movement should look, likely they will fail.

A Clear Description of Tasks Required

The definition and design of the church-planting task will significantly influence the church planter's success. Ferdinand Fournies (2000, 94) surveyed twenty-five thousand managers and supervisors from around the world regarding the poor performance of their employees. He listed sixteen of the top responses he received.

- Employees don't know what they are supposed to do.
- Employees don't know how to do it.
- Employees don't know why they should do it.
- Employees think they are doing it (lack of feedback).
- There are obstacles beyond their control.
- Employees think it will not work.
- Employees think their way is better.
- Employees think something is more important (priorities).
- There is no positive consequence to them for doing it.
- There is a negative consequence to them for doing it.
- There is a positive consequence to them for not doing it.
- There is no negative consequence to them for not doing it.
- Personal limits (incapacity).
- Personal problems.
- Fear (they anticipate future negative consequences).
- No one could do it.

The majority of these problems relate to the managers/supervisors not doing something right in supervising their employees. There are also a number of problems that can be traced back to a lack of clear direction and/or a lack of feedback, similar to the points that Thomas Gilbert made in his human competence model (1996).

Fournies' study relates to the question, "Does the employee know what is supposed to be done?" He reports, "The most common missing information which causes project failure is they don't know what finished is supposed to look like" (2000, 120). Another way to say it is that there is confusion concerning the process and tasks involved in doing the job. Failure to know what a good finished product looks like emphasizes the need for job descriptions and performance outcomes. Fournies states,

> Every business consultant and professor I have ever heard talk about increasing worker productivity has preached, "Tell people what you want them to do; give them good job descriptions." And business has flubbed that advice because most job descriptions don't describe the work; they describe the job responsibilities. Unfortunately, you can't do a job responsibility. (2000, 121)

The worker doesn't know how to do his or her job; he or she is confused and it shows in his or her performance. This problem is equally significant for church planters—they need a description of their work to help them in achieving agreed upon outcomes.

The church planting survey findings indicate that the church planter's perceived lack of a definition for the criteria for success in church planting does lead to more dissatisfaction. Also, if the church planters perceive that they have received a poorly defined task description, this leads to increased discouragement. Statistically, this was one of the most highly significant findings in the overall study.

Training, Coaching, and Mentoring

While following sound wisdom and principles learned along the way, church planters work hard and depend on Christ and his Spirit to provide the increase. The practical issue that frequently emerges is the mission agency's inability to achieve the success it desperately longs to see. They do not adequately educate their church planters concerning how to achieve their purpose.

Gilbert posits that when results are not being achieved, the ultimate cause lies in the organization's management (1996, 81). His table for "Creating Incompetence" (1996, 87) graphically tells the story of how organizations desert their people by lack of information, instrumentation, and motivation. Obviously, the supporting environment affects behavior positively or adversely. Gilbert's framework also takes into account the person's knowledge, skills, and attitude he or she needs to succeed. The following steps (1996, 179) help in organizing information for clear criteria for success.

- Identify the expected accomplishments: mission, responsibilities, and duties.
- State and explain the requirements for each accomplishment.
- Describe how performance will be measured and why.
- Set exemplary standards, preferably in measurement terms.
- Identify exemplary performers and any available resources that people can use to become exemplary performers.
- Provide frequent and unequivocal feedback on how well each person is performing; usually expressed as a comparison with an exemplary standard with good and bad consequences made clear.
- Supply backup information to help people troubleshoot their own performance and those for whom they are responsible.
- Relate various aspects of poor performance to specific remedial actions.

The results of the church planter survey indicate a strong correlation between the preparation and ongoing training and coaching of the church planter and a subsequent sense of support and direction experienced. When church planters did not feel supported by their mission agency, they almost always felt discouraged enough to leave the field.

Consistent Encouragement

Team leaders and supervisors are critical in forming and maintaining strong church-planting teams. Marcus Buckingham insists that supervisors are key to building a strong workplace environment (Buckingham and Coffman 1999, 32). In fact, immediate leaders may be the single most significant factor in determining whether employees have a successful experience in the working environment. Employees are likely to leave the organization if their experience with their immediate supervisor is poor. Buckingham states,

We have discovered that the manager—not pay, benefits, perks, or charismatic corporate leaders—was the critical player in building a strong workplace. The manager was "key." Competent leaders are needed. If you have a turnover problem, look first to your managers. (1999, 32-33)

Paul McKaughan agrees that attrition is often related to management inefficiencies. He says,

> Often, rather than evaluate and admit our organizational guilt or ineptness, we mission leaders abdicate our responsibility and too easily write off the individual as somehow not having measured up—another casualty of missionary attrition. Individuals become the problem, not the management or system which misused them. (1997, 20)

This is the proverbial elephant in the room that everyone sees, but no one is willing to talk about or deal with directly. Mission field team leaders may believe they are too busy with their own work to give assistance to church planters. Jerry Gilley states,

> Performance standards also are not used because managers are too busy managing and workers are too busy working. They don't have the time to identify the standards. Quality is another thing jeopardized during this period. (Gilley and Boughton 1996, 8)

Too little time is spent thinking about what the end product should look like (in this case, a healthy church). As a result, church planters learn how to do the job through the school of hard knocks. Gilley states,

> Distress and confusion are words connected with periods of growth and expansion. Managers may miss opportunities to reduce employees' distress by not clearly communicating expectations. They should also provide feedback while employees perform their jobs. (1996, 9)

According to Gallup research, *only twenty percent of people in the workplace believe they are in the right role where they are doing what they do best every day.* This likely means there are a lot of frustrated people, and this phenomenon affects missionaries as well. Missionaries are often called on to do numerous activities, some of which are not their area of strength. If missionaries end up with too many tasks that they are not good at, then they will become frustrated. It is important to know where the missionaries' talents and gifts lie and capitalize on these.

Recommendations

Below are four recommendations for mission agencies and team leaders as they think about success and church planting.

1. Mission agencies and team leaders/supervisors must provide a clear definition of the criteria for success. Since the study indicated that church planters are more likely to be encouraged if they have a clear definition of the criteria for success, mission agencies and team leaders/supervisors must provide those definitions. Do church planters know what a successful church plant looks like? If not, this needs to be described and defined for church planters as they take up their ministries. One church planter I surveyed commented: "The job description is vague at best. There is absolutely ZERO accountability when jobs are changed, both before arrival on the field and during time on the field. The expectation is that we all need to be 'flexible.'"

Mission agencies dare not neglect to provide up-to-date job descriptions. It is also true that certain mission fields are more difficult than others, but that is not an excuse for unclear task descriptions. The church-planting ministry I visited in India had simple, but very clear, descriptions of what church planters needed to do in order to plant a healthy church. This fostered confidence in the church planters. It gave them cause to celebrate, and they deliberately took time out to praise God for what he was doing among them.

2. Mission agencies need to provide a clear description of tasks required to plant a church. Mission agencies should take the time to study the most basic and important tasks necessary to plant healthy, biblical churches. That will help them describe these tasks to church planters. For example, what does evangelism look like in the context in which the missionaries are working? When church planters understand the tasks and desired outcomes to be achieved, they will be more confident and motivated.

3. Mission agencies need to provide training, coaching, and mentoring in tangible church-planting principles. Church planters are likely to be more confident and motivated if they receive training, coaching, and mentoring in church planting. One church planter commented, "Early on in my ministry I was discouraged because of the lack of mentoring given and because of the lack of vision that was evident in the church planters."

On the job training is vital, and it is one of the key components of the church-planting movement I saw in India. Mission agencies should assign new church planters to a mentor/coach. They must take care to ensure that church planters receive training throughout their missionary careers. Providing effective training requires studying the criteria for success and the tasks required to plant healthy, biblical churches. If the organization provides mentoring and adequate training for church planters, they will be more likely to perform well and more likely to experience job satisfaction.

4. Mission agencies and team leaders/supervisors need to provide consistent encouragement and feedback. Finally, church planters are less likely to be discouraged if they receive support from the mission agency and team leader/supervisor. In this study, the highest statistical correlation between whether a missionary felt dissatisfied to the point of leaving the field depended upon whether he or she felt supported by the mission agency. If he or she didn't feel supported, he or she was much more likely to be discouraged, and to possibly leave the mission field.

Team leaders, supervisors, and managers are crucial to forming and maintaining strong teams on the mission field. This seems obvious, yet it is often overlooked. This is part of the genius in bringing the church planters together once a month in India. Thomas Peters speaks of the importance of what he calls "transforming leadership," which is evident in great companies:

> But transforming leadership ultimately becomes moral in that it raises the level of human conduct and ethical aspiration of both the leader and the led, and thus has a transforming effect on both....Transforming leadership is dynamic leadership in the sense that the leaders throw themselves into a relationship with followers who will feel "elevated" by it and often become more active themselves, thereby creating new cadres of leaders. (Peters and Waterman 1982, 83)

Mission agencies can lead well by showing interest in their missionaries and being willing to listen. They have valuable insights to offer. One discouraged missionary I surveyed commented:

> When the mission agency insists on using methodology from other parts of the world and tries to impose it on our ministries, it becomes ridiculous and irrelevant. Thus the leaders appear to be friendly, but at the same time unwavering. This brings frustration, and the church planter, who is indeed the only one who truly knows his field, feels obligated to accept and go along with the new system or resigns and goes back home. This is indeed sad.

Another church planter commented:

> Most of my frustration has come from lack of communication in the midst of massive change. I have made my issues known, and I have been able to have some dialogue with my leadership. My feeling is that they still don't understand how I feel. The strategy and objectives are what seem to be more important than the people implementing them.

When agencies and team leaders involve church planters in the process of making changes and important decisions, it is easier for missionaries to accept these changes. This process will prevent an "us versus them" mentality and create a healthy environment in which church planters will thrive. Feedback to church planters is also important. They want to know how they are doing, and their progress should be acknowledged in appropriate ways. One church planter commented, "There is little feedback (either good or bad) and little opportunity to bounce ideas off fellow church planters."

Peters offers a positive way to reward people for a job well done: "The systems in the excellent companies are not only designed to produce lots of winners; they are constructed to celebrate winning once it occurs. Their systems make extraordinary use of non-monetary incentives. They are full of hoopla" (Peters and Waterman 1982, 58).

Mission agencies can celebrate milestones of individual and corporate accomplishments. For missionaries who work in difficult places where there are few tangible results, faithful service and new innovations can be rewarded. The Bible teaches that some people plant and others water, but God gives the increase. Each of these endeavors can be celebrated.

Summary

I have found that little serious study has been made among Christians in the areas of discouragement, criteria for success, and the tasks required to plant healthy, biblical churches. This present study shows a correlation. Based on the findings of this study, it is recommended that leaders in mission agencies study and define expectations for church planters, define criteria for success, develop the necessary training, and create avenues to give and receive feedback from church planters. These practices will serve the mission agency, church planter, and the kingdom with the hope that fewer church planters will leave the field discouraged, and encourage church planters to be more effective in their ministries.

Endnote

1. 180 missionaries from fourteen agencies were involved: 64% of the church planters served in Latin America, 6% in Africa, 10% in Asia, 12% in Europe, 1.4% in the Middle East, and 3% in the United States.

References

Buckingham, Marcus and Curt Coffman. 1999. *First, Break All the Rules: What the World's Greatest Managers Do Differently*. New York: Simon & Schuster.

Diaso, David Anthony. 2006. "The Relationship between a Cross-Cultural Church Planter's Discouragement of the Mission Field, and the Criteria for Success, and the Task Descriptions Required for a Healthy Biblical Church Plant." DMiss dissertation. New Geneva Theological Seminary.

Fournies, Ferdinand F. 2000. *Coaching for Improved Work Performance*. New York: R. R. Donnelley & Sons Company.

Garrison, David. 2004. *Church Planting Movements: How God Is Redeeming a Lost World*. Midlothian, Va.: WIGTake Resources.

Gilbert, Thomas F. 1996. *Human Competence: Engineering Worthy Performance*. *Tribute Edition*. Silver Spring, Md.: International Society for Performance Improvement.

Gilley, Jerry W. and Nathaniel W. Boughton. 1996. *Stop Managing, Start Coaching! How Performance Coaching Can Enhance Commitment and Improve Productivity*. Chicago: Irwin Professional Publishing.

McKaughan, Paul. 1997. "Missionary Attrition: Defining the Problem." In *Too Valuable to Lose: Exploring the Causes and Cures of Missionary Attrition*. Ed. William D. Taylor, 15-24. Pasadena, Calif.: William Carey Library.

Peters, Thomas J. and Robert H. Waterman, Jr. 1982. *In Search of Excellence: Lessons from America's Best-Run Companies*. New York: Harper & Row, Publishers, Inc.

Power Encounter and Church Planting

Ken Baker

In the context of biblical teaching and compassionate witness, a ministry of power encounter can have a profound effect on a people group.

Early in January 1982 the elders of Fasavolo were considering a proposal from our church-planting team. This Gbandi village is nestled in the mountainous rain forests of northern Liberia near the Guinea border. For quite some time different missionaries on our team had spoken to the men about the deplorable, unhealthy way the women drew their water. Many people in the village were sick and dying from waterborne diseases.

About one hundred yards beyond the village muddy spring water flowed over the face of a rock. The flow was so slow that it took a woman about ten minutes to fill her jug. Groups of women, children, goats, and dogs trampled around the spring and added to its contamination. Another five hundred yards away was a rarely used free-flowing spring.

We made a simple proposal: cap the good spring and pipe the water to a reservoir. The village would have a safe, efficient water supply. We would provide the materials if the villagers did the work.

We had been there only a few months, so none of us spoke Gbandi. Consequently, we couldn't figure out why it took so long for the elders to reply. We thought they would jump at our idea. Finally, the elders came to us and said that although they liked our idea, the answer was no. The women had voiced a unanimous veto on spiritual grounds. The dirty spring was sacred for fertility rites and sacrifices; if they disturbed it, they would become barren. That settled it; there was nothing we could do.

Frankly, I was both appalled and angry at the outcome. As a new missionary I filtered this experience through my Western Christian grid, and it all seemed ridiculous. This was just another example of backward fear and superstition triumphing over modern reason. I just could not believe the village would reject such an obvious improvement for such reasons.

As I write years later, I can see how my thinking has changed. My subsequent experience in West Africa has helped me to develop new perceptions of culture, worldview, ministry, and spiritual warfare. Back in Fasavolo in 1982, did our team miss an opportunity to confront the powers of darkness that held those people in bondage? I can't say, because I didn't stay there very long. However, I tell the story to point out my growing awareness and understanding of spiritual warfare. Back then, power encounter against the forces of evil would not have crossed my mind.

What Is the Problem?

What was my problem, which I'm sure, is not unique to me? Evangelicals believe Satan is real and that he engages us in spiritual battles. But what is our response? The Apostle Peter tells us to "be on the alert" (1 Pet. 5:8), but for the most part we seem to be dull and naive when it comes to spiritual conflict. It's not a prime concern to us.

During my youth and education, the active role of the demonic was not emphasized. We didn't deny it, we just gave it a minor touch in our teaching. Yes, Jesus cast out demons and I was told to put on God's armor against temptation. But problems, whether spiritual or physical, always had explanations other than the demonic. We looked askance at people who delved too deeply into this area.

It seems that the average evangelical admits the growing impact of the occult in Western culture, but doesn't see that it affects him or her. The evangelical Church, generally, is unaware of its huge blind spot about the pervasive reality of spiritual warfare. As Unger has said so well, the Christian's response to satanic activity "tends to be theological and theoretical rather than biblical and practical."

Only in recent years has the full reality of spiritual conflict caught my attention. Why did my evangelical environment treat the demonic as unimportant, or as something limited to "pagan lands?" Because of the way we perceive and understand reality, which is Western and scientific. Our problem is perception and worldview. The way westerners in general perceive reality is the way most Christians do. That's why we have failed to grasp the significance of spiritual warfare.

When East Meets West

One time in Monrovia, Liberia, a young fellow in my discipleship group came to me. He wanted to return to his village to see his mother, but he had learned that his uncle had placed a curse on him because he had become a Christian and would no longer participate in the bush (Poro) society. In view of his fear and nervousness, we prayed briefly and I told him that he did not need to worry about the curse because he was a believer in Jesus. (My response still haunts me.) However, my answer did not satisfy him.

I did not see him again for more than three months. When he came back, he told me that he had become extremely ill and had almost died. All along, he had feared that he would never leave the village alive. Well, I thought, he must have drunk some contaminated water or something. With my Western, scientific worldview, I interpreted the events the only way I knew how: by rational deduction. But this incident, and many others like it, forced me to conclude that my teaching and counseling were totally inadequate.

My experience in this regard is not atypical. Many missionaries struggle with their response to animistic beliefs and practices. Because we are not adequately trained and experienced, we either deny the reality of the demonic, or fail to appreciate its power and influence. Worse, we say it is all superstition and fear. We believe in the natural and the supernatural, but, practically speaking, we deny the role of the Spirit (angelic) World that functions in between, and which is such a dominant factor in the lives of animists. Paul Hiebert calls this "the flaw of the excluded middle."

The Inherent Danger

When an animistic villager asks a missionary, "My dead grandmother is tormenting me. What should I do?" our first response springs from our Western mindset and we answer, "Don't be afraid. At death, the spirit is separated from the body and goes into eternity. Your grandmother's spirit no longer has an existence in our world." Such an answer is theologically correct, but insufficient to deal with the problem. There's great danger here, because the questioner is not satisfied (even though he or she may show it outwardly). Rather, he or she is confused because he or she knows the torment is real. What that person does not know is that his or her affliction is demonic, an evil deception in the guise of a dead relative.

John Mibiti, an African writer, comments:

> Every African who has grown up in the traditional environment will, no doubt, know something about this mystical power which is experienced, or manifests itself, in the form of magic, divination, witchcraft, and mysterious phenomena that seem to defy even immediate scientific explanations....This mystical power is not fiction; whatever it is, it is a reality, and one with which African peoples have to reckon.

Traditionally, we in the West have relegated such experiences to the level of primitive superstitions, and the people who hold them have yet to be enlightened through empirical data. But Christians, of all people, should give animists credit for acknowledging and fearing a realm of reality that we largely ignore. The animist is not stupid, that is to say, fearing something that does not exist. He or she fears because it is real and powerful.

Animists must have satisfactory answers about this reality before they can truly profess Jesus as Lord of their lives. If not, they are in danger of syncretism and living a divided life. They will revert to where they have always found solutions.

Missionaries who avoid, or even deny, the demonic in daily life create a perplexing problem for the indigenous churches. On the one hand, they teach how Jesus cast out demons, but on the other they refuse to incorporate the problem of demonization within the scope of the church's ministry.

Therefore, animists find their own solutions and operate in both contexts. They look to the church for forgiveness of sin and eternal life, but go to the shaman or diviner to receive solutions to problems that the church, or the missionary, cannot answer. Unfortunately, they think that Jesus and the church are impotent in the very area where he exercises supreme authority and dominion.

All too often, missionaries tend to approach people and expect them to meet on their level of understanding. We expect them to repress their worldview and experience. Unless missionaries answer their questions and deal with their problems on the receivers' level, they may never see Jesus as Lord of their whole lives.

Power Encounter and Ministry

When power encounter is mentioned, many images spring to mind, especially the classic example of Elijah and the prophets of Baal (1 Kings 18). Or we may think of Jesus casting the demons out of the man among the tombs (Mark 5). Others might consider a person being transformed from darkness to light upon receiving the gospel. But we need to be more specific. I find Timothy Warner's definition to be comprehensive and practical.

> Power encounter is the demonstration by God's servants of God's "incomparably great power for us who believe" (Eph. 1:19), based on the work of Christ on the cross (Col. 2:15) and the ministry of the Holy Spirit (Acts 1:8), in confrontation with and victory over the works of Satan and demons (Luke 10:19) in their attacks on God's children, or their control of unbelievers, resulting in the glory of God and the salvation of the lost, and/or the upbuilding of believers.

Perhaps it is best to identify this subject in the plural (i.e., power encounters). This emphasizes the specific instance where God's power is demonstrated in confrontation with the forces of evil. This confrontation may take different forms, but each would be understood as a power encounter. Each incident is one battle within the larger scope of spiritual war.

Such an encounter, no matter what the form, proclaims and establishes the truth that God has absolute authority, and that the evil forces must submit to it and obey. Satan and his demonic servants cannot stand in the presence of truth. He is the father of lies and the master of deception, perverting all that is good.

In a power encounter, the demon is exposed for what he is and called to account in the face of truth. On the basis of his or her position in Christ, every believer has the delegated authority and responsibility to call the demons to account, and to proclaim the sovereign power of the Lord over the forces of darkness.

To have a power encounter ministry, one must have a keen sensitivity toward spiritual conflict. I do not mean that we should be consumed by the subject, but rather that we should be "tuned in" to recognize the presence of demonic influence or activity. As you come to understand the biblical perspective—the three realms of reality: God, angels, and humans—and allow it to transform your thinking, you will begin to see your ministry in a new way. Spiritual warfare will come into sharper focus like the image in your camera lens as you adjust it.

My own thinking has been transformed by this process. I had acknowledged the existence of demons, but in practice I was oblivious to their activity and to my relationship to them as a believer. My experiences in West Africa forced me out of my naivete, because I had to reckon with the obvious presence of demonic power and the fear it generated.

My Western worldview was tested and came up short. Not only could I not explain the demonic realm, I did not know how to deal with it. I came to realize how much Western rationalism had clouded my understanding of the Spirit World. As I integrated a biblical worldview, I also understood my spiritual authority in Christ.

Jesus commanded us to go in his authority and make disciples. He assigns us the task of moving into Satan's territory to confront the power that holds people in spiritual blindness. As was the Apostle Paul's, our task is to turn people "from darkness to light and from the dominion of Satan to God" (Acts 26:18). This verse proves that evangelism is one of the primary forms of power encounter.

God wills that the evil powers be resisted and their evil schemes exposed by the truth. On the basis of Christ's victory over Satan through his death and resurrection, believers can have firm confidence in resisting the forces of darkness. In any confrontation, the demonic spirits will know that you know they are subject to God's authority. Such conviction delivers us from fear of Satan and any of his evil desires.

Conclusion

I have sought to demonstrate the role of power encounter in a church-planting ministry, especially among animists. Because power encounter is not part of the usual evangelical teaching agenda, missionaries face serious obstacles. The root of their problem is the Western worldview that excludes demonic spirits from functional reality. By contrast, the animistic worldview sees the Spirit World as the dominant force in every aspect of life. When these viewpoints clash, there is considerable misunderstanding on both sides.

The solution to this cross-cultural dilemma is a biblical worldview that sees demons and angels as functioning elements in daily existence. The Bible is quite clear in its teaching about the believer's relationship to the opposing forces of the demonic realm. Satan and demons have been defeated by Christ's work on the cross; believers have been raised and exalted with him. Therefore, Christians can share in Christ's authority over all the forces of evil. We can stand firm in resisting Satan and in confronting his schemes.

The Apostle Peter warns us to be alert for the prowling enemy (1 Pet. 5:8-9). Resisting and confronting demonic power should be normal for all Christians, no matter what their culture. However, this ministry focus is particularly necessary for missionaries working in animistic societies. In the context of solid biblical teaching and a loving, compassionate ministry, a ministry of power encounter will play a significant role in the conversion of animists.

2 1/2 Percent: Church-planting Movements from the Periphery to the Center

Dwight McGuire

Harnessing the power of anomalies can become a gateway to spreading the gospel through media.

The U.S. Census Bureau states that the average height for an American adult male is 5'9", with the normal range being 5'2" to 6'4". Statistically, most people are grouped around the average (mean), with the population tapering up and down from the average to create a bell curve in height. Yet if a man from a European country happened to go to a professional basketball game and meet the players, and the players were his only exposure to Americans, he could naturally conclude that Americans are very tall people, since his sample of ten people all exceeded the normal range of 6'4".

He could report to friends and family back home that although he had heard that Americans were not much different in height than his fellow Europeans, this information must be incorrect since everyone he met was incredibly tall. In reality, our friend had measured an anomaly in society (basketball players), who happened to be gathered in one central location.

In research, anomalies make up five percent of a population, and in this case, include 2½ percent excessively tall people and 2½ percent excessively small people, both outside the range of 5'2" to 6'4". Anomalies tend to cluster together for various reasons. Harnessing the power of anomalies could become a gateway to spreading the gospel in a new area.

Characteristics of Aberrant Groups

Armed with an understanding of anomalies, both statistical theory and social research observe that at least 2 ½ percent of any society are open for religious change, no matter how resistant the whole society (Marasculio and Serlin 1988). In fact, John Wesley capitalized on the fact that resistant peoples experience times of openness to the gospel, noting that their openness is fleeting and he needed to capitalize on this while the openness existed (Hunter 1987, 72-77).

Westerners often consider evangelism to be individualistic, but in fact much research demonstrates that in many societies, "aberrant" individuals—those willing to go against the prevailing local religion—collect into small "aberrant" groups (Hesselgrave 1991, 193-285). Researchers of radical Islam call these small pockets a "bunch of guys" who collectively develop a radical ideology and even take steps toward becoming a terrorist cell (Sageman 2004, 157). Often, these small groups discuss the dissatisfaction with their prevailing religion (Fiske and Goodwin 1994).

Characteristics of Aberrant Group Members

From two different perspectives, Everett Rogers (1995) and Malcolm Gladwell (2000) identify certain roles within these social groups. Rogers is concerned with social movements and the adoption of an innovation; Gladwell is concerned with the spread of an adoption of a product or idea by using theories from epidemics. Rogers concentrates on two roles within those who first adopt an innovation, which he identifies as *innovators* and *opinion leaders*. Gladwell concentrates on the concepts of *mavens, connectors,* and *salesmen.*

Innovators are gregarious individuals who have more social participation (and hence, greater connecting points) with outsiders, are social change agents, are highly connected into interpersonal networks, and have greater exposure to media channels (Rogers 1995, 262-264). Like the men of Athens who gathered at the Areopagus (Acts 17:16-34), innovators are interested in "what's new, what's cool."

It is not uncommon to find them to be multi-lingual and to be more Western-minded than their contemporaries. Rogers points out that innovators will more readily adopt a new innovation; the downside, however, is that they are more often seen as "deviants" (i.e., anomalies) of the social norms and have low credibility (trust) with other members of their social group (1995, 26). They are interesting individuals who pursue all sorts of new things, but "normal" members of society take what they say with a grain of salt.

Opinion leaders are individuals who are considered leaders within a large or small social group. Since they are leaders, they often look to innovators for current ideas, yet are more reserved in adoption. Adopting an innovation too early or too late could be politically detrimental to their leadership role, so they are both observant and cautious.

For this reason, opinion leaders, compared to innovators, have higher credibility with the social group, and are seen as being in the center of interpersonal communication networks in a social system (Rogers 1995, 27). For example, those who brought Paul to the Areopagus were innovators, whereas many opinion leaders graced the audience.

Gladwell notes that mavens are collectors of information. For different reasons than opinion leaders, mavens also connect with innovators. They are media savvy, yet choose media that is information-driven, including content-driven Internet sites. Maven-ness will often have a specialty focus, and if mavens do not know the answer, they generally know where to get one. Innovators and opinion leaders look to mavens to validate the introduction of an innovation into their small group.

Connectors overlap with innovators in the way that they interact within the group—they are channels of networking (Barabasi 2002). They are different than innovators, who are more connected to the outside world. Salesmen are those who often help the small group adopt an innovation through persuasion, moving them from talk to action.

A New Look at John 1:35ff: Jesus Inspires an Aberrant Group

John 1 provides an example where we can see some of these roles played out. Jesus recruited this "bunch of guys" to become the core of his ministry team. John 1:37 records how two of John the Baptist's disciples heard him identify Jesus as something new and important: "Behold, the Lamb of God." Observe that two of John's disciples (Andrew and John) went from following him to following Jesus—a typical innovator trait. Jesus accommodated their innovativeness and invited them to spend the day with him.

The conversations led Andrew to go to Peter (the group opinion leader) "first thing" and announce that he had located the Messiah. Peter went to Jesus, and Jesus, recognizing him as the group leader, commissioned him as such by giving him the name Cephas. John MacArthur (2002) argues that the nicknaming of Simon (his given name) to Cephas (Aramaic) or Peter (Greek) was the distinguishing mark of acknowledgement of Peter's leadership among this "bunch of guys." In this case, the innovator connected the opinion leader to the change agent (Jesus).

Observe that Jesus did not embrace the innovators—the more worldly/sophisticated members of the bunch of guys. Peter was the rock of the group. Andrew and John had their places, but not as the glue that held the team together. Networks and bonds already existed, and Jesus merely commissioned what was already a natural group and its leader.

The text records that the next day Jesus found Philip in Bethsaida. Philip then located Nathanael (a connector activity) and stated, "We have found the one Moses wrote about in the law" (vs. 45). Who is the "we?" I would argue it is the Andrew, Peter, John, and James gang. Bethsaida was a small fishing village; everyone knew everyone. Note that Nathanael was introduced to Jesus by way of the messianic idea, giving the appearance that a thread of conversation between this "bunch of guys" focused on this topic. But who was the maven of the group—the collector of information and the thinker? Look at the exchange in verses 46-51. But before proceeding, it is important to discuss the concept of the fig tree. Scholars generally agree that persons who spent time meditating on the Torah were described as people who sat under the fig tree (cf. Ridderbos 1997, 90). Formal learning often occurred in the temple, but self-taught seekers sought informal methods, retreating under the boughs of the fig tree.

Nathanael's first impression of hearing Philip's news was that of a skeptic: "Nothing good can come from Nazareth." But in their meeting, Jesus affirmed Nathanael with the words that "he was a true Israelite in whom there is nothing false" (vs. 47). Jesus affirmed Nathanael's maven learning style by acknowledging that his "sitting under the fig tree" was an honorable style of learning.

Several observations can be made from this passage. The first is that Jesus' initial contact with the group was through the innovators John and Andrew. These were men who had fluid contact with the outside world. Innovators are quick to jump from group to group, thing to thing, but are stable in friendships within their own network. In that friendship network, innovators can direct one to the "rock" of a network, the opinion leader—in this case, Peter.

The second observation is that Peter's authority is affirmed within the network. Note that he may not have been the "smartest" member of the group (that was Nathanael, the maven's role), nor was he the most outreach-oriented (those were John and Andrew as innovators and Philip as a connector), but he had the charisma to be recognized as a leader just the same. A third observation is that Jesus pulled in the whole "bunch of guys." Had Jesus focused on one team member, say, Andrew, then the dyadic relationship with the rest of the "guys" would have been broken. Andrew would have experienced persecution because of his new belief, but more importantly, he would have been persecuted because the new belief broke the bonds of fellowship.

Keeping the group together as a group is key. As persecution comes, the group can collectively thwart the attacks and come out stronger in the end. Social research demonstrates that individual members will become progressively stronger in their beliefs if they are part of a fellowship of like-minded persons (Drury and Reicher 2000; McCauley and Segal 1987).

Case Study: LETMI

LETMI was a media ministry of Pioneers in a Muslim majority country. Initially, the group was comprised of an expatriate missionary and a small team of nationals whose objective was to use media in distributing evangelistic material.

Initial projects were geared toward "getting the gospel out" using products such as the Jesus film, radio programs, and various locally-produced media. But getting mass distribution was expensive and difficult, and the response rate was often minimal. As LETMI was researching a small people movement in a strong Muslim area, it became apparent from the data that people were coming to Christ not so much from what they learned from the media, but from the fact that media gave a chance for responders to locate a Christian.

In essence, the content of the media was less consequential than the offering of an opportunity to respond to the media. This conclusion is supported by research in what has become known as the media "limit effects" model (McLeod, Kosicki, and Pan 1991). From these findings, LETMI shifted its focus from gospel presentation-oriented media to developing follow-up/response systems for media products. In other words, media used as pre-evangelism to identify seekers was more productive than direct presentations of the gospel if a good response mechanism was built into the media strategy.

Not feeling the constraint to be directly evangelistic in media products and providing ways for seekers to contact the organization gave LETMI more media options that secular national mass media organizations found acceptable to air. LETMI worked with a local television producer to develop several "specials" that highlighted social problems and how the love of God through Isa (Jesus) could help people to overcome those issues. For example, in 2000, LETMI was part of the Jesus Millennium film project, where the gospel was clearly presented on national television. Yet in a country of over 100 million inhabitants, only one hundred people responded. Applying the new strategy in 2002, LETMI and its partners did a television special about a woman who was impregnated after a rape and the shame that resulted from this event—and that God through Christ could meet her deepest felt need. The respondents from Muslim backgrounds exceeded 117,000. LETMI's role was to do the follow up with the Muslim respondents.

We, Not I

After being engaged in correspondence with the group, it became apparent from the content of the respondents' letters that less than two percent of the respondents had theological questions, whereas over twenty-eight percent just wanted to know that God cared for them, and twenty-four percent were people looking for prayer to overcome health or family matters. Clearly, LETMI was touching a hurting audience.

Also, as LETMI reviewed the content of the correspondence they received, roughly half of the letters had questions or statements in which the writer used the word "we" instead of "I." In the local language "we" is sometimes used as a polite "I"; yet, the LETMI leaders were curious—who were the "we?" They sent ministry teams to meet several of the writers who had invited them to hear their stories.

LETMI was surprised to find that the writer functioned as the innovator who was bold enough to contact the outside world, and "we" was indeed a small band of respondents. Some were from the same family who watched the program together, and some were an aberrant "bunch of guys" who did not feel Islam was giving them the answers that met their hearts' desire. Many groups had at least one member who had experienced a dream or vision (cf. Scott 2008).

After years of tweaking the model, LETMI began to shift its follow-up methods to try to keep groups meeting and discussing biblical truth. Several factors led to this, but the greatest was the fact that they simply did not have field church planters who were able to go to remote areas. LETMI later added to its methods an identification of the "opinion leader," whom LETMI then invited to meet other group leaders in a secure location. For some of these, this was the first time they had contact with a church planter since they had believed in Jesus (Isa al Masih).

Three Suggestions for Field Leaders

Use media properly. The principle is: "People use media; media does not use people." Significant research has shown that mass media is a poor persuasion tool (Bamberg and Schmidt 2001; Petty and Priester 1994; Popkin 1994). Another way of stating this is that media products used for persuasion among resistant peoples will most often fail in converting them to Christ, but media products can be used effectively to identify the 2½ percent who are open for religious change (Rogers 1995, 17).

Remember that innovators will be first responders. As argued, innovators will be greater media consumers than the population at large, and will be more open to new ideas. They will be attracted to the foreign missionary since the innovator thinks in broader categories than the average person. The innovator can be confused as the "person of peace" since he or she obviously "gets it." Yet many missionaries know well the heartache that comes as these innovators quickly grow spiritually and then lose focus because they lack roots (Matt. 13:1-23). But innovators can be a gateway into a network of a "bunch of guys." Spending time with them can be strategic, but mainly for seeing them as a link to the opinion leader.

Teach them as a group. As noted earlier, the aberrant group finds their restlessness in the fact that the majority religion does not satisfy their soul. These groups are looking for someone to help them make sense of their restless soul. Helping the group as a group keeps the bonds tight and the vision alive. They are more often able to handle persecution as a group and also use their gifts in a natural way to expand the work. The missionary should concentrate on the "group leader," who will then teach others (2 Tim. 2:2).

Conclusion

This article has looked at the use of media to identify people who are open for religious change. Harnessing the fact that in any given population there are individuals and small groups who, as "anomalies," are persuadable, church planters can put wind to their sails by using media to identify these people. By using media as an identification tool (rather than a persuasion tool) coupled with intentional follow-up systems, we can work from the periphery to the center in reaching a resistant population to create church-planting movements.

References

Bamberg, Sebastian and Peter Schmidt. 2001. "Theory-driven, Subgroup-specific Evaluation of an Intervention to Reduce Private Car-use." *Journal of Applied Social Psychology* 31(6):1,300-1,329.

Barabasi, Albert-Laszlo. 2002. *Linked: The New Science of Networks.* Cambridge: Perseus Publishing.

Drury, John and Steve Reicher. 2000. "Collective Action and Psychological Change: The Emergence of New Social Identities." *British Journal of Social Psychology* 39(4):579-604.

Fiske, Susan and Stephanie Goodwin. 1994. "Social Cognition Research and Small Group Research." *Small Group Research* 25(2):147-171.

Gladwell, Malcolm. 2000. *The Tipping Point: How Little Things Can Make a Big Differ-*

ence. London: Little, Brown, and Company.

Hesselgrave, David J. 1991. *Communicating Christ Cross-culturally: An Introduction to Missionary Communication*. Grand Rapids, Mich.: Zondervan.

Hunter, George. 1987. *To Spread the Power: Church Growth in the Wesleyan Spirit*. Nashville, Tenn.: Abingdon Press.

MacArthur, John. 2002. *Twelve Ordinary Men*. Nashville, Tenn.: Thomas Nelson.

Marasculio, Leonard and Ronald Serlin. 1988. *Statistical Methods for the Social and Behavioral Sciences*. New York: W.H. Freeman and Company.

McCauley, Clark and Mary Segal. 1987. "Social Psychology of Terrorist Groups." In *Group Processes and Intergroup Relations*. Ed. Clyde Alvin Hendrick, 231-255. New York: Sage Publications.

McLeod, Jack, Gerald Kosicki, and Zhongdang Pan. 1991. "On Understanding and Misunderstanding Media Effects." In *Mass Media and Society*. Eds. James Curran and Michael Gurevitch, 235-266. London: Edward Arnold.

Petty, Richard and Joseph Priester. 1994. "Mass Media Attitude Change: Implications of the Elaboration Likelihood Model of Persuasion." In *Media Effects: Advances in Theory and Research*. Eds. Jennings Bryant and Dolf Zillmann, 155-198. Hillsdale, New Jersey Hove, U.K.: Lawrence Erlbaum Associates.

Popkin, Samuel. 1994. *The Reasoning Voter: Communication and Persuasion in Presidential Campaigns*. Chicago: University of Chicago Press.

Ridderbos, Herman. 1997. *The Gospel According to John: A Theological Commentary*. Grand Rapids, Mich.: William B. Eerdmans Publishing.

Rogers, Everett M. 1995. *Diffusion of Innovations*. 4th edition. New York: Free Press.

Sageman, Marc. 2004. *Understanding Terror Networks*. Philadelphia: University of Pennsylvania Press.

Scott, Randal. 2008. "Evangelism and Dreams: Foundational Presuppositions to Interpret God-given Dreams of the Unreached." *Evangelical Missions Quarterly* 44(2):176-185.

Seven Phases of Church Planting and Activity List

Dick Scoggins

A general, step-by-step guide for church planters, particularly those in Muslim contexts.

PHASE 1: Launching the Team

Definition: Preparing the team. Initial church-planting plans and strategies.

When begun: When the aspiring team coordinator has officially been "knighted" by the general director to become a designated team coordinator.

1. Research best information available on language, history, and culture of country and target group.
2. Prepare a vision statement.
3. Develop memorandum of understanding.
4. Get church approval, support for each team member.
5. Plan a strategy paper.
6. Each team member secures adequate prayer, financial support.
7. Recruit a team.
8. Get the team to own the vision and strategy for church planting.
9. Complete team coordinator checklist.

PHASE 2: Preparing to Sow

Definition: Learning the language, adjusting to the culture, becoming "belongers" in society.

When begun: Most of the team is on-site (and, usually, engaged in aggressive language learning).

1. Team members "land," secure suitable housing, arrange for their initial entry strategy.
2. Resolve conflicts arising in the home.
3. Address team conflicts.
4. Develop a team life which spiritually sustains members.
5. Set goals and plan for the team.
6. Team members work hard at learning the target language.
7. Make sure language-learning program and accountability are in place.
8. Learn how to survive in area chosen, get comfortable, and enjoy life in the country.

9. Enable a family to do the same.
10. Start residency procedure on basis of strategy.
11. Develop multiple relationships of varying depth with target persons.
12. Enable family members to develop relationships with target persons.
13. Bring redemptive elements into your relationships.
14. Enhance character through the stress of adapting personally, as a family, and as a team to culture.
15. Discover and collect any evangelistic tools available in your target language.

PHASE 3: Sowing

Definition: The noble work of evangelism.

When begun: Most members of the team are spending most of their ministry time on evangelism, as opposed to language learning.

1. Memorize parts of the Bible (e.g., parables, miracles, etc.) in the target language.
2. Learn to share biblical truths in the language.
3. Develop a sympathy for the gospel in friends.
4. Develop a strategy for reaching receptive people and their closest relationships (family or friends) as a group.
5. Begin evangelistic Bible studies.
6. Encourage contacts to bring some committed relations.
7. Prayerfully evaluate your friends for a prospective person of peace: can he or she bring others with him or her?
8. Prayerfully identify one or more potential men or women of peace among your relationships. (You may more readily identify women, especially where men are not responding but women are.)
9. Lead someone to commit to follow Jesus.

PHASE 4: Discipling Begins

Definition: Discipling one or more Muslim Background Believers (MBBs) from the target group. Both parties should recognize this as a process toward the maturing of the MBBs in character and service for Christ.

When begun: Begin regular discipleship with a MBB, regardless of how he or she came to Christ.

1. Challenge one or more believers (man or woman of peace, if possible) to be discipled by you or other team member, so he or she might grow "unto the full measure of Christ."
2. Model Christ's lifestyle before this man or woman and his or her network.
3. Have the believer include some of his or her family or friends in the discipling.

Disciple the believer(s) to:

4. Fully understand his new identity as a child of God by faith, not works.

(Are there tendencies to return to the "works" mindset of Islam?)

5. Understand the purpose of baptism as an outward sign of the death of self and rebirth in Christ.
6. Relate Bible stories that will impact life.
7. Develop a regular habit of turning to scripture to deal with specific problems as they arise.
8. Recognize sin in personal life and respond by repentance, confession, and developing new patterns.
9. Live out Christ's life in extended family (e.g., Matt. 5-7).
10. Develop godly patterns of a loving spouse (e.g., resolving conflict, forgiveness, reconciliation).
11. Develop godly patterns of child-rearing.
12. Implement godly patterns of conflict resolution with others.
13. Understand the place and function of suffering in a believer's life and be able to apply it to your life.
14. Practice godly response to those hostile to his or her faith (e.g., government, family, employer, friends).
15. Understand the biblical perspective on local occult practices and godly alternatives and responses.
16. Be ready to give a reason for the faith in a non-fearful, non-combative way.
17. Share the good news with family and friends.
18. Begin to identify gifts and calling.
19. Become familiar with God's plan for the extension of his kingdom in the Book of Acts.
20. Team women to begin discipling women in Titus 2:3-5 skills.

PHASE 5: Beginning the Church

Definition: The ministry of gathering MBBs together. Growing the fellowship into a church, or having such work with more than one group. During this phase, the church planter exerts significant influence in the community.

When begun: Three or more MBBs begin meeting regularly for fellowship, teaching, prayer, etc. (with at least two from the target group).

1. Family and friends begin to explore the good news together.
2. Three or more believers agree to follow Christ in a committed community.
3. Church planter shares God's plan for forming kingdom communities among family and friends.
4. Believers embrace God's plan for forming kingdom communities and, together with church planter, decide on a culturally meaningful pattern for regular gatherings.
5. Believers learn to recognize and maximize spiritual gifts in the emerging community of believers.
6. The older believers understand the "one another" verses of the Bible and

how they define Christian community.

7. Older believers have settled on an appropriate way to determine fellow-ship in their community (e.g., covenant).

8. Community has become identifiable (e.g., via covenant).

9. The community celebrates the Lord's table.

10. The community meets together regularly for meaningful worship, in-struction, and prayer.

11. The believers do the work of evangelism.

12. Community gatherings are culturally relevant.

13. Church planters begin to phase out; responsibilities between church planter and leaders defined.

14. Most of the church planters withdraw from meetings.

15. Withdrawn church planters focus on starting new communities of believ-ers (Phase 4).

16. Remaining church planters take lower profiles in meetings.

PHASE 6: Training Leaders

Definition: Last steps so that the MBB fellowship is a complete church. Mainly leadership development and installation. In this phase, any remaining church planters will target leadership development.

When begun: Leadership development is now the main work of the team. Team expects to conclude its role in the appointment of plurality of biblically-qualified elders in six months or less. Any elder appointed after that is the re-sponsibility of existing elders (in whatever decision-making model they choose).

Leaders Emerge

1. Older believers have baptized new believers.

2. Older believers are discipling new believers.

3. Older women teach younger women Titus 2 skills.

4. Older, more mature men are trained to take leadership of community gatherings.

5. Believers take responsibility for biblical instruction.

6. Older believers preside at the Lord's Table.

7. Initial leaders emerge and function as shepherds.

8. Growth in godliness in their homes sets pace for others.

9. Gifts are encouraged and developed for edification.

10. Peacemaking skills are exercised by the community; forbearing and for-giving one another.

11. Erring members are confronted, exhorted, reproved.

12. Those persisting in sin are shunned "dis-fellowshipped."

13. Train and recognize leaders; character developed in context of marriage.

14. Team leadership concepts are taught and implemented.

15. Discerning the will of the Lord by leaders and community is taught and practiced.

174 Extending God's Kingdom: Church Planting Yesterday, Today, Tomorrow

16. Leaders' place in conflict and peacemaking in the community is taught and practiced (peacemaking, Phase 6).
17. Emerging elders are recognized (provisional leadership).
18. Mature women are recognized in ministry.
19. Conflicts about leadership appointment are dealt with.
20. Leaders begin shepherding and church discipline.
21. Leaders look for new men to develop as leaders.
22. Leaders begin discipling new leaders. (See discipling, Phase 4 and above, this phase).
23. Church planter is often absent from community meetings; leaders lead.
24. Church planter is often absent from leadership meetings.
25. Elders are formally ordained.

PHASE 7: Reproducing and Exiting

Definition: Developing church reproduction and other new church-planting efforts, or assisting the new church for a temporary period. The church planters are not making a career out of working with the one church they have planted, but are working with national believers to plant more churches.

When begun: Plurality of biblically-qualified elders have been recognized and installed in the first church, which is of sufficient "critical mass." Local authority and responsibility for shepherding that church rests solely in the hands of indigenous leaders.

Reproduction Begins
1. Intense teaching is stated regarding reproducing communities.
2. Community embraces goal of reproducing.
3. Members begin to look for new men of peace around whom to start another community.
4. New gathering (Bible study) is started or owned by church (if started by other church planters).
5. Leaders begin to network with emerging leaders of new gathering and take some responsibility for their training.
6. Leaders formally recognize newer emerging leaders (provisional elders).
7. Leaders of two communities start meeting regularly.
8. Elders take more responsibility to develop leaders in the new community.
9. New community meeting is started.
10. Communities care for each other; resources are shared.
11. Peacemaking skills among leaders (of different communities) is practiced.
12. Elders (possibly with church planter) lay hands on new elders in the newer community.
13. Relationship between communities and leaders is worked out and formalized (e.g., covenant).
14. Peacemaking skills between communities and leaders of different communities is exercised.

15. Church planter commits the old community to God and leaves community meetings. May sometimes visit.
16. Church planter redefines relationship to leaders as coach. No longer attends leadership meetings unless invited.
17. New churches are started without at a church planter.

Great Commission Vision

18. Vision is developed to plant churches beyond local area.
19. Vision includes recognizing, training, and sending national church planters to other cities and countries.
20. Vision is given by leaders to congregation.
21. Means of sending teams of nationals is devised.
22. Church planters are sent out either with Frontiers team or other teams.
23. New clusters of communities are started.
24. National teams of church planters are sent out.

Church Planting Tracking and Analysis Tool

Scott Breslin

Chart helps church-planting teams get a snapshot of their progress, areas of strength, and ongoing challenges with people to whom they are seeking to minister among.

I'd like to introduce a tool that we have found helpful in enabling church-planting teams (and their supervisors) to get a snapshot of the team's progress in the church-planting process. This tool consists of a simple one-page visual summary. It was designed with bivocational expatriate church planters in mind, especially those focused on establishing networks of house churches in restricted access countries. Although this tool is not perfect, many of my colleagues have found it to be helpful.

I first used this tool with the church-planting team I was leading. Later, when I began to oversee other teams, I used it to help me understand their ministry, track their progress, discern bottlenecks, and pray intelligently. The "columns" or "phases" used in the chart help identify different benchmarks in the church-planting process.

In spite of the fact that a given church-planting situation may not follow a clear, linear sequence, this tool can help a supervisor get enough understanding to ask the right questions. Church-planting teams almost always find the task of completing the tracking chart a very useful and stimulating exercise. Most are encouraged and edified when they step back and see a snapshot of the progress they have made and/or begin to identify bottlenecks in the process.

Normally, I collect the data during a one to three-hour session (depending upon the size of the team) with all members of the church-planting team participating. Using a white board or flipchart, I draw the chart (see Figure 1) and fill out the columns from left to right by asking the team questions. We later transfer the data to a Word or Excel document.

The teams usually update their chart every six months and send me a copy. This helps me track their progress from a distance. I do not use the tracking chart with teams that are primarily in language learning or in the midst of conflict resolution. The tool helps me understand what is happening on the ground so I can appropriately coach and encourage church-planting teams in their work. I do not write down the real names of people, but instead use initials or pseudonyms. I also try to be sensitive to those team members who are negatively predisposed to this type of analysis which can seem in their eyes as

Figure 1

CP Tracking & Analysis Tool					

Month _____ 200__

1 Positioning Hearer	2 Sowing Seeker	3 Watering Believer	4 Reaping Disciple	5 Keeping	
Meeting the messenger	Tasting the Kingdom	Hearing the Word	In Christ	In Community	
Context	**Crowd**	**Community**	**Congregation**	**Committed**	**Core**
Project/Platform/Activities				Covenanted	(Co-workers)
1.					
2.					
3.					
4.					
5.					
6.					
7.					
8.					
9.					
10.					
	Total =	Total =	Total =	Total =	Total =

cold, impersonal and arbitrary.

The chart consists of six columns, each representing a different phase of the church-planting process. I have given the columns multiple names to demonstrate their similarity to the different phases of evangelism written about by Laurence Singlehurst (1995) and church growth by Rick Warren (1995). It is my hope that most church planters and overseers/supervisors will find the process used here generic and self-evident.

1. Positioning column. In this column, I write the names of platforms or contexts in which team members meet and bless the lost. These are ministries that help position team members to develop relationships and be a blessing to those they are trying to reach. For example, it may be a business platform, community service, special event, humanitarian project, or daily activity like shopping, traveling, or visiting neighbors (see column 1 in Figure 2).

Some activities in this column will be proactive and deliberate and some will be spontaneous and unplanned. For example, Jesus' visit to Jacob's Well near the Samaritan town of Sychar (John 4:1-6) is an example of a column 1 activity as it provided the context in which Jesus met the Samaritan woman. Samuel's peace offering (a heifer) in 1 Samuel 16 allowed him access to the sons of Jesse in Bethlehem so he could anoint David.

The primary goal in the "positioning" column is to list the activities that position the messenger to make contact with the lost. This will be different in different contexts; however, by "contact" I do not mean just physical or geographic proximity (although that is part of it). It also has to do with winning the right to be heard and trusted. It has to do with being close enough to introduce different aspects of the Kingdom of God to the lost. For the expatriate living in restricted access countries, this can be quite difficult and requires

Figure 2

CP Tracking & Analysis Tool					
				Month __xxxx__ 200x_	
1	2	3	4	5	
Positioning Hearer►	**Sowing** Seeker►	**Watering** Believer►	**Reaping** Disciple►	**Keeping**	
Meeting the Messenger	Tasting the Kingdom	Hearing the Word	In Christ	In Community	
Context	Crowd	Community	Congregation	Committed	Core
Project/Platform/Activities				Covenanted	(Co-workers)
1. Office (Paul, Ed, Sam)					
2. English class (Bill)					
3. Apartment teas (Mary, Jill)					
4. Dinner party (Sally & Sam)					
5. X-mas party (all)					
6. Soccer game (Sam)					
7. Neighbor (Sam & Sally)					
8.					
9.					
10.					
	Total =	Total =	Total =	Total =	Total =

planning, patience and God's provision.[1]

2. Sowing column. In the second column, I write the names (and draw stick figures) of people who in the past month (or six weeks) have been exposed to some witness of the Kingdom of God (see column 2 in Figure 3). This may be a verbal or nonverbal witness. It would include the names of people who watched the Jesus film or heard part of the gospel or a personal testimony.

In addition, it would include the names of people with whom team members have prayed with and the names of people who witnessed a healing or deliverance or had a dream from God or other miraculous testimony of the

Figure 3

CP Tracking & Analysis Tool					
				Month __xxxx__ 200x_	
1	2	3	4	5	
Positioning Hearer►	**Sowing** Seeker►	**Watering** Believer►	**Reaping** Disciple►	**Keeping**	
Meeting the Messenger	Tasting the Kingdom	Hearing the Word	In Christ	In Community	
Context	Crowd	Community	Congregation	Committed	Core
Project/Platform/Activities	♦ ♦ Medet & Fama →→			Covenanted	(Co-workers)
1. Office (Paul, Ed, Sam)	♦ Alui →				
	♦ Amma				
2. English class (Bill)	♦ Denti →				
3. Apartment teas (Mary, Jill)	♦ ♦ Ameto & Filib →←				
4. Dinner party (Sally & Sam)	♦ ♦ Alui & Sema				
	♦ ♦ Baan & Enki				
5. X-mas party (all)	♦ Hesin →				
6. Soccer game (Sam)	♦ Bos				
7. Neighbor (Sam & Sally)	♦ Anan ←				
8.	♦ ♦ Bera & Poner →				
9.					
10.	♦ Detrim				
	♦ Ourb				
	♦ Ulusu				
	Total = 19	Total =	Total =	Total =	Total =

Kingdom of God. Some aspect or witness of the Kingdom of God has been "sown" into the person's life. Jesus' discussion with the woman at the well (John 4:7-26) is an example of a column 2 activity. You do not need a personal relationship with a person to sow into their lives. Without broad sowing, it is pretentious to expect a season of broad reaping. Sowing takes place from the initiation of members of the church-planting team.

Sowing activities help identify people who need immediate follow-up. It helps identify whom to invite to "watering activities" (column 3). Often, a person does not get enough content in a sowing activity to come to faith, but sowing activities help identify potential seekers in the crowd.

Sowing activities serve as spiritual filters or sieves. They help you identify who is ready for more. They help create curiosity, thirst, and goodwill toward the Kingdom of God. An arrow pointing to the right next to the person's name indicates if he or she is a likely candidate to be invited to watering activities (column 3). Of course, a person can move from column 2 (sowing) to column 5 (keeping) in one day; however, this is not yet the norm among most unreached peoples. It may be better to expect a longer process...and be pleasantly surprised when God moves a person along faster. When many people are moving rapidly (say in days or weeks) through this process, it may be a sign that a church planting movement is close behind...and this chart will quickly become obsolete.

3. Watering column. In column 3, I write the names of people who are being regularly exposed to God's word, often via a seeker's Bible study and Bible storying (see Figure 4). The watering column attempts to identify "seekers." We consider people "seekers" when they take initiative to hear more or experience more of the Kingdom of God. While in column 2 (sowing), it is the church planter (or God himself, in the case of dreams) who takes the

Figure 4

CP Tracking & Analysis Tool				
			Month __XXXX__ 200 X	
1 **Positioning** Hearer Meeting the Messenger **Context**	2 **Sowing** Seeker Tasting the Kingdom **Crowd**	3 **Watering** Believer Hearing the Word **Community**	4 Reaping Disciple In Christ Congregation	5 **Keeping** In Community Committed Core
Project/Platform/Activities 1. Office (Paul, Ed, Sam) 2. English class (Bill) 3. Apartment teas (Mary, Jill) 4. Dinner party (Sally & Sam) 5. X-mas party (all) 6. Soccer game (Sam) 7. Neighbor (Sam & Sally) 8. 9. 10.	♦ ♦Medet & Fama →→ ♦ Alui → ♦ Amma ♦ Denti → ♦ ♦ Ameto & Filib →← ♦ ♦ Alui & Sema ♦ ♦ Baan & Enki ♦ Hesin → ♦ Bos ♦ Anan ← ♦ ♦ Bera & Poner → ♦ Detrim ♦ Ourb ♦ Ulusu	♦ ♦ Emit & Guvi →← ♦ ♦ Barti & Tantu →→ ♦ Kaba → ♦ Hsan →		Covenanted (Co-workers)
Total = 19		Total = 6	Total =	Total = Total =

initiative; in column 3 (watering), I list the names of people who are taking initiative to hear more.

These are people who not only say yes to an invitation to participate in a seeker's Bible study, but who show up. Since "faith comes from hearing" (Rom. 10:17), no one comes to faith without taking some initiative to listen and be exposed to God's word. Jesus' two days of teaching at the Samaritan town of Sychar was a watering activity (John 4:39-42) because the townspeople were coming back for more content.

An arrow pointing to the right or the left next to the person's name indicates if he or she appears to be moving toward faith or losing interest. Church-planting teams must develop watering-type activities (like chronological Bible storying) to invite seeking friends. Whenever possible, we do seeker studies in small groups rather than one-on-one. A small group of seekers studying the Bible can develop into a house church.

4. Reaping column. In a perfect world, this column would not exist. We purpose for people to move directly from column 3 (watering) to column 5 (keeping). In reality, it is often not the case. There are those who have confessed Jesus as Lord but are clearly not yet disciples of Christ. In this column, we write the names of people who have made a profession of faith but for one reason or other are not actively ministering to others and are not committed to the community of believers (e.g., local house church).

This column would include believers who are in our team's sphere of ministry (even if they are backslidden or under church discipline). An arrow pointing left next to the person's name indicates if the person has been falling away. An arrow pointing right indicates the person is still growing in the faith.

5. Keeping column. This column (see Figure 5) includes all believers who are members of the local church (in our case, house church). It is subdivided into the "Committed" (or Covenanted) column and the "Core" (or Co-workers) column. In the church-planting model I use, I often encourage the house churches to define their membership by covenanting together; however, many of the teams I supervise do it a different way.

In any case, we write the names of believers who are both baptized and have made a membership commitment to the community of believers in the "Committed" column. An arrow right or left next to the person's name indicates if the believer is growing toward becoming a co-worker or if he or she is backsliding.

In the co-worker column, we write the names of believers whom we consider co-workers. These are people who are involved in ministry. Our primary goal for all the people we work with is to become co-workers. Co-workers have the potential of transforming a single house church into a network of house churches and into a church-planting movement. This whole chart is about the initial stages of finding and equipping co-workers.

Analysis of the Chart

After the names[2] and directional arrows are put on the chart, you have a

Figure 5

CP Tracking & Analysis Tool				
			Month __XXXX__	200__X__
1 **Positioning** [Hearer] Meeting the Messenger **Context**	2 **Sowing** [Seeker] Tasting the Kingdom **Crowd**	3 **Watering** [Believer] Hearing the Word **Community**	4 **Reaping** [Disciple] In Christ **Congregation**	5 **Keeping** In Community **Committed Core**
Project/Platform/Activities 1. Office (Paul, Ed, Sam) 2. English class (Bill) 3. Apartment teas (Mary, Jill) 4. Dinner party (Sally & Sam) 5. X-mas party (all) 6. Soccer game (Sam) 7. Neighbor (Sam & Sally) 8. 9. 10.	♦♦ Medet & Fama → ♦ Alui → ♦ Amma ♦ Denti → ♦♦ Ameto & Filib →← ♦♦ Alui & Sema ♦♦ Baan & Enki ♦ Hesin → ♦ Bos ♦ Anan ← ♦♦ Bera & Poner → ♦ Detrim ♦ Ourb ♦ Ulusu	♦♦ Emit & Guvi →← ♦♦ Barti & Tantu →→ ♦ Kaba → ♦ Hsan →	♦♦ Batu & Lale →← ♦ Gigkan ← ♦ Immo → ♦ Okan → fallen away ♦ Aykut ← ♦ Ece ← ♦ Bertel ← ♦ Barsel ←	Covenanted (Co-workers) ♦ Kaan ♦ Adnan ♦ Banli ♦ Kudi ♦ Vural ♦ Roman ♦ Nurb ♦ Metr ←
Total = 19	Total = 6	Total = 5+4=8	Total = 5	Total = 3

snapshot (imperfect though it may be) of what is going on at the ground level. There are dozens of ways to analyze and use the information. Here are a few of the things I look for.

1. What kinds of "positioning" activities (column 1) are producing people for sowing activities (column 2)? I draw a line from the names in column 2 (sowing) to the activities in column 1 (positioning). This can show what activities are really bearing fruit and which are not.

2. I ask which team members are associated with which positioning activities (column 1). This must be done sensitively so as not to embarrass or dishonor anyone on the team.

3. I ask which team members are associated with which names in columns 2-5 (Figure 6).

a. Depending upon the situation, it is a sign of good team dynamics/health when more than one team member is involved with each name. I also like to hear if national believers from columns 4 and 5 are involved in sowing and watering. This should be the norm. If not, it could be a sign of sterility that needs to be investigated.

b. I like to see if any team members are not involved in sowing (column 2) and watering (column 3) activities and find out why. These are activities we can equip team members to do. Teams need to be deliberate and proactive in implementing activities in columns 1-4.

c. I like to see which team members excel in sowing and watering. This sometimes helps identify the evangelists on the team.

d. I have noticed that the amount of sowing in a team exponentially increased when teams hold special "sowing" events like parties, dramas, concerts, and seminars where testimonies and/or Bible stories are shared. Some team mem-

Figure 6

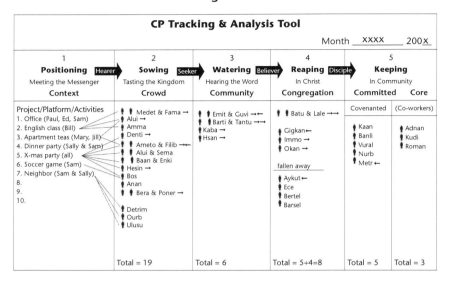

CP Tracking & Analysis Tool

Month ___xxxx___ 200x

1 Positioning [Hearer]	2 Sowing [Seeker]	3 Watering [Believer]	4 Reaping [Disciple]	5 Keeping	
Meeting the Messenger	Tasting the Kingdom	Hearing the Word	In Christ	In Community	
Context	Crowd	Community	Congregation	Committed	Core
Project/Platform/Activities	⚥ ⚥ Medet & Fama →	⚥ ⚥ Emit & Guvi →←→	⚥ ⚥ Batu & Lale →←→	Covenanted	(Co-workers)
1. Office (Paul, Ed, Sam)	⚥ Alui →	⚥ ⚥ Barti & Tantu →←→			
2. English class (Bill)	⚥ Amma →	⚥ Kaba →	⚥ Gigkan←	⚥ Kaan	⚥ Adnan
3. Apartment teas (Mary, Jill)	⚥ Denti →	⚥ Hsan →	⚥ Immo →	⚥ Banli	⚥ Kudi
4. Dinner party (Sally & Sam)	⚥ ⚥ Ameto & Filib →←→		⚥ Okan →	⚥ Vural	⚥ Roman
5. X-mas party (all)	⚥ ⚥ Alui & Sema →			⚥ Nurb	
6. Soccer game (Sam)	⚥ ⚥ Baan & Enki →		fallen away	⚥ Metr ←	
7. Neighbor (Sam & Sally)	⚥ Hesin →		⚥ Aykut←		
8.	⚥ Bos		⚥ Ece		
9.	⚥ Anan		⚥ Bertel		
10.	⚥ ⚥ Bera & Poner →		⚥ Barsel		
	⚥ Detrim				
	⚥ Ourb				
	⚥ Ulusu				
	Total = 19	Total = 6	Total = 5+4=8	Total = 5	Total = 3

bers excel at organizing or hosting the event and others excel at inviting people.

4. I like to see how many people are in each of the columns (columns 2-5). In order to get six people in column 5 (the church), you normally need to have dozens (sometimes hundreds) of people in columns 2-4. If little sowing is going on, church planting will not happen.

5. I look at past charts and see what progress is being made.

6. I use the chart in my prayer for the team.

7. I may ask a team to set more aggressive goals for the number of people they are sowing into. I will work with them on strategies to increase their sowing. We believe it is good and reasonable to hold teams accountable for the amount of sowing they do, as it is one of the few measurable outcomes within their direct control.

8. I teach the teams how to use this chart with their team. Many teams show local believers how to use the tool as part of their leadership development. It helps cast vision by explaining to the local believers a church-planting process.

9. In many cases, there will be multiple church-planting efforts going on simultaneously within one church-planting team's sphere of ministry. Often, the division of who belongs where will not be clear. Several people may be involved with several efforts.

Figure 7 shows an example of where three separate house church efforts are in various stages...the Riverview Church being the furthest along. In our example, Ahmet is developing a third group through his own relational networks (which he is not enfolding into the Riverview Church). In this case, no one from our expatriate team would be directly involved with Ahmet's group;

Figure 7

CP Tracking & Analysis Tool

Month ___ XXXX ___ 200 X

1 Positioning [Hearer] Meeting the Messenger **Context**	2 Sowing [Seeker] Tasting the Kingdom **Crowd**	3 Watering [Believer] Hearing the Word **Community**	4 Reaping [Disciple] In Christ **Congregation**	5 Keeping In Community **Committed**	**Core**
Project/Platform/Activities Westend group	Modet & Fama →→ Ago → Brando Oli & June →→ Soaper ←	D&L ←→ Finer →	Win & Lake →→	Covenanted	(Co-workers)
Riverview Church	Carl & Tank Harp → Carl & Tank Harp → Light New one	Ahmets family → Kako2 → Kako → Suto ← Temple →	Peace → B-C Ablet Flura ←	Freedom Helper Fame Pearl	Manly Ahmet
Ahmet's group	Bingo & Puder → Dako Obi Canons Harmi	Ahmets sister's family Hoker Kapo Ahmets brother's family			

however, someone would be coaching or shadow-pastoring Ahmet off-stage. In fact, this is the goal of our ministry. By God's grace, men and women like Ahmet will help move networks of house churches into rapidly multiplying church planting movements.

Summary

This tool helps you take a snapshot of a team's progress in the church-planting process. In a one to three-hour meeting, the group facilitator can complete the chart with the team. This focused meeting is almost always an edifying and professionally stimulating experience for all participants. Many more stimulating hours can be spent analyzing the findings. As an overseer of expatriate church-planting teams (working among unreached peoples), I have found this a very useful tool in my ministry toolbox. You can download a blank copy of the form at www.fcpt.org. Please feel free to adapt and improve it in any way you like.

Endnotes

1. For more discussion on the topic of positioning in restricted access countries, see "The Heifer Principles (Thoughts from 1 Samuel 16)" at www.fcpt.org.

2. I usually draw stick figures with the names for a more "pictorial" view. This also helps me visualize the gender make-up of the people the team is working with as I may not be able to recognize the gender by the name.

References

Singlehurst, Laurence. 1995. *Sowing, Reaping, Keeping.* Colorado Springs, Colo.: YWAM Press.

Warren, Rick. 1995. The *Purpose Driven Church.* Grand Rapids, Mich.: Zondervan.

Section 5

Partnership and Church Planting

Although we all understand **"partnership"** to be a buzzword today not only in missions, but also in secular work, we also know it to be a biblical concept. For too many years, silos were built and "lone rangers" went about their work, sometimes successfully, sometimes not. Today, however, with the changing face of the missional church, globalization, and technology, making strong relationships is more important than perhaps any time in recent memory. Partnership simply must be a cornerstone in any mission effort. This includes church planting. In this section, our authors move us closer to making partnership not only doable, but having the ability to see flourishing results in both relationships and outreach.

David Dunaetz begins by reminding us that a unified church-planting community will have both high relationship and high task cohesiveness. **Floyd and Christine Schneider** offer five rules for working with church planters from other agencies.

Frank Allen shares an analysis of seven areas often overlooked in church-planting seminars and literature. **Rick Kronk** concludes with an example of how missionaries and native French Christians united to reach out to North Africans in France.

Transforming Chaos into Beauty: Intentionally Developing Unity in Church Plants

David Dunaetz

A unified church-planting community will have both high relationship cohesiveness and high task cohesiveness.

The first few years were great. Young Christians were excited about the gospel, Christians who lived in the region were enthusiastic that there would be a church in their area, and seekers were happy to talk with Christians who had personally met God. There was a sense of unity, camaraderie, and solidarity in the young community. In spite of the multitude of diverse cultural origins, French, Americans, Irish, Congolese, Ivorians, Caribbeans, and various individuals from another ten or twelve cultures were getting along.

Then reality hit. While the missionaries were leading all the activities, there was no problem with unity. But once we started handing over responsibilities to various people in the church, KABOOM!

But this was to be expected. Even in mono-cultural church plants, where the ethnic make-up of the young community is fairly homogeneous, unity does not come naturally. In any group, individuals come from different backgrounds and have different capacities and spiritual gifts. Each individual has had different experiences with the gospel and has different expectations for the community.

Today, however, there is an unprecedented cultural blending occurring in world-class cities such as Paris, where we worked. Many church planters today are confronted with new problems due to this multiculturalism. Unity does not come naturally to these young churches!

The Importance of Unity

On a practical level, unity is extremely important. First of all, a church characterized by internal strife is not going to grow, especially if it is small enough for everybody to know one another. Non-Christians come to Christ in order to find peace and love; they do not want to become Christians to join a church where leaders are fighting one another. Conflict will push them away from the gospel rather than draw them toward it.

From a theological angle unity is also extremely important. A major theme of Jesus' prayer the night before his crucifixion was the unity of his disciples (John 17:21-23). A sign of a healthy church is unity (Acts 2:42-47; 4:32-35).

If a person is truly regenerated through Jesus Christ, he or she should seek unity with fellow believers (Phil. 2:1-4; Eph. 4:1-6) by modeling Christ-like attitudes (Phil. 2:5-8). The basis for unity is a common commitment to Christ's teaching (Rom.16:17-18; 1 Tim.1:3-4) and the work of the Holy Spirit in the believer's life (Eph. 4:3).

Understanding Cohesiveness: Two Dimensions

One of the most important aspects of unity in a church-planting situation is what social scientists call "cohesiveness." This is a measure of the forces and factors that cause people to stay in a group. If there are not enough reasons for people to stay in a young church, they will leave. However, if they have plenty of reasons for staying in the church, they will stay—and hopefully grow spiritually and serve the Lord with their gifts. Without cohesiveness, it is impossible for a church to experience unity. There are two basic reasons people will stay in a group.

1. The relationship factor. They like at least some of the people who are in the group and have positive relationships with them.

2. The task factor. They like what the group stands for and does. They understand what the group is trying to accomplish and believe it is moving in the direction it should go.

These two factors can be present in various degrees in any young church. They can be thought of as two dimensions of cohesiveness. A church that is high in relational cohesiveness will have many healthy relationships among its members. Most people in the group will know several other members and have positive interactions with them regularly. If people can find others in the group who are very similar in background, personality, and culture, these relationships will develop more naturally and require relatively little effort.

On the other hand, a church that is low in relational cohesiveness will have many people who have few significant relationships with other people in the church. Many will have little or no significant interaction with other members, even when they are present at the activities. Interaction outside of church activities might be non-existent. The only people recognizable to many in the church are the individuals up front.

The other dimension, task cohesiveness, can be present in various degrees as well. In an evangelical church, this cohesiveness should be based on the gospel. In a church high in task cohesiveness, the members will know what the church believes and what it is doing in response to these beliefs. The majority of the members will have a clear vision as to why they are meeting together and what they hope to accomplish. The purpose of the church is clear and, ideally, each person knows what role he or she should be playing to accomplish this purpose. In a church with low task cohesiveness, it would be less clear what the church believes or what its purposes are.

These two dimensions can be represented on a grid, resulting in four quadrants (see Figure 1 on page 188). If the vertical axis represents task cohesive-

Figure 1

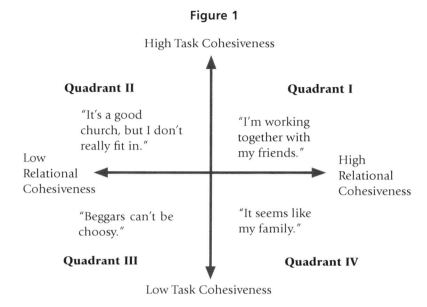

ness, and the horizontal axis represents relational cohesiveness, we can see how different combinations of cohesiveness can manifest themselves in the church.

Quadrant I represents a church that has both high relational cohesiveness and high task cohesiveness. People enjoy being with each other and they both understand and are committed to the task of the church. When they think of the church, they believe, "I'm working together with my friends." Both the vision of the church and relationships between members are understood, relatively unambiguous, and valuable to the vast majority of people in the church. This is the optimal condition for developing biblical unity within the church.

Quadrant II represents a church where members might feel that although they are in a good church, they do not really have a place in it or are "just a number." The church has a well-defined vision that is supported by the members in general (high task cohesiveness), but the relationships among people in the church are weak (low relational cohesiveness).

Quadrant III represents a church least likely to have biblical unity. Either the vision of the church and its task is not clear, or the people in the church do not really believe in it (low task cohesiveness). In addition, most people do not have good friendships with others in the church and are not especially attracted to them (low relational cohesiveness).

Quadrant IV represents a church that is slightly healthier. Although there is a lack of clarity or commitment concerning the task and vision of the church (low task cohesiveness), people have developed healthy and enjoyable relationships with one another and, in general, enjoy being together (high relational cohesion). People might say, "It seems like my family." Sometimes the church grows, sometimes it shrinks. What counts is making everybody happy and keeping the situation stable.

Moving toward Quadrant I: Increasing Relational Cohesiveness

I would like to present five basic, but often overlooked, ideas to increase relational cohesiveness. All have been studied by psychologists and sociologists and have been shown to help people develop positive relationships with one another. Most importantly, all are also either prerequisites or manifestations of biblical love (John 14-17; 1 Cor. 13; Phil.1).

1. Repeated contact with the same individuals. It is only through repeated exposure to one another that people can experience mutual recognition, a condition that is absolutely essential for a meaningful relationship to develop. If two people cannot recognize each other, their understanding of one another is very limited and there is no basis for a biblical relationship where love is manifested.

For example, if a newcomer is greeted in a friendly, loving way each time he or she comes to an activity, it does not count for much if it is always different people he or she is meeting. In fact, it would be a far more positive experience for him or her to talk to the same Mr. Ordinary four times in a row than to meet a new Mr. Charisma each time he or she visits the church.

A key for repeated contact with the same individuals is physical proximity. People need to be near each other to have contact. This can be facilitated by having activities which enable people to meet and interact with one another regularly. The smaller the group is, the more likely each of the participants will have meaningful interaction with someone. Early in the church-planting process the church planter should invest much time in leading small groups and finding and training appropriate leaders. In larger group situations (e.g., worship services) opportunities must be created to allow people to meet the same individuals over and over.

For example, people can be encouraged to sit in the same area of the meeting room each week or to greet all the people they have previously met once the meeting is over. In one of the churches we started we found that asking people to stack the chairs immediately after the worship service gave people a reason not to flow out of the room as soon as it was over, and it provided enough space for people to freely mingle and have contact with whomever they desired. After we began this, we found people stayed nearly twenty minutes longer.

2. Pleasant interactions with people. In order to develop a sense of relational cohesiveness, it is not enough simply to have repeated contact with a group of individuals. These interactions must be pleasant, creating positive emotions in both parties. Often, the agreeableness of an interaction is based on fairly superficial things such as: the way a person dresses, physical attractiveness, and race. Other factors that make interactions pleasant include: expressive, animated behavior; laughter; and participation in group discussions.

Factors that produce disagreeable interactions include: lack of self-revelation, arrogance, sadness, very distinctive unusual physical features, hypocrisy, and inconsistent behavior. Certainly, some of these factors can be controlled; others cannot. In general, however, people manifesting the fruit of the Spirit (Gal. 5:22-23) will appear more attractive.

In one of our churches, a dynamic, joyful, caring, African teenage girl started coming to the young church. As she grew in her faith, she invited her friends and we were able to start a youth group which became the most dynamic group in the church. Simultaneously, we had two somewhat gruff, poorly-dressed, older men who also invited people. Their ministry was less effective, possibly due to their inability to have consistent, pleasant interactions with others.

3. Fulfillment of affiliation needs. Just like we need food and water for our physical well-being, we also need to be with others and be accepted by them for our psychological well-being. This need is called the need to affiliate. From a biblical point of view, our need to affiliate is a reflection of God's tri-

IN MANY CULTURES, eating together is the **primary means** of social bonding and developing friendships; therefore, meals together or in one another's homes should be encouraged as much as possible.

une nature and motivates us to create Christ-centered communities characterized by love. People vary in their affiliation needs.

Some need to be with people all the time. Others need to be alone more often. All of us, to some degree or another, need to be associated with a group as well as have close, personal friends. The more these needs are met in a church, the stronger will be the church's relational cohesiveness. Closer friendships and fellowship cause one's commitment to the group to grow.

On the practical side this means church planters need to encourage friendships among members. Church activities need to provide significant social interaction that allows these friendships to develop. In many cultures, eating together is the primary means of social bonding and developing friendships; therefore, meals together or in one another's homes should be encouraged as much as possible. This can partially explain the success of Alpha Groups and youth groups who eat together regularly.

4. Perceived similarity with others. People prefer being with people whom they perceive as being similar to themselves. If they see themselves as different, they tend to feel like an outsider. In modern, multicultural situations, this presents a major challenge. The ethnicity of a group's members is among the first things people notice when considering joining a group. People also tend to seek out people of similar educational backgrounds, personalities, and interests.

To combat the human tendency to withdraw from highly diverse groups, the church planter needs to make sure that the group members have something in common, specifically, a commitment to the gospel. Putting the gospel and its implications for today's world at the center of the church's activities will create a context where this shared understanding will allow those committed to Christ to find much in common. The ministry of teaching is not distinct from fellowship building—it is, in fact, an essential element of it.

At the same time the church needs to encourage affinity groups to form. There need to be Christ-centered groups for women, men, youth, young couples, etc. The more the groups can be based on a common situation in life (middle schoolers, recently divorced, teachers, etc.) or common interests (music, fishing, ministering to the homeless, etc.), the greater the bonding will be to the whole church. People want to be in a place where they feel they belong.

5. Expression of mutual appreciation. One powerful way to help people feel part of the group is to express appreciation. People need to know they are valued and appreciated. The more people express their appreciation to a person, the more the person's commitment to the group increases. Similarly, if one individual expresses his or her appreciation and positive evaluation of another, the personal attraction between the two increases and a friendship is more likely to develop. A church planter would do well, then, to express genuine appreciation often and to encourage others to do so as well. Public expressions of appreciation (during announcements, in a newsletter, etc.) show that people are valued by the leadership. Small group activities that encourage members to say what they like about others allow appreciation to be expressed on an individual level.

Moving toward Quadrant I: Increasing Task Cohesiveness

Unity in young churches will not be biblical if it grows only through closer relationships; the unity must also be founded on accomplishing God's purposes (including worship, evangelism, and discipleship training) for the church. Some cultures might naturally put an emphasis on relationships and some might naturally put an emphasis on task accomplishment. The responsibility of finding a culturally relevant, biblical balance falls soundly on the missionary church planter and the leadership team that he or she chooses and trains. I would like to present three elements of church planting that are essential for task cohesiveness.

1. Clear vision. The essence of leadership is moving a group toward goals or purposes. If these goals and purposes are not clear, there is little a missionary can do besides maintain the status quo or try to make people feel good. The effective church planter has a doubly difficult task. Not only must he or she lead the church to a clear understanding of its purposes (such as those formulated in Rick Warren's The Purpose Driven Church [1995]: worship, ministry, evangelism, fellowship, and discipleship), but he or she must also instill a vision for the church to become independent of missionary presence and support, and to become a sending church rather than a receiving church. No matter where the young church is in its life history, it will always be easier to maintain the status quo than to move ahead in these areas. However, that is no excuse for not knowing what God wants for the church and doing everything possible to move in that direction.

2. Culturally relevant leadership. Most cross-cultural church planters want to follow the Apostle Paul's example of planting one church, putting leadership into place, and moving on to plant another church. But we also need to follow Paul's advice not to turn responsibilities over to the wrong people (1 Tim. 5:21-22). Poor leadership allows the church to lose its focus. No matter how willing people in the new church are to lead, if they are not gifted in essential leadership skills relevant to their culture, they will not be able to lead the church to where it should be going. Task cohesiveness will be minimal.

First Timothy 3 and Titus 1 give various requirements for being a leader. It is especially important to find out about the potential leader's reputation with outsiders (1 Tim. 3:7), a concept closely related to cultural relevancy. For insights as to whether a potential leader has culturally relevant leadership skills, it is appropriate to look at his or her career path.

If a young person is on a career path that will lead to a position of influence within his or her culture, this indicates leadership potential. If the person has had a career which has not led to increasing leadership responsibilities, this could indicate that leading the church is not within his or her gifting. The church planter needs to find out as much information as possible to see how naturally gifted and culturally relevant potential leaders might be. An abundance of these qualities, however, will never make up for a lack of true, Christ-centered spirituality which manifests itself through the fruit of the Spirit (Gal. 5:22-23).

3. Leadership training. North American missionaries tend to be quite egalitarian. We are often sorely aware of our foreignness (which can be seen by the color of our skin or heard by our accents every time we open our mouths). In addition, because we so much want to get the young church into the hands of locals, we may think, "If I can do it, then surely a local person can do it just as well." We might not think of all the years of education and training we have received, especially when we are working primarily with the poorly educated who have had little or no training.

Leadership training must be based on high standards and high accountability. Poorly trained, low-skilled leaders will provide poor leadership. God certainly uses the weak of this world to confound the strong (1 Cor. 1:26-27), but church leaders must be able to master and teach God's word (1 Tim. 3:2), a requirement that excludes most Christians (James 3:1).

Training must be both theoretical (what to say and do if such and such a situation arises) and practical (carrying out responsibilities under the direction of and with feedback from the church planter). It must be complete, covering all essential areas of biblical teaching and dealing with all elements of the host culture. Anything less will not enable leaders to stay focused on the biblical task within the cultural context; task cohesiveness will fall by the wayside.

Young churches are often chaotic in nature. Diverse people with a multitude of backgrounds coming together to worship and serve God can be beautiful; however, it can also be a formula for conflict and confusion. If the church planter is aware of the dangers, many of them can be avoided. Instead of chaos, the church can grow in both relational and task cohesiveness, producing a unity that is not only beautiful to the members in the church, but also to those who are outside and, more importantly, to God.

Reference

Warren, Rick. 1995. *The Purpose-Driven Church*. Grand Rapids, Mich.: Zondervan.

From Rivals to Allies

Floyd and Christine Schneider

Five rules for working peacefully with church planters from other agencies.

Marshall was a fellow soldier who liked to boss people around. Because I outranked him by a few weeks, he informed me that he hated me. I avoided him after that. A few weeks after we arrived in Vietnam, we were ordered to lead our squads in taking a village from the Vietcong. Within the first few minutes of the battle, men were dying all around us. Although no words passed between us, I remember the look in his eyes: "If we're going to come out of this alive and complete our mission, we have to set aside our differences and work together." I nodded.

During the entire battle, Marshall protected my back, while I and my squad pushed forward. The losses to our entire platoon were appalling. But although Marshall and I never became close friends, we learned on the battlefield that sometimes we have to set aside personal differences in order to accomplish our job.

Ever since Paul and Barnabas argued about a co-worker and their missionary team consequently fell apart (Acts 15), missionaries and their sending agencies have been trying to "work in unity." Although a worthy enough goal, many of these attempts to avoid conflicts between co-workers have failed miserably because of non-biblical definitions.

Christians often confuse organizational unity with spiritual unity. Bringing missionaries together through organizational unity does not automatically lead to spiritual harmony. Too much organizational unity can be counterproductive if it keeps us from spending enough time with the unsaved.

Two things are vital for spiritual harmony. First, *we need to have similar goals*. We hope that we all want to see people get saved. If we insist that everyone submit to our authority and evangelize "our way," we have overlooked spiritual gifts and replaced evangelism with uniformity.

Second, *we need a supportive attitude toward one another*. Speak good of the other missionaries. This is crucial for the spiritual harmony (not organizational unity) which Christ spoke of in John 17. If we cannot sincerely say something good about another's work, then we should say nothing. Nowhere in scripture do we read that Paul or Barnabas criticized one another, or one another's ministries, even after their disagreement. Later on, Paul's evaluation of Mark changed to praise, even though Mark had been the center of the controversy. Satan is the accuser of the brethren (Rev. 12:10). He doesn't need our help.

Achieving unity is not easy, especially when ideas, methods, personalities, and even results differ. People are not robots, and the creativity of a starry-eyed beginner can be the spark to begin a vibrant new ministry or to blow up an old one. In contrast, the steady faithfulness of an incumbent missionary can be the glue which holds a team together, or keep it from moving at all. An even more sensitive issue is achieving some sort of a working relationship between mission boards. They probably have the same goals—to win souls—but they also have their theologies, traditions, and darlings to help them reach their goals.

How can missionaries—both the incumbents and the starry-eyed beginners—peacefully work alongside one another in their separate church-planting ministries? Perhaps these guidelines can help.

Guideline 1: Communicate with other missionaries who live in your city or region about your plans

Paul tells two believing women in Philippians 4:2 to "live in harmony." He did not command them to necessarily agree with one another. If we do not agree with other missionaries, but we desire to live in harmony with them, then we must have open lines of communication; we must let them know what we are doing.

Find out what is already being done in the area you want to work in. Don't condemn what others have or have not done, and don't offer suggestions for improvements unless you're very sure the incumbent missionaries or other mission boards will appreciate your viewpoints. Exchange information. You might even modify your plans and choose a different method or different segment of society to work with.

As time and energy allow, visit and pray with missionaries from other groups. This may be difficult for a missionary to do if he or she has lots of contacts and friends among the unsaved, and if you want to spend as much time as possible working with them. Beware of forming a Christian clique, but do your best to nurture peaceful co-existence with other missionaries.

Guideline 2: Gain an understanding of the concept of "neighborhood" in your mission field

Anthropologists usually define a neighborhood in most Western countries as a specific segment of society, instead of exclusively as a geographical area. Each person has his or her own "neighborhood": a unique set of acquaintances, bus lines, local grocery stores, school, work, and recreation areas.

Look for people who are open to the gospel, regardless of where they live. Then concentrate on their specific "neighborhoods." With this mindset, even missionaries who live near one another will work in different "neighborhoods" and will be supportive of one another.

Arguing over who "owns" the people in a given area is wrong. When problems sprang up between the herdsmen of Abraham and Lot, Abraham—with more rights, and yet with more wisdom than Lot—asked Lot to choose an area for himself and leave. The reason: "The (unbelieving) Canaanites and the Perizzites then dwelt in the Land . . . (and) we are brothers" (Gen. 13:7-8). In some cases, the best way to avoid a conflict with other believers is to spend less time together. The more mature brother will not demand his rights from another brother for the sake of their testimony before unbelievers.

After I had been in Austria for a few years, a missionary from another mission board moved into the same city. We met and he wanted to assure me that he didn't want to "step on my toes." I told him that we had been trying to lead our next door neighbors to the Lord for four years and had had no breakthroughs. If he could do so, we would be overjoyed—and he was welcome to begin a church in their apartment. However, I reserved the right to do the same with his neighbors. He laughed and heartily agreed.

Guideline 3: Don't steal sheep from other churches

Paul wrote to the Romans, "And so I have made it my aim to preach the gospel, not where Christ was named, lest I should build on another man's foundation" (Rom. 15:20). In most countries, the unsaved far outnumber the believers. Missionaries don't need to fight over a handful of people. There are enough people to go around.

In many cities in Europe, many of the missionaries are working mainly with believers and have little, if any, contact with the unsaved. Given this situation, sheep-stealing is an obvious problem.

Keep friendly relationships with any other churches and agree to inform each other when church hoppers come to visit. When believers from other churches come to you, tell them that you would rather they attended their own churches. Say something like, "It was nice that you came today. Please greet your pastor when you return to your own church next week. I'll be calling him this week, and I'll mention that you dropped by." Then contact the leaders of the other church and inform them.

If the people still want to change churches, ask them if they have spoken to their church leaders. They may be under church discipline, or perhaps everyone involved wants them to change churches. Find out why. Remember: church hoppers are sometimes problem children, and they will bring their troubles with them into the new church. A church planter is far wiser to evangelize the unsaved and build a church from them than to accept sheep from other folds.

Guideline 4: Work together in various public evangelistic efforts

Paul tells the Philippians to be like-minded, having the same love, of one accord, of one mind (2:1-3). He then goes on to talk about the Lord's basic attitude of selflessness and humility. The Lord esteemed others better than himself, but he did not always agree with what others did. Paul is not advocating that believers always agree with one another, but that they recognize God's built-in worth of each believer. This attitude can greatly improve our chances of working together, especially in joint evangelistic efforts.

Here are some ideas for such efforts:

1. Invite a speaker for a city-wide evangelistic campaign.
2. Show a film at one of the churches.
3. Pool financial resources for a special evangelistic project that would be too expensive for one church alone to handle.

In every case, members of each church are responsible to bring their own friends and relatives and follow up with them afterwards.

In the winter of 1993 the 400 evangelical believers in Graz, Austria, came together and rented Austria's largest movie theater for the purpose of bringing Billy Graham's evangelistic messages via satellite to that city of 300,000. The cost was over $20,000 for the theater. The few churches involved were not all in agreement in every point of theological doctrine. The Lord was glorified, however, in their cooperation and he allowed the theater to be paid for completely in advance. Many unsaved went forward every evening at Billy Graham's invitation. What a magnificent testimony to the unity of the Spirit in the midst of diversity.

Guideline 5: Pray for the unity of the Spirit at all times

Praying for it will remind us of our own attitudes and motives in touchy situations, and perhaps we can at least avoid a conflict, even if we can't work in unison. Pray with others from other mission boards and ministries and you might make friends for life, and together—in different ministries—you may see the Lord bring many to himself through you both. "Now he who plants and he who waters are one, and each one will receive his own reward according to his own labor" (1 Cor. 3:8).

Missionaries are in a war with much more at stake than the political fate of a few people living in a Vietnam jungle. We should never forget who the enemy really is. Surely as we struggle to persuade immortal souls to abandon Satan's kingdom, we can put the Lord's mission first and our personal feelings last.

Your Church-planting Team Can Be Booby-trapped

Frank W. Allen

Seven areas often overlooked in church-planting seminars and literature.

Like the thousands of Iraqi landmines strewn across the desert, potential booby traps can blow up in the faces of church-planting teams that take to the mission field with high enthusiasm but little knowledge of the territory. To avoid disaster, I've addressed some key issues that too often fail to appear in our church-planting seminars and literature.

National Leaders

Most missionary candidates today realize they will have to work under national leaders. But what will the team face when it sets foot on foreign soil?

1. Lack of leadership training. Most likely, the national team leader has little leadership training. Often, he is younger than the missionary and does not have as much formal education. It's a false assumption that he can be a good leader because he knows the language and the culture. The team either bypasses him or the work stagnates, and both the leader and team are frustrated.

Young, untried missionaries need direction. If the mission cannot provide it under a national leader, it must quickly remedy the problem. To ignore it is to risk casualties.

2. Leadership styles. Expectations degenerate into conflicts because of misunderstandings over leadership styles. Leadership styles are neither sacred nor fixed in concrete. They vary from culture to culture and place to place. People from other countries note how much Americans are chained to Roberts Rules of Order in our business meetings. Sometimes the nationals, whom we have taught, are even more badly addicted to Roberts, and meetings can be run into the ground over parliamentary distinctions.

Some leaders grow up with a hands-off leadership style. This is just about as frustrating as working under a leader who lacks training and experience. In other cultures, the team leader is an autocrat who makes all the decisions and the team knuckles under, or else.

Obviously, we cannot simply criticize different cultural leadership styles. Rather, we must recognize that they exist and that people preparing for team ministries must prepare ahead of time to face them. Unless we clearly understand and accept distinctive cultural dynamics, we may be programming our teams for unbearable frustrations and eventual failure.

3. Nationalism. Until more recent times, missionaries have not encountered full-blown nationalism, which can be either wholesome or destructive. It's no use fighting it or rejecting it; it's a fact of life.

Wholesome nationalism is essential to the selfhood of any people and to the growing churches. If we fail to prepare missionaries for it, they could fall into some huge difficulties. Here are some guidelines to avoid the booby trap of nationalism:

- Downplay our own ethnocentrisms
- Learn to more fully appreciate the host culture
- Encourage rather than criticize national leaders
- Bow out before resentment sets in

Missionary team members can respond positively to nationalism by:

- Remembering they are servants
- Avoiding defensiveness
- Reminding themselves that much resentment is aimed at their nationality, not at them personally
- Acting in love
- Speaking biblically, if nationalism degenerates into bitterness and hatred

Economic Implications

Team membership carries with it certain economic implications. Team members frequently encounter lifestyle questions. The lower living standards prevalent in many countries may demand a much simpler lifestyle than most missionaries are used to. The close relationships within a team often exacerbate economic disparities.

Therefore, missionaries must be willing to deprive themselves of some things that may be right and proper in other circumstances. We cannot continue to rationalize the differences given the economic facts of life.

Cultural Differences

Our Western concepts of teaming are not necessarily understood or appreciated in some cultures. For example, prior to our mission's going into Hong Kong, we strongly backed the team concept to Chinese pastors and other church leaders. Their response was less than enthusiastic. They couldn't see all the supposed advantages we talked about.

That's probably true in other cultures as well. Some pastors and leaders see our team concept as a threat, not as a help. Therefore, we must assure them of our desire to be servants, and of our willingness to modify our plans and procedures.

Our American team ideal doesn't fit in some societies. We're supposed to be pals, equals, and enjoy first name status with everybody. But in Japan, for example, leaders expect to be addressed formally. These men are used to listening to team members and then deciding unilaterally. In some teams, where several missionaries work under a pastor, the pastor's major relationship is with one of the missionaries. After a team discussion, the Japanese leader decides on his own and passes down the word through the one missionary he is closest to.

In Spain, pastors welcome missionary teams, but the Americans soon meet some subtle nuances peculiar to Spain. When we think of a team, we think of a number of people working together. But the Spanish pastors, like those in Hong Kong, see so many needs that they can't conceive of several people bunching up in one place.

In some countries, where anti-Americanism may run high, the presence of too many foreigners in one place makes the pastor uncomfortable. He also worries about too much of his work—and perhaps his authority—being taken over by missionaries. He sees them cutting his own members out of their ministries.

Some pastors resent having outside teams assigned to them. They rightly want some time to assess these people and to build trust and friendships with them. In the end, the team's success or failure will largely depend on relationships, not on skills and training. This fact should be stressed on our U.S. campuses, where there is such a keen interest in church-planting teams.

Role of Women

We must recognize the roles that women have in team leadership. In our mission we have many women with high leadership abilities. I believe our teams would be stronger if we accepted the fact that the Holy Spirit has given women all of his gifts, just as he has to men.

If we continue to ignore gifted women on our teams, and if we place ungifted men in leadership roles to the exclusion of gifted women, we risk losing the women on the team and the work will be handicapped. Not all men are willing to work under women and problems arising from this attitude must be handled on a case-by-case basis.

Conflict Resolution

Some members' personalities do not always neatly mesh with others. Personal idiosyncracies become irritants. More aggressive types can easily aggravate consensus types. Conflicts arise and team members must be shown that there are ways of solving them, other than "grin and bear it," or "pray about it."

Team leaders must be taught how to resolve conflicts. The mission itself must be prepared to act if the leader either does not recognize the conflict, or is unprepared to handle it. The mission must plan for possible changes in team leadership and in the team's make-up, for the sake of harmony.

Multinational Teams

On a recent trip to Asia I discovered once again how much trouble springs from national differences. In one conference, during our discussion about objectives, it became clear that not everyone agreed on the process of setting objectives and goals. One non-North American couple felt that objectives should grow more out of prayer than out of discussion.

Prospective team members must realize that respect for national and cultural differences is absolutely essential. Being different is not the same as being wrong. Thus far, our approaches to multinational teams have been far too simplistic.

Team Purpose

We need to be clear about our teams' basic purposes. Are they doing evangelism and church planting, or church maintenance? From my perspective, the greatest service we can render to the churches is to make sure that our teams are leading them outward in new ventures of evangelism and church planting. When we recruit students for our teams with the dream of evangelism and church planting, we have to make sure that this is what they do when they get to the field. Sadly, sometimes that fails to happen.

We have to accept, of course, that sometimes our new teams arrive with unrealistic expectations. So on the home end, we have to do as much as we can to prepare them for those awful booby traps. Part of their preparation should include not only lectures about the potential pitfalls on the field, but also some real life experience working through mine fields at home.

Unfortunately, some teams arrive on the field like rookies. They haven't had much experience in evangelism and church planting at home, and, for the most part, they have never lived in such close quarters with other people as they will be doing on the field.

Therefore, we need to develop more "practice fields," or pre-field internships in team living and evangelizing, even though this might mean a longer preparation time. We might put new teams under apprenticeship to older, more qualified leaders on the field.

Our mission has used teams successfully, especially in Kamuning, Quezon City, and Makati, Metro Manila, the Philippines. Over the last decade or so, many students have flocked to this church-planting concept, but they have not been forewarned about some of the booby traps and failures. In the interests of working together more effectively, we have to call for perhaps fewer, but better qualified team members.

Successful Partnership: A Case Study

Rick Kronk

An effective partnership between a group of missionaries to North Africans in France and a local French church led to the foundation of a ministry model for the future placement of teams in France.

No matter what happens, Rick, we want you to do what you came here to do." Such was the counsel of the elders of the local French church with which we had come to work. We, a team of two couples and a single, had moved to Grenoble, a medium-sized French city of approximately 400,000, in late 1999, after completing an in-house demographic study which included a search for a local church which shared our burden: to reach the North African immigrant community—men and women from Algeria, Morocco, and Tunisia. Our demographic study involved compiling census data from the 1990 census in an effort to determine the French cities with the ten largest populations of North Africans.

Although several years had passed by the time of our study, we made the assumption that immigration patterns had not changed significantly enough to throw off our conclusions: in effect, the top ten cities in 1990 would still be the top ten cities ten years later. Grenoble weighed in at number seven in terms of North Africans. There were nearly fifty thousand, with an additional several thousand students of North African origin at the local university.

Identifying a local French church which shared our burden was not as simple. Church history, coupled with popular political opinion, predisposed many to uncertainty with regard to establishing a focused North African ministry as part of, or alongside of, current church activities. Not that any were out-and-out opposed, but the question of what happens when several of these Arabs become Christians and begin to bring their friends and "date" young people from the church made some uncomfortable.

Prayer and conversation with prominent church leaders in various cities in France eventually led us to a local Brethren church in Grenoble. Initial contact with their lead elder, JLT, resulted in an invitation to discuss our vision and consider a possible partnership. In our presentation, we explained that we had an interest in partnering with a local French church to see a local North African church implanted which would be a sister church and eventually led by North African leadership. We explained that we were preparing to work with a team of five (the two couples and one single noted above) initially, that we were more than happy to include church members who would like to participate in the ministry, and that we were willing to coordinate our ministry such that it complemented and did not compete with the ministry of the local church. Apparently, our vision was sufficiently palatable that JLT felt inclined to offer us an invitation to discuss our vision with the elders. A short time later we met with the church elders to present our vision and to propose a partnership. Seeing that the vision was compatible with where this church wanted to go, the elders invited us to begin our work.

As a first step, and indication of their commitment to the cooperative effort, they proposed a meeting at which they would invite specific individuals from the church whom they knew would be predisposed to support our work. This included a mixed North African-French couple and a North African believer, both of whom had been in the church for several years. From the point of view of the church, JLT said,

> We were happy to have someone on the "inside" to work with us to try to reach these people who were all around us. We also knew that we had a need for both the resources and the know-how that this team brought. Because we had good experiences with missionary partners in the past, we were more than willing to enter into a partnership with them.

Expectations and Concerns

Inevitably partnerships, like marriages, bring both blessings and challenges, joys and disappointments, as both sides discover who the other person(s) really is (are). Our experience in Grenoble was no different. Our first expectation as an American team was for the establishment of a formal relationship that we could "contractualize," complete with a mission statement, strategy proposal, list of written expectations, and other terms giving both parties a clear delineation of who was responsible for what, where the boundaries of authority lay, as well as a signatory block committing representatives from both sides to the partnership.

To our surprise (a rather pleasant one, as it turned out), our French partner didn't think such a contract was necessary. Instead, they insisted on a "contract" of communication and visibility, which they boiled down to two things for the team: (1) be involved in the life of the church beyond our own ministry niche and (2) be represented at elder and other church meetings as requested.

Their history with missionaries in the past had helped them see that if these two conditions were faithfully met, then a formal contract was not necessary. Eventually, however, we found it helpful to create a visual image of how we related to the church in terms of ministry and lines of authority. The diagram below, which we referred to as "a church within a church," was our best attempt to picture this relationship. The large circle represents the host church membership. The central, smaller circle represents the church leadership, in this case, elders and pastors. The large triangle represents the North African group which has a number of particularities.

Church within a Church

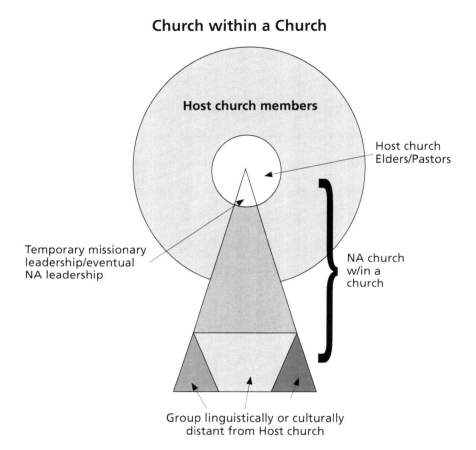

Host church members

Host church
Elders/Pastors

Temporary missionary
leadership/eventual
NA leadership

NA church
w/in a
church

Group linguistically or culturally
distant from Host church

The North African leadership is represented by someone (or several persons) as part of the host church leadership. Initially, this role was filled by one or two missionaries who would eventually be replaced by qualified North Africans.

That part of the large triangle which extends beyond the large circle represents those of the North African group who are associated with the host church, but may or may not attend regularly.

The smaller triangles within the large triangle represent those North Africans who are associated with the North African group, but who have little or no contact with the host church because of major language or cultural barriers.

As time went on, a second challenge reared its head and threatened to distract certain members of our team. This challenge is called the "we need you" challenge. In short, the French local church is in need of competent contributors at all levels. Increased lay-training is helping the local church respond to ministry needs, from worship to Christian education (i.e., Sunday school), but the presence of a team of equipped and trained church workers is hard to overlook. So whereas we were willing and ready to contribute to the life and ministry of the church, we were encouraged by the local church elders not to get so involved that we gave up the work for which we had originally come to France.

In practical terms, those on our team who were competent in preaching would preach from time to time. Those who had music skills assisted in worship leading. Others helped in the children's Sunday school or took turns on the church cleaning rotation. Everyone on our team participated in city-wide outreach events or special events in the life of the church, and we were always ready to provide training tools (e.g., understanding Islam, how to reach Muslims) to local churches—whether in a church-wide event, small group, or one on one.

A third challenge we faced was cultural. The North African Muslim in France faces a host of challenges due to the fact that his or her culture, religion, and family life is so different, and in many ways, opposed to that of French culture, religion, and family life. Despite wishful thinking, these differences do not automatically disappear for the North African once he or she becomes a Christian. Although he or she may be a new creature and not unequal to others in God's eyes (Gal. 3:28), the fact of the matter is that he or she will still struggle to eat the ham offered at the church potluck dinner and drink the wine served at communion. He or she will still prefer to come uninvited to your home and expect to stay as long as needed. Schedules, clocks, appointments, etc., are secondary; relationships are primary.

Thankfully for our partnership, the leadership and membership of the church caught on to this quickly and from the start made a point to minimize the non-essentials and cultural obstacles that could have inhibited our North African friends. For example, they always made sure grape juice was available for communion and that many non-pork items were served at church potlucks.

Benefits Received

JLT put it like this when asked what the church received from this partnership:

> The missionary team brought energy to the overall life of the church. Their focus on a particular ministry and the results that we saw as North Africans came to faith and began to participate in the church helped us see that it was possible to reach this community. This is something for which some of us had been praying for many years.

One joint decision we made early on was to arrange for worship services to be led by the missionary team focusing on North African ministry. These services would include music led by the mission team (often bilingually in French and Arabic), a sermon by a trained North African pastor, and testimonies. Such a service was always followed by a large meal to which everyone was invited. The result of these services helped the church not only to see people from a part of the world of which they were not fully aware, but also to be spiritual recipients—overturning some of the prejudices and healing from the scars of the colonial era.

As the missionary team, we gained invaluable experience in partnering. One of the most important aspects was the role history played in ministry. By history, I mean the collective efforts and results of the missionaries who had come before us in the same location. We, as a team, were not conscious of the historical and religious-political context into which we were arriving with our grand ideas and idealistic ministry plans. We had little knowledge of what had happened missiologically prior to our arrival, and we were ill-equipped to respond to the complex web of inter-church and church-government relationships.

Fortunately, the local church leaders took us by the hand and helped us meet the right people, represented us before local officials, and defended our rights as foreign workers in their country. They also took the time to tell their story and that of the missionaries who had come before us, careful to instruct us as to the "dos and don'ts" so that we would have the best experience possible.

The Result: A Ministry Model for the Placement of Teams in France

Our experience in Grenoble has resulted in formulating a ministry model for the future placement of teams in France. Confronted as we had been by the cumulative (and not always positive) experience between churches and missionaries—together with the sometimes complicated prevailing political and popular opinions of North Africans (and later, during the Iraq War, attitudes toward Americans in particular)—we soon recognized the necessity of finding a "friendly" partner with whom we could work: a partner who would bring legitimacy to our efforts and be able to carry on the effort after our departure. If we were to summarize our ministry model for partnership in France, it would look like this:

Step one: Identify a local church that is willing to allow missionary-directed ministry which is integrated into the local church ministry or cooperates by not competing with local church ministry. The key to this is prayer: prayer to identify possible local churches that might be willing to explore a partnership; prayer with and for the potential local church partner to see if the partnership should be entered into; and prayer all along the way to keep God's purposes the primary ones.

In addition to the active necessity of prayer, finding such a partner should involve understanding the ministry history of the local church as well as prevailing attitudes and experiences with the proposed ministry venture. What we learned in France was that we, as the incoming mission, were not working from a clean slate. Rather, we were only the next ones in line of a considerable history of mission efforts before us. We were in part evaluated initially through the lenses of what had transpired in the past.

Our "glorious" vision was for many a very foreign idea that would require time and evidence that what we envisioned would be valid for the local church as well. Because of this mix of history, culture, missiology, and church polity, not only was patience a fundamental ingredient, but even patience had to take a backseat to humility and respect for the host local church. With regard to our partnership with a French church, whatever criticism we may have had of them, France was and still is their country. As international foreign workers, we had to realize and accept the fact that we were on their turf, and whatever we did—in the name of the gospel—they would have to live with it...even after we were gone.

Step two: Establish a working agreement, whether formal or informal, which both parties understand and which outlines at least levels of cooperation, communication, authority, and terms of continuation. Such agreements will inevitably vary from situation to situation but should be maintained in all good faith. Despite our desire to establish a partnership complete with written objectives and clauses and detailed lines of authority in keeping with what we saw as "normal," the local church was much happier to work instead off of a relational basis.

This relational agreement involved significant potential risk on their part, but their experience as a missionary-friendly church gave them confidence that it could work. All they asked was that we would be involved in the life and ministry of the church outside of our ministry niche, and that we would be represented as requested at regular elder meetings—two conditions we were more than eager to meet.

Step three: Propose a transition or trial period during which initial ministry is carried out and integration of local church members is attempted. Such a transition period allows for learning the local context, building trust between the local church and the missionaries, and identifying hidden "surprises" that may turn out to be accelerators or obstacles to the ministry and call for a "re-think" of the ministry plan. A trial period also allows both sides to determine if this is a good ministry fit and if the partnership should go ahead.

In Grenoble, as part of our coming to terms with a partnership, we built in a trial or transition period to our early phases. For nearly one year prior to actually moving team members into Grenoble, we made trips to Grenoble for the purpose of ministry with the church approximately once a month. Over the course of that year we built credibility, developed relationships with church leadership and church members, and began to forge a clearer picture of how to proceed.

Step four: Make time to evaluate relationships, plans, strategies, and results—both positive and negative. Such efforts to be vulnerable provide opportunities for mutual prayer and encouragement, and for the humble of heart, the possibility of learning something important from the local church partner. Another thing we learned was that evaluation does not always have to be formal and serious. We enjoyed a number of great celebratory moments with our French brothers and sisters around the table, following a baptism or other special event.

Conclusion

"Rick, what you (and your team) have been able to do here has been nothing short of amazing. We could have never imagined that we would be so encouraged as a church by the contributions of the North African brothers and sisters that you have helped us get to know and love." Our time in Grenoble was a successful experience due in large part to the partnership with the local French church. They valued our presence and demonstrated it by praying for us and inviting us to plan church-wide events that would highlight our North African ministry.

They gave us access to their facilities, people, and resources. They joined with us in celebrating when things went well and grieving when things went poorly. But mostly, they got personally involved with us. Many gave hours and hours to helping those struggling with immigrant/refugee issues. Many gave financially to our North African friends in need. Several participated with us in evangelistic outreach and discipleship. And they never stopped encouraging us to continue to do what we had come there to do.

SECTION 6

Case Studies

Theory, strategy, teaching, equipping. All are important. But, practically, what does successful church planting look like? In this section, we present four examples of top-notch church planting based in real-life situations.

Dan Brown details how Frontiers has worked to successfully plant churches among Muslims. In looking at case studies of twelve churches, **David Greenlee** shares why some churches have continued to thrive in difficult areas. **Todd Jamison** looks at why house churches in Central Asia have produced much fruit. **Mark Johnson** takes a look at how a church-planting team in Venezuela knew it was time to leave the field.

Is Planting Churches in the Muslim World "Mission Impossible?"

Dan Brown

A description of Frontiers' Seven Phases of Church Planting among Muslims.

Two half-truths: (1) church planting among Muslims is an impossible task and (2) God must intervene in a special way to reveal how to do it. First of all, in a sense it is impossible. When you consider all that's stacked up against seeing a movement of Muslims coming into the kingdom, it seems almost ludicrous. Second, who can debate that without the miraculous work of the Holy Spirit in a person's heart, no one's eyes are opened. Yet in our brief experience, Frontiers' ninety-one teams across North Africa, the Middle East, Central Asia, South Asia, and Southeast Asia are seeing churches planted. God is forming his Church out of Muslim Background Believers (MBBs) in nearly every country. So is it impossible? No.

God does not expect us to make this up from scratch. Sure, we depend on him to lead in specific ways and to provide the keys that will "unlock the doors" in each location. But we now see that he has already revealed in the Bible most of what we need to know about getting the job done. Much of it comes down to a steady aim.

We see a strong correlation between the narrowness of a team's objectives and its eventual effectiveness. When a team goes into a Muslim city with the singular aim of planting a church among the Muslim majority—and is committed to doing nothing else except what will lead to that goal, and having some clearly understood stages in mind—then usually MBB fellowships emerge.

Where teams go in with broad multiple goals, having only a vague notion of how to get there—and conflicting views on strategy within the team—then usually there are little or no results. When you see a church among an un-reached people group, it's like finding a turtle upon a fence post: clear intentionality from an outside party was involved.

Our "Seven Phases of Church Planting" has grown out of such a context. While some may object that there is no magic plan in the Bible for church planting, we believe that in fact there are definitive stages indicated in the New Testament. Common sense tells us that before you can have a church, you probably first have a gathering or fellowship of believers that may not yet have the minimum New Testament characteristics of "church."

Before that you must have at least one from the target group who has come to Christ, and into whose life you are building the faith. And that presumes you have been evangelizing. So it's no surprise that we find these basic stages (with some variation) in each of Paul's church-planting situations.

Multi-stage church-planting models are not new (for example, David Hesselgrave's "The Pauline Cycle"). Other models have certainly influenced our seven phases, which have been contextualized to our Muslim church-planting teams and agency ethos.

To illustrate, Frontiers' teams (including those in pre-field preparation) are currently at these phases:

Phase 1, "Launching the Team"—19 teams
Phase 2, "Preparing to Sow"—16 teams
Phase 3, "Sowing"—9 teams
Phase 4, "Discipling Begins"—12 teams
Phase 5, "Beginning the Church"—26 teams
Phase 6, "Training Leaders" — 4 teams
Phase 7, "Reproducing and Exiting"—5 teams

This shows a healthy movement up the ladder. Also, our sister agencies who are likewise working to plant churches in the Muslim world are seeing similar progress. It's been our privilege to cross-pollinate with them and share resources, and therefore we rejoice together.

Promoting and using the seven phases widely in our organization has proven invaluable. Some examples:

• When a team has a clear picture of what the next one or two steps are, it is able to work with greater confidence and intentionality (e.g., language learning). Simple tools work best, and much time can be saved from always needing to figure out the next step.

• When a new team is formed in Frontiers, it is linked with 90-plus other teams working at the various phases 1 through 7. This provides a great milieu for peer-to-peer coaching, and faith is energized that the new team, too, will eventually be at Phase 5, 6, or 7, by God's grace.

One of the biggest causes of conflict and ineffectiveness on field teams is mismatched ideas about goals, strategy, methods, time allocation to specific tasks, etc. The "Seven Phases of Church Planting" provide a common vehicle that the team can use to discuss all those crucial aspects of team planning. Using it reduces conflicting expectations, and individual team members can more readily see where they fit into the bigger picture.

The seven phases also give us a common language across the whole organization to identify progress levels, strategy, and activities.

What the Church-planting Phases Are Not

They are not a cookbook: "Just do A, then B, then C, add three pints of Bible, then voila! you'll have a church." In seeking to establish communities of believers in some of the most hostile, unreached, and dangerous places of the world, nothing is so easy or automatic. Of course, there is spiritual battle, persecution, ingrained sin, false conceptions of God, falling away, and betrayals. And it never goes as you expect it to. Our teams still require help and course corrections from leaders and coaches.

Likewise they are not a precise road map. There remains great need for the team's creativity and Spirit-led ingenuity. As someone has said, *church planting is an art, not a science*. Frontiers comprises wide diversity in evangelical theology, philosophy of ministry, and ideas about "church."

That's okay, as this is certainly not intended to be a cookie-cutter approach to missions. The seven phases are intended to encompass a variety of church-planting models. For example, one team intends to plant house churches. Another a cell church. Another team will plant a large traditional or normative-type church. Specific philosophies of ministry have been kept to a minimum for the sake of broad applicability.

What the Church-planting Phases Are

They are a good tool to show where a team's work is at, where it needs to go, and to give many specifics on what the team should work on in each phase. Each phase has four parts.

1. The Phase Title. E.g., Phase 5 is "Beginning the Church."

2. Definition. A brief thumbnail of what the phase is. E.g., Phase 2 is "Learning the language, adjusting to the culture, becoming 'belongers' in society."

3. When Begun. One of the crucial aspects of the seven phases is to differentiate between one phase and another, so that a given team can unambiguously know which phase members are in—like a mark on a yardstick, to clearly distinguish between 35 3/4 inches and 3 feet. E.g. in Phase 4, "Begin regular discipleship with an MBB of the target group (regardless of how he/she came to Christ)."

4. Activities. Very specific objectives or tasks that should be accomplished during the given phase. However, let me hasten to clarify that these are suggestive only. Not every activity needs to be done in each situation.

Specific activities and styles are going to vary greatly from ministry to ministry. For example, Activity #19 in Phase 4 is "Disciple the new believer to become familiar with God's plan for the extension of the kingdom, from the Book of Acts." That may be perfect. Or it may be that the discipler has a different way to teach those truths. Also, they're not comprehensive, as other things will usually come up that are not anticipated in our list.

Some Real Life Examples

We have a team of three families in a large Indonesian city. Having started a growing MBB fellowship, they are in Phase 5. The fellowship has around twenty adult believers, plus children. A spiritually mature, middle-aged MBB couple gives primary leadership within the group. The expatriate team leader and wife are very close to this couple and are discipling them, now focusing largely on ministry and church matters—a fine example of 2 Timothy 2:2.

But the situation is far from being one-dimensional. Various team members must work hard at discipling MBBs, training other leaders, learning the language further (especially for newer members), carrying out the necessary governmental work related to projects and other logistics. Also, some of the team members are not highly involved in the MBB group, as the cultural dynamics don't allow for too much of an expatriate presence. So they focus mainly on evangelism and training some Christian background believers in Muslim evangelism.

All the while the team needs to pay attention to its own life and growth. So under the Phase 5 umbrella, they still remain active in many facets of previous phases (e.g., language learning, evangelism, discipling, etc.). Nonetheless, this team needs to move on toward Phase 6 (later aspects of work just prior to full "church-ship," such as majoring on leadership development) and also keep an eye on Phase 7 (appointing elders, ensuring a mode of reproduction, and exiting). Keeping these two later phases in view prevents the team from straying into cul-de-sacs or nice ministries that don't contribute to the main thing: church planting.

A very large team in Kazakhstan has planted a large MBB church and some satellite groups in other cities. As in the previous example, lots of work remains, with much variety, so that team members can operate in areas of their gifts, whether they be teaching the Bible, discipling, evangelizing, serving, counseling, leading, music, youth work, administration, etc. Being at Phase 7, the work concentrates on multiplication—starting new fellowships and churches.

Another team has worked for years in a major Arab capital. After experiencing many setbacks and waves of opposition from the government, the MBB fellowship they started has grown in size and maturity. This church is comprised of around twenty adults plus children, and two MBB men have been recognized as elders through their active leading and teaching.

However, one of these elders, highly gifted as a church planter, is yearning to move his family to a new city and start afresh. So this ministry must focus on both Phase 6 and Phase 7 priorities.

Diversions

Phases 2 and 3 in particular are difficult to persevere in. There's usually a strong temptation to give up. More commonly there's the danger of getting diverted into other good things: heavy tentmaking involvement, working with ethnic Christians, creating media, "computer work," lots of team activities, or simply spending time with Muslim friends, but never challenging them to a decision point for Christ.

All these may be worthwhile pursuits, but they do not really lead toward planting a church. Therefore the seven phases are a constant reminder and discipline to pull them back toward the main thing, and hopefully give some good ideas of what to do within Phases 2 and 3.

Finally, Frontiers has several teams at Phase 5; that is, they have started and are giving leadership to an MBB fellowship in their target city. But some are tempted to conclude, "Great, we've accomplished what we came here for. We're done. Praise the Lord." The seven phases force them back to realize that in fact the work is not at all done. Much is still required if they are to leave their work in a similar ecclesiastical condition as Paul and Titus left the churches in Crete, i.e., as real "churches" under a plurality of qualified elders in each place.

Three Signs of a Church

This begs the question, "What is a New Testament church, and how do we know when we've planted one?" Such an issue is beyond the scope of this paper. However, I believe that by New Testament examples and criteria, three things must be true for the church planter to be able to walk away and say, "I planted a church there":

1. There must be some "critical mass"—in other words, some minimal size and social makeup. A group of three single men is not a church. A fellowship of fifteen adults plus children may be. The New Testament doesn't give us a magic number, and that's probably because what is a minimal critical mass will vary from one situation to another.

2. There are two or more men who meet the qualifications for eldership and are willing to serve as such. I say two because I believe the New Testament teaches a plurality of elders in a given church; and again, no number is given. Three or more is usually a whole lot better than two.

3. These elders are installed and assume the leadership authority and responsibility. If the believers are still looking to the foreigners to call the shots, the church planting is not yet done.

As we stand near the close of two millennia of the Church's efforts in obeying the Great Commission, clearly the task remains unfinished. Yet the signs are that God is pouring out his mercy on more and more unreached people groups, and pioneer church-planting teams are seeing results that in many cases are unprecedented. We believe that the main thrust of the Church's work to extend the gospel to "those who were not told about him, and those who have not heard" needs to be church planting. Tools such as the "Seven Phases of Church Planting" can aid in this task.

Growing Churches in Resistant Areas

David Greenlee

Case studies of twelve churches reveal characteristics of why vigorous churches have continued to thrive in difficult areas.

How do churches grow? From Paul's basic yet profound explanation (1 Cor. 3:6) to Christian Schwarz's statistical studies (1996), many have attempted to explain the principles that affect the growth of churches, and wondered how they could foster greater growth in and of the church.

Many books have been written born from research in regions such as India (McGavran 1955) and sub-Saharan Africa (Braun n.d.). Less attention has been paid, at least in terms of formal research, to the recently emerging churches in the Muslim world. Greg Livingstone (1993) provided a global survey but indicated the absence of research on conversions from Islam to Christianity (1993, 154). My dissertation (Greenlee 1996) was an attempt to start bridging that gap.

In early 1997, a regional church development working group asked what could be learned from existing churches to benefit those planting new churches of Muslim background believers (MBBs). Those discussions led to the collection of case studies of twelve churches in the region. Analysis of the cases points to certain tendencies and patterns among the churches.

These findings, we should remember, arise from descriptive studies; we must be very careful in moving from them to prescriptive statements. What I have written is true about these churches. As you read, I encourage you to bracket these findings with a question mark and allow them to stimulate reflection on your own ministry setting.

Categorizing the Churches

Case studies were provided for twelve churches. *Church* refers to a group of Christian believers who regularly meet for fellowship, teaching, worship, and the sacraments. Eleven are located in a setting dominated by Islam and with no significant Christian presence in recent centuries. The remaining church is in a neighboring country with a historic Christian presence, but these MBBs have had virtually no contact with Christianity except through a small number of Western expatriate missionaries or other national MBBs. Eight of the churches continue to function today; one ceased in the 1980s and three in the 1990s.

Of the eight churches functioning today, I have classed five as *vigorous*, two as *plateau* and one as *struggling*. These groupings are based on the case studies themselves, not on an external scale. Although admittedly somewhat subjective, the factors affecting my categorization include numerical growth, vitality of fellowship, response to opposition, and strength of national leadership.

At least two of the churches which have ceased meeting, could have been called vigorous at one time. In looking at the case studies, I tried to learn lessons from those ceased groups when they were at their best as well as the factors leading to their decline.

Burden Bearing

Galatians 6:2 gives practical instruction on how to put John 13:34-35 into practice: bear one another's burdens. My earlier work on individual male believers in one country revealed a disturbing lack of commitment to "burden bearing" (Greenlee 1996, 159-161).

In this study, it is encouraging to find that all of the vigorous churches report a strong sense of community demonstrated in specific instances of burden bearing. Caring for the sick, helping the unemployed, and encouraging those in various struggles were some of the examples reported.

The two plateau churches referred to burden bearing, but it seemed to have occurred more in the past. The struggling church gave no indication that burden bearing was a part of the fellowship.

Of the ceased churches, one had gone through a vigorous phase in which it did have a time of significant burden bearing. The only other reference among the ceased churches to burden bearing was to the absence of this practice in one group before its demise. The informant reported that the decline of the church "might have been that everyone was exhausted with some people always giving and not being able to give any more while others were always receiving and not willing to give."

Evangelism and Welcome of New People

Missionaries should evangelize. But the vigorous churches tend to be those in which the national believers have taken on an active role in evangelism. Schwartz argues that, although "it is indeed the responsibility of every Christian to use his or her own specific gifts in fulfilling the Great Commission... the gift of evangelism applies to no more than ten percent of all Christians" (Schwartz 1996, 34).

How then does a church characterized by evangelism emerge? Much, it seems, depends on the founder, or a leader who has come in at a time of revitalization. Robert Coleman's classic work (1993) points to eight principles Jesus did beyond simply evangelizing. He produced evangelists through selection, association, consecration, impartation, demonstration, delegation, supervision, and reproduction.

Of the two vigorous churches most strongly characterized by evangelism, the founder of one and the revitalizing leader of the other clearly exemplify the principles Coleman presents. Their own commitment to evangelism, close association with a select few, training, and demonstration has led to several others being equipped and involved in evangelistic ministry.

What should be done with seekers and new believers in an environment where betrayal may bear serious consequences? Welcoming new people to the church is a critical issue. Several churches had experienced negative repercussions from welcoming an insincere person; most of the rest were fearful of what could happen. Various strategies were adopted by the vigorous churches, but it is clear that finding some plan to welcome seekers and new believers, a workable plan which the church as a whole adopts, is very important.

Spiritual Gifts

It is not surprising that the vigorous churches indicate that the members are, in one way or another, using their spiritual gifts. Some churches which were weaker, or ceased, also made such reports, although the reports tended to indicate this had to do with teaching and not a broader range of spiritual gifts that contributed to the life of the body.

Two of the ceased churches were characterized by the unwillingness of some to get involved, leaving a heavier load on a small number. This contributed directly to the demise of these churches.

Leadership Transitions

Leaders are vital. Finding qualified national leaders is very important to long-term growth. How those leaders are appointed appears to be crucial.

In the countries of these twelve churches, national politics is characterized by a strong, central figure. Where an attempt had been made at free elections, the result was years of civil unrest. The people tend to accept the situation but when crops fail or the economy turns sour, tension on the streets can become acute.

Intercultural relations expert Geert Hofstede (1997) describes the countries of this region as having a very high power distance. That is, in this region inequality is accepted, hierarchy is needed, superiors are often inaccessible, and power-holders have privilege.

Having visited most of these countries myself, I would agree with Hofstede's description of society as a whole. But what applies to successful national politics and social structure does not apply within these churches. In fact, it could be that two sets of values are competing, those described by Hofstede and a more biblical, egalitarian, servant-leader approach to Christian community.

All of the vigorous churches have made a transition to national leadership. For some it was a bumpy process as leaders failed in one way or another, leading to a turbulent period. Failure in the leadership transition contributed to the decease of two groups and is a continuing problem for one which is struggling.

In one setting, an expatriate who had helped found a church appointed a leader with apparently adequate gifting. When the expatriate left the country the church fell apart. The others in the church did not place confidence in the new leader and were not in agreement with his appointment. In other cases, appointing people to leadership prematurely, or taking leadership back out of their hands, were reported as negative influences on church development.

Our cases do not provide definitive answers for this thorny issue of transition from an expatriate founder to national leadership. It appears, though, that a consensus-building approach to decision-making and leadership issues is helpful. Having leadership gifts alone is not enough; building trusting relationships is vital. The failure of leaders to develop relationships and build consensus run counter to the health of the church. On the other hand, good leadership must be complemented by the rest of the church sharing the load, using their spiritual gifts and bearing one another's burdens.

Persecution

Persecution, as experienced by these churches, ranged from the general social pressures and intimidation from family and employers to harassment and, at times, torture at the hands of the police. The only specific death threat reported was directed at an expatriate by friends of a fundamentalist who had come to faith. Perhaps the most common characteristic among the churches was the problem of fear of what might happen.

Among the twelve churches studied, the only pattern I find linking the cases is that persecution tends to push the believers inward, to curtail witness, and to cause them to be cautious in relationships. The specifics of their responses vary greatly. Some struggle with fear, while at least two of the vigorous church-

THE DEMISE OF THE CHURCH which ceased **in the 1980s** was, in part, a result of severe police intimidation and arrests of several believers.

es want to avoid unnecessary trouble and so have measured their (somewhat) open evangelistic activity accordingly.

The demise of the church which ceased in the 1980s was, in part, a result of severe police intimidation and arrests of several believers. Another church seemed to be growing well, but fear linked to one man's open evangelism led to division and eventual break-up of the group. In another short-lived church, quite strong police intimidation helped prevent the group from being solidly grounded, leading to its demise.

Since the cases were gathered, I have been aware of serious police intimidation of two of the vigorous churches. The believers made it clear that they were Christians, making no attempt to emulate Muslim religious practices (cf. Green 1989). I have been informed that, when the intimidation subsided, both groups saw significant numerical growth or multiplication in the formation of other groups.

Singles or Families?

One mission agency's definition of an autonomous, functioning local church includes the presence of Christian families in the fellowship (Livingstone 1993, 170). Although doubtless we all long for the incorporation of entire families in the churches, no clear pattern emerged linked specifically to the question of singles-only churches.

One group started by two single men, involving just single men, thrived and eventually, through marriage of the members, included families. Another similar group struggled. A group started by couples involving singles eventually fell apart as a result of police intimidation and inadequate leadership transition when the expatriates had to pull out of participation. At the same time, presence of families in a church was no guarantee of the church's vigor.

It is evident that families can add a measure of stability to a church, but single men at times give the needed leadership and evangelistic drive to a church made up of singles and families together. At other times, the married man (and his wife) provide leadership as well as a secure place to meet. Study of the roles of Philemon, Onesimus and Epaphras among the New Testament churches in the Colosse-Laodicea-Hierapolis triangle may help to illuminate this point further.

One important finding is a confirmation of the role of single missionaries as church planters in the Muslim world. One of the older churches was blessed for many years through the ministry of a godly single woman missionary who, perhaps due to her age and longevity in ministry, held the respect of both men and women. Another of the vigorous churches was planted by two single men. As singles, the two did not attempt to bring in women but when a church member married, followed some time later by the marriage of one of the missionaries, the group was able to transition to mixed membership in the church.

Place

It seems that having a secure, regular place to meet which is identified more with nationals than missionaries is an aid to growth. Too much dependence on the missionaries for a place to meet appears to be unhealthy.

Alternatively, it seems that the weaker churches tended to be dependent on the missionaries for a place to meet, or that the meetings took place outside the normal environment of the national believers. One exception is a house that has been known as a Christian place for decades and has been somehow tolerated by the authorities (although with waves of persecution over the years). Another vigorous church comprised of singles did meet initially in the single missionaries' apartment. Its location and the lifestyle of these men, however, reflected their close bonding to the local culture.

Conferences and Special Events

Mathias Zahniser (1997) suggests the importance of symbol and ceremony in the cross-cultural discipling process. In an Islamic setting, MBBs may struggle with their response to Ramadan and the various Islamic feasts, all the while wondering how to incorporate such Christian celebrations as Christmas and Easter.

The case studies I have considered remind us again of the importance of special events in building up the church. Summer Bible camps, Easter and Christmas events and other opportunities to gather believers for celebration, fellowship and teaching make a major, positive contribution, especially among the vigorous churches. Even some reporting on churches that have now ceased, in looking back at better times, consider these gatherings of great importance.

Conclusion

There is no simple key, no recipe, for planting thriving churches of MBBs. Suggested success principles and practices developed in countries with significant freedom for open church life may not prove relevant to our setting. Schwartz's excellent work must be applied with care since his extensive surveys involved few churches in settings dominated by Islam (1996, 19). We may even find that practices developed in one region of the Islamic world are irrelevant among MBBs elsewhere. Joshua Massey (2000, 12-13) helps us understand the reason for this by reminding us of the diverse attitudes Muslims hold toward Islam, not just their diverse theologies.

The research project giving rise to this paper grew out of the disquiet of a group of MBBs and missionaries concerned to see churches growing and thriving in their region. Broader research might help us refine these findings and extend the range of their validity. The hard work will not be further studies, surveys and analysis; the real challenge is in creatively, contextually bringing these principles to life in ourselves and in the people entrusted to our care and training.

References

Braun, Willys K. n.d. *Evaluating and Escalating Church Growth in the Third World*. Kinshasa: International Center of Evangelism.

Coleman, Robert E. 1993. *The Master Plan of Evangelism*. Grand Rapids, Mich.: Fleming H. Revell.

Green, Denis. 1989. "Guidelines from Hebrews for Contextualization." In *Muslims and Christians on the Emmaus Road*. Ed. J. Dudley Woodberry, 233-250. Monrovia, Calif.: MARC.

Greenlee, David. 1996. "Christian Conversion from Islam: Social, Cultural, Communication and Supernatural Factors in the Process of Conversion and Faithful Church Participation." PhD diss. Deerfield, Ill.: Trinity International University.

Hofstede, Geert. 1997. *Cultures and Organizations: Software of the Mind*. New York: McGraw-Hill.

Livingstone, Greg. 1993. *Planting Churches in Muslim Cities: A Team Approach*. Grand Rapids, Mich.: Baker.

Massey, Joshua. 2000. "God's Amazing Diversity in Drawing Muslims to Christ." *Inter-*

national Journal of Frontier Missions 17(1):5-14.

McGavran, Donald A. 1955. The Bridges of God. New York: The Friendship Press.

_____. 1970. *Understanding Church Growth,* 3rd ed., rev. and ed. by C. Peter Wagner. Grand Rapids, Mich.: William B. Eerdmans Publishing Co.

Scharwz, Christian A. 1996. *Natural Church Development Handbook.* British Church Growth Association. www.CundP.de/international provides a list of international distributors.

Zahniser, A.H. Mathias. 1997. *Symbol and Ceremony: Making Disciples across Cultures.* Monrovia, Calif.: MARC.

House Churches in Central Asia: An Evaluation

Todd Jamison

For many Christians in Central Asia, house churches are the best church-planting strategy.

David Garrison (2004) and Rad Zdero (2004) have demonstrated both the biblical and missiological basis for house church methodology. The amazing advance of the gospel in places such as China and parts of India are clear evidence for the validity of this approach, even in an Asian context. Zdero and others believe that a second reformation is occurring as we enter the twenty-first century, a reformation of basic ecclesiology (Zdero 2004, 1-5).

So what about Central Asia, an area encompassing some 220 million people, the vast majority of whom are Muslims?[1] Is it possible to see a Church Planting Movement (CPM) of house churches in this region? Are there any documented cases of CPMs in this area? What are the current attitudes and efforts toward house churches? What does the future hold? In this article, I will seek to evaluate these questions.

For the person unfamiliar with the Central Asian context as it relates to the spread of the gospel, a brief summary is in order. Christianity in its Nestorian form existed in Central Asia for almost one thousand years. In the fourteenth century, due to a number of factors, including large-scale persecution by the Turko-Mongolian ruler Timur, Nestorian Christians disappeared from Central Asia.

Various Protestant denominations sent missionaries to Central Asia during the nineteenth century, with limited or no success (see Foltz 1999). The remoteness of the region, combined with hostile governments that restricted missionary access, contributed to the difficulty. Today, Central Asia percentage-wise is the most unreached place on earth. The total number of believers is thought to be only .03% of the population.

The number of evangelicals increased discernibly in the past decade. This was mainly due to three factors. First, the collapse of the Soviet Union in 1991 contributed to a new wave of religious freedom and expression. Second, various mission agencies developed new ways of entering previously restricted regions, thus enabling direct evangelism and church planting to take place. Third, the composition of the mission force of the last decade of the twentieth century was also quite different from the previous century's efforts. Missionaries from Korea, Singapore, South Africa, Latin America, and India entered the region, along with large numbers of westerners. The rapid and exponential increase in the number of laborers resulted in a rich harvest.

CPM experts have noticed this growth, especially among the Kazakhs (Garrison 2004, 107-110). Because Garrison listed an advance among the Kazakhs, some have wrongly assumed that a CPM is taking place there. Garrison never admits this, but says there are "encouraging signs" (2004, 110). Others have also declared that a CPM was taking place because their definition of CPM could more accurately just be called "church planting" as opposed to a movement of rapidly multiplying churches.

So why has Central Asia not seen a CPM? That question has multiple answers, not the least of which has to do with God's timing. Space prohibits consideration of many factors; however, the lack of access to scripture is probably the major reason why a CPM has not broken out in Central Asia. Closely behind this is the fact that until recently there has been no major effort to plant house churches among the peoples of Central Asia.

Current Status of House Churches in Central Asia

Modern mission efforts in Central Asia only began in earnest around 1990.[2] Almost without exception, congregations planted during this period started in private homes and apartments. It was not uncommon for missionaries to have their first gospel conversations with Central Asians over tea in relaxed, home settings. Central Asian hospitality provided a natural setting for warm conversation and the exchange of ideas. Small groups worshiped Jesus in homes and apartments of every major city of Central Asia within just a few years.

Such church planting, however, did not occur in a vacuum. While the number of Muslim-background evangelicals in many of these locations prior to 1990 could be counted on one hand, Russians, Germans, and other Slavs had been in the region worshiping in their building-based churches for almost 120 years.

Most of the newly-independent republics maintained many governmental ministries that regulated religion from the Soviet era. To varying degrees, these republics have allowed religious freedom; however, all of them still require registration of churches. All "real" churches are to have a written charter and an address, and if they are not to be identified as sects, they need their own church building with a sign. This building-based mentality is predominant throughout the culture of Central Asia; thus, legitimacy is often determined by whether or not a church has a building.

From the beginning, most Central Asian believers seemed to instinctively believe that the logical progression of church growth resulted in the purchase of land and a building. Many of the churches that got their start in a Soviet-style apartment quickly began the quest for a larger location.

Foreign missionaries, agencies, and churches have been only too happy to oblige in meeting financial needs for the construction or renovation of buildings. If local Central Asian churches could not build, they sought to rent public facilities such as schools or university auditoriums. Small congregations meeting in homes were removed from their natural setting of community and family for the sake of the legitimacy of being a "real" church.

Foreign missionaries have contributed to the architectural hunger further by setting the standard of success as the large mega-church. A few years ago, during a gathering of some sixty Central Asian pastors, a well-known Korean missionary-pastor, who had grown a very large congregation of approximately five thousand people, said to the group, "One day, if you have enough faith, your church will be larger than mine."

Many of these pastors came from villages whose population was less than five thousand! Additionally, the members of this missionary-pastor's congregation were predominately indigenous Koreans or Russians, with a much smaller percentage being from a Muslim background. Yet this distinction was lost on the pastor's gathering. For them, the standard for success became the mega-church.

While the vast majority of Central Asian churches started in homes, it almost universally served as a launching pad to "real" church, with the goal of a large, building-based organization. The reality is, however, that this standard of "ideal" church can be found in very few places in Central Asia, and there is almost no congregation of more than one hundred people that is led by a local.

THE CURRENT STATUS OF THE CHURCH
and church planting in many parts of the region now suffers under extra burdens that new believers and their young leadership cannot carry.

Even after more than a decade of labor, the largest churches are still pastored by foreign missionaries. Existing local Muslim-background pastors are often burdened with the weight of not having a "large church" and have no previous experience in leading a group much larger than their immediate family.

The current status of the Church and church planting in many parts of the region now suffers under extra burdens that new believers and their young leadership cannot carry. The concept of biblical servant leadership, already difficult enough to grasp from a human perspective, is especially alien in a context where dictatorial, communistic and Asian models prevailed. Administrative skills that westerners handle naturally as a part of their culture, such as keeping a checkbook, can seem highly complex for leaders whose average education levels are not much beyond high school. We must return to the simple and go back to the house church, the very core of Central Asian culture.

The ancient *oikos* (Greek for "household") is the closest model we find in scripture to the idea of house churches (see Gehring 2004). Often, I have heard nationals mention how the traditional customs so closely mirror the scriptures. It is time for our Central Asian brothers and sisters to return to the simplicity of the small and relational, and for missionaries to quit trying to turn them into large-scale people-managers who mimic professional business-persons trying to raise the bottom line of their growing enterprise.

New Efforts toward Intentional House Church Planting

In parts of Central Asia, house churches are the only way that the Church can continue to grow, particularly in Uzbekistan, Turkmenistan, and Afghanistan. Yet in the former two countries, such church planting is often viewed as less than ideal. Some of the Russian and indigenous Korean congregations have been able to build structures, and Muslim-background churches have used their facilities.

Yet in the last few years, due to rapid growth, some local church leaders are beginning to see the advantage of house churches. This is particularly true in Karakalpakistan and the Ferghana Valley, both locations in Uzbekistan where house churches and cell groups have steadily increased.

While restrictions and persecution in these locations have caused some to consider house church methodology, the embracing of house churches as a valid church-planting strategy came when Garrison visited Kazakhstan and Uzbekistan in 2003 and 2004. During his visits, he spoke to both Eastern and Western foreign missionaries and local pastors. His presentations defined more clearly what a CPM is and also demonstrated that house churches are one of the universal elements of all CPMs (Garrison 2004, 191-193).

While not accepted or understood by all those he spoke with, Garrison's impact was unmistakable. Within a year's time in Kazakhstan, many Western missionaries in particular began planting house churches. One local seminary started offering the option of house church planting to its leaders in training.

In 2004, some local leaders in southern Kazakhstan gathered to learn more about house churches. The gathering represented ten to fifteen small groups that considered themselves to be either churches or the beginnings of churches. They heard testimonies from Kazakh pastors who had already begun house churches. Increasingly there is an understanding of CPMs and the role of house churches.

Uzbek church leaders recently discussed the need for gathering their house churches into a network. The same is true for five house church pastors in Tajikistan. Some Uighur pastors in Kazakhstan began intentionally starting house churches. In Kyrgyzstan, one missionary led seminars for Kyrgyz pastors in his Pioneer Evangelism method, a discipleship program that stresses the gathering of converts into house churches.

House church-planting efforts are underway among the Muslims in the Caucasus in Russia, Azerbaijan, Turkey, and other areas highly-restrictive to the spread of the gospel. The intentional planting of house churches is gaining momentum, and while there is no evidence of rapid multiplication, many locations seem to be positioning themselves for such.

Advantages for Planting House Churches in Central Asia

Zdero has provided several reasons for the advantages of planting house churches (2004, 56-57, 76-78). Many of those same advantages apply to the Central Asian context. This section seeks to highlight these advantages.

1. Advantages in contextualization. Over the past decade I have assisted Central Asian church leaders in contextualizing their building-based services to better fit the culture. Whether it concerned worship music, preaching, or dress, long hours of discussion were devoted to creating a setting that seemed more Kazakh, Kyrgyz, or Uighur. Such efforts often came up short, as the Central Asian believers merely copied what they observed from foreigners. Newspaper articles still appear from time to time, lamenting how meetings and music of a "foreign religion" are destroying the culture.

When the church meets in a home, it enters the most basic level of culture. The cradle of cultural traditions is the family unit. If a church is meeting in

THE HOME IS THE BASE for family **gatherings** and the average Central Asian family with extended relatives is quite large. People gather to drink tea, enjoy a meal, and sing as a part of daily life.

a home, it more easily takes on the characteristics of the surrounding culture and language of the home. As mentioned above, biblical parallels exist in the homes of Central Asians.

2. Advantages during persecution. "Everyone in our church has a birthday, so we have many birthday celebrations." This was the answer one Central Asian church leader gave as to how they could continue to meet for worship despite governmental restrictions on religious meetings in homes. The home is the base for family gatherings and the average Central Asian family with extended relatives is quite large. People gather to drink tea, enjoy a meal, and sing as a part of daily life.

House churches can also easily change location. Such gatherings are so stealthy that a house church pastor recently asked if registering his network of churches in a fairly restrictive area was even necessary because their house meetings attracted no attention of government officials. House churches by no means guarantee that persecution will not occur.

The Bible reveals the certainty of persecution (Acts 8:1-3; Matt. 24:9). Someone with the zeal of a Saul of Tarsus had to persecute the Church in order to have a detrimental impact. Uzbekistan and Iranian governments have demonstrated such zeal in recent crackdowns, yet they have not been able to prohibit all house churches from meeting.

3. Advantages in leadership. Leadership is the biggest problem in the Central Asian Church today. Foreign missionaries are still leading the largest building-based congregations. While this article cannot examine all of the reasons that Central Asian church leaders have so slowly emerged, one major factor has been the decades, in some cases centuries, of colonial rule.

In many parts of Central Asia, male passivity and obeisance was the only way to ensure survival. War, famine, oppression, and fractured families contributed to the decimation of male leaders. Additionally, older males are the most resistant to the gospel. Most Central Asian male believers are still young, inexperienced, not well-educated, and living in a culture that promotes passivity. Is it any surprise that so many young pastors struggle in leading a group of more than thirty people?

Such leadership requires management skills derived from training and education. The pressure to perform and produce church growth contributes to the burden that has caused some leaders in a Central Asian seminary to report widespread burnout among the pastors they have trained.

I have personally seen the joy return to some pastors who embraced the house church model. Instead of wilting under administrative duties that often await building-based church pastors whose goal is to manage hundreds of people, these leaders focus on people and on multiplying small, manageable house churches. Their energy is directed toward building people instead of structures.

4. Advantages with finances. To date, there are no known self-financed evangelical church buildings among Muslim Background Believers in the former Soviet Central Asia. Foreign sources have either totally or partially financed all current structures. Many Central Asian governments now prohibit churches from renting public facilities, thus increasing pressure for building-based churches to find their own facilities.

As these countries advance economically, land and construction costs climb steadily. The majority of Central Asian evangelicals come from the population's lower socio-economic strata, where monthly salaries average $50 to $250. In the political, cultural, and economic climate of the region, the building of a church structure is a daunting task and next to impossible apart from foreign assistance.

What about house churches? Financial needs are no longer a major concern when a church's goal to build or purchase a structure is not a priority. The ability of the members to care for one another and to use their money for genuine felt-needs becomes a reality for even the smallest and poorest congregations.

Potential Pitfalls for House Churches in Central Asia

House churches are not the "magic silver bullet" that will solve all the problems of church planting and the expansion of the Kingdom of God in Central Asia. As long as churches are filled with human beings, problems will exist. Christians meeting in a house does not guarantee that genuine fellowship, evangelism, disciple-making, and God-encountering worship will occur. There are pitfalls to house churches in Central Asia. Below are four.

1. Confusion with Islamic fundamentalist groups. Islamic fundamentalism is the greatest fear for the governments of Central Asia. Particularly in former Soviet Central Asia among governments still run by former Communists, the inability to distinguish between the various religious groups and their nuances has led to policies that are restrictive of all religions.

Although the vast majority of the countries have constitutional provisions protecting freedom of conscience, government officials, particularly on a local level, often ignore or are ignorant of their constitutions. It is not unusual for fundamental Wahabist groups to meet in houses or cell groups. Therefore, when evangelicals meet in house churches, authorities can associate them with fundamental Muslims whose intent is to overthrow the governments in the region.

ONE DISTINCT DISADVANTAGE that small house churches may have is the inability to draw from a larger pool of sound theologians.

In Uzbekistan and Turkmenistan, religious gatherings in homes are illegal. Even in Kazakhstan, local officials have fined unregistered religious groups who gather in homes, although such actions are unconstitutional.

As a way of overcoming this obstacle, some house churches have come under the registration of existing building-based congregations. Also, because large social gatherings in homes are not unusual, Christian gatherings are hard to distinguish from other social events. In most cases where house gatherings have been raided by authorities, it is due to disgruntled neighbors who inform on them rather than to a random discovery on the part of the secret police.

2. Promotion of tribalism. The expression "blood is thicker than water" applies to Central Asia. In lands where blood feuds and massacres have occurred periodically throughout the centuries, and particularly in areas touched by Stalinism, only relatives are fully trusted. House churches that naturally form around family relationships can become too inwardly focused.

While this problem is not unique to house churches, house church-planting methodology could easily make the problem worse. From the beginning, house church planters should emphasize the need to make disciples of all nations by starting new house churches among all the people groups of Central Asia.

3. False teaching. While false teaching is most certainly a potential pitfall, I have yet to see or hear of a specific example of false teaching emerging from a house church in Central Asia. The same cannot be said of building-based congregations. So it may be more accurate to say that this is a pitfall of the Church among all generations in all countries at all times (Matt. 24:11, 24; 2 Pet. 2:1).

One distinct disadvantage that small house churches may have, however, is the inability to draw from a larger pool of sound theologians. It is very important that house church planters instill in the DNA of the church complete reliance upon scripture. The best antidote to false teaching is when house churches and their elders are trained to go to the Bible for answers (Garrison 2004, 182-186, 269-270).

4. Polarization of the larger Body of Christ. God is using traditional, building-based churches in Central Asia. House church planters and the members of these new churches must not become prideful and criticize or distance themselves from their brothers and sisters in Christ who have chosen not to be a part of house churches.

Throughout the history of the Church, critics have assailed movements that have promoted small groups and house churches (see Bunton 2001). House church planters, elders, and members should expect criticism and misunderstanding (Luke 5:37-39); however, an attitude of defensiveness fails to enhance outreach and usually promotes disunity.

Conclusion: House Church Networks—The Next Step

A necessity in overcoming the pitfalls house churches in Central Asia face is developing house church networks. Again, Zdero and others have explained the important role that house church networks can play in any movement (2004, 106-109; Kreider 2001). Intentional house churches in Central Asia are just emerging and only recently starting to link together via common leadership meetings. As of yet, there is no example of a full-fledged, formalized network that uses a common covenant or confession.

If house churches in Central Asia are going to remain and continue multiplying, networks must develop. Missionaries and local church planters can assist in this process by bringing various leaders together for fellowship, prayer and instruction. The sharing of ideas and resources via conferences could greatly increase the pace of house church planting and growth. Central Asian believers and missionaries involved with house churches need to provide case studies so others can learn from their successes and failures.

Endnotes

1. The boundaries of Central Asia, sometimes referred to as Inner Asia, are rarely one of uniform agreement. Our definition of Central Asia encompasses what would be considered the majority of the Turko-Persian world, starting in the west with Turkey and incorporating the former Soviet republics of Azerbaijan, Turkmenistan, Tajikistan, Uzbekistan, Kyrgyzstan and Kazakhstan. Turkico-Persian peoples can also be found in several parts of Russia, particularly the Caucasus and the Ural regions. Iran, Afghanistan and

even parts of northwest China, with its large Uighur population, fall under our definition of Central Asia.

2. This is mainly true for the Central Asian republics of the former Soviet Union. Efforts outside of these parts of Central Asia (i.e., Turkey, Afghanistan, Iran) have a different history with various times of openness and varying levels of missionary activity.

References

Bunton, Peter. 2001. *Cell Groups and House Churches: What History Teaches Us*. Ephrata, Pa.: House to House Publications.

Foltz, Richard C. 1999. *Religions of the Silk Road: Overland Trade and Cultural Exchange from Antiquity to the Fifteenth Century*. New York: St. Martin's Press.

Garrison, David. 2004. *Church Planting Movements: How God Is Redeeming a Lost World*. Midlothian, Va.: WIGTake Resources.

Gehring, Roger W. 2004. *House Church and Mission: The Importance of Household Structures in Early Christianity*. Peabody, Mass.: Hendrickson Publishers.

Kreider, Larry. 2001. *House Church Networks*. Ephrata, Pa.: House to House Publications.

Zdero, Rad. 2004. *The Global House Church Movement*. Pasadena, Calif.: William Carey Library.

April 2001

Learning to Leave

Mark Johnson

A case study from TEAM's work in Venezuela offers advice on how to know when it is time to leave the church in the hands of national believers.

Reggie **White plays football.** He had a very well-defined task as defensive end—to tackle the guy with the ball. The sooner, the better. He has done well enough to lead the National Football League in quarterback sacks for his career. But Reggie was responsible for more than just tackling the quarterback. The game plan for a particular opponent might demand different types of alignments, and each player has specific responsibilities, depending upon the defensive play that had been called. Each player has to know exactly what to do and when to do it. Before leaving the Green Bay Packers, Reggie trained a replacement, a rookie drafted in the first round. He trained by example. In his last year, Reggie was named NFL Defensive Player of the Year.

Reggie is also an ordained Baptist preacher who says what he thinks. Some of his more famous comments are related to major career changes he has faced. When he went to Green Bay from Philadelphia a few years ago, he said God told him to go. Once he retired, and then came out of retirement a few hours later. "Why?" he was asked. God told him to do it, he said.

Now, what does this have to do with a church planter completing the task? First, we must know our team and our role. We must know our purpose, and develop a game plan for the particular situation we are confronting. We must pursue excellence. As missionaries, we must remind ourselves that we are not called to stay, but to think in terms of finishing the task, and of training someone to take our place. And we must hear the Lord's voice telling us when it's time to move on. In Venezuela, The Evangelical Alliance Mission (TEAM) is learning to discern God's voice in this very area.

Let's start with a broad principle for defining a church-planting plan for a given country. A church planter should have a plan for leaving at the beginning of a church-planting project. It is amazing that after ten years of work in four provinces of the Roman Empire, Paul could speak as if his work there was done. The churches that he planted were truly established, and not just left to their own devices when Paul moved on to another city (Allen 1962, 3).

This is a shock to us as we consider the amount of time many missionaries, including my wife and I, spend in one location trying to get a church established. Paul was an exceptional man in exceptional times, but others on his teams and those that followed in his footsteps applied the same principles, the most important of which was dependence upon the Holy Spirit.

Tom Steffen proposes a gradually decreasing role for the church planter even as he or she maintains a role, first as a participant, then a resident advisor, and eventually as a non-resident advisor. He cites Paul as an example, as he changed roles from that of evangelist and on-site teacher to that of writing letters to churches he established and returning periodically to visit them.

Steffen advocates a "church-planting model that does not bog us down with unnecessary details, but instead keeps us focused on a phase-out departure." He says,

> Knowing when to leave a church plant is just as important as knowing when to begin it. Phase-out establishes the parameters for the entire church-planting movement because it defines a strategy for closure toward which all earlier strategies are directed. (Steffen 1997, 6, 215)

As a church-planting mission agency, TEAM has used the criteria of completion of our church plants to help us determine when the mission should phase out of Venezuela.[1]

TEAM's purpose is to help churches send missionaries to plant reproducing churches in other nations. It has missionaries in more than forty countries around the world. In Venezuela, we work with two associations of churches. A few years ago the home office in Wheaton, Illinois, started asking some disturbing questions: *are the churches in the two associations planting other churches? Well, yes,* we answered, *they are.* So, they returned: *how much longer do you think TEAM needs to be in Venezuela?* We've been working on the answer to that question ever since.

The first thing we did was to gather information from the principal "stakeholders." These included TEAM missionaries in Venezuela and in the home office, retired missionaries from other fields who had gone through a similar process, supporting churches, and the national church associations. We asked them these questions:

1. What information do you think we should seek, and from whom, in order to develop criteria for eventual departure from Venezuela?
2. What do you think should be the criteria for the completion of TEAM's task in Venezuela?

Our supporting churches were, for the most part, quite positive about TEAM leaving Venezuela—assuming we could establish solid criteria for why we should be leaving. They gave us excellent ideas for establishing criteria. The TEAM Venezuela missionaries had extensive input in three regional meetings held in different parts of the country, in TEAM Venezuela's annual meetings, and by phone and Internet. Some of the retired missionaries we heard from had the most difficult time with the concept of TEAM leaving Venezuela.

"There is still so much to do," they told us. They are right, of course. The question we asked ourselves, in light of TEAM's purpose statement, was, "Which of the many things to be done should be done by TEAM?"

The two national church associations had quite different answers to our questions. The president of one, the older association, told us that we would be bad parents if we left Venezuela in the near future. This association is more than seventy years old, and we had to ask ourselves how much longer we'd have to stay for this dear brother to construe us as a good parent when we left! The other church association helped us initiate the thought process that has led us to the criteria for leaving.

We decided that TEAM will leave Venezuela when we have established strategically located impact churches throughout Venezuela. This is certainly not new. Roland Allen said,

> Paul's theory of evangelizing a province was not to preach in every place himself, but to establish centers of Christian life in two or three important places from which the knowledge might be spread into the country around. This is important, not in showing that he preferred to preach in a capital rather than in a provincial town or village, but because he intended this congregation to become at once a center of light.

He goes on to say that churches in the city can be made "graves of mission" as easily as churches in rural towns" (Allen 1962, 12). It is essential, then, that a church be a "source of light" or it is not worth the effort to locate it in a strategic city.

The church association with which TEAM works in eastern Venezuela, ASIGEO, has had this vision for several years. When we asked them what TEAM should do in Venezuela before leaving, they spoke to us in terms of establishing some model churches in the cities. The evangelical church has been fairly well established in rural parts of Venezuela, but has yet to effectively reach the large cities and especially the middle class and up. ASIGEO felt that none of their one hundred churches could be considered well established. We were incredulous, and named some churches with good-sized congregations with church buildings and full-time pastors. They said that one must first define what an "established" church is, and proceeded to do so for us. This became the basis for our definition of a well-established church.

An established church is a local body of believers that is characterized by the following biblical principles:

1. It is known for its dynamic worship of God.
2. It assumes responsibility for one another as a family, ministering to one another in love and humility.
3. It has a vision for reaching the world for Christ.
4. It relates to other churches of like mind.
5. It is directed by leaders who are recognized as meeting the biblical re-

quirements for leadership.

Beneath each of these points are practical ways these principles were fleshed out in the early Church, with corresponding biblical references. We recognize that there are other definitions of the established church that are more comprehensive than this one. The purpose of our definition is to give us a basis for evaluating how far a church is down the road toward becoming a well-established church.

This evaluation will give us valuable information as we seek to determine which churches are candidates to become real impact churches.[2] Our definition of an "impact" church is an established church which: (1) has a congregation of at least two hundred people; (2) provides resources to other churches; (3) has an adequate locale for worship, training, and outreach; and (4) reaches all social classes, especially the middle and upper classes.

The first criterion, then, for determining the cities in which to invest TEAM Venezuela's resources is the existence of a church in that city which is well on the way to becoming an established church, as we've defined it. We also look for missionaries and Venezuelans with a vision for establishing the impact church in that city.

WE MUST BE CAREFUL not to impose our criteria on the church. Neither should a pastor, no matter how well intended, force the church to accept change just because he believes it is right.

The city itself should be a growing city of at least one million people with a low percentage of evangelicals, and an unreached middle and upper-middle class.[3] We have sought consensus among the leaders of the two national church associations, and TEAM Venezuela's Field Council, regarding the choice of the cities. Most importantly, we are actively praying and seeking the direction of the Holy Spirit. We have given him veto power! He may also direct us to cities we have not yet considered.

The above criteria are not mutually exclusive. We will look at all issues when determining what will qualify as a potential impact church. It may be that we have a very qualified missionary or pastor with a vision for a city that may not otherwise meet our criteria. We'll be open to the Lord calling us to invest time and resources in that place.

We must also be careful not to impose our criteria on a church. Neither should a pastor, no matter how well intentioned, force the church to accept change just because he believes it is right. Rick Warren recognized how important it was to allow the leaders of his church, Saddleback Church near Los

Angeles, to arrive at their own conclusions regarding biblical principles of the church. He says,

> Leading your congregation through a discovery of the New Testament purposes for the church is an exciting adventure. Don't rush through the process. And don't spoil the joy by simply telling everyone what the purposes are in a sermon. Wise leaders understand that people will give mental and verbal assent to what they are told, but they will hold with conviction what they discover for themselves. You're building the foundation for long-term health and growth. (Warren 1995, 96)

A strong leader can impose his or her will on a congregation, but all too often it is just that: his or her will. A plan to establish a church God's way, using biblical principles that the congregation discovers for itself, will result in God's church.

As we've progressed toward evaluating the target cities for potential impact churches, we've learned from the experience of others. For example, Pastor Samuel Marcano became convinced that some changes needed to be made in his church, Dios Es Amor, in Maturin, Venezuela. Several key people supported his initiatives, including TEAM missionaries Danny Carpenter and Sheila McNaughton, who live in Maturin.

But it soon became clear that this 70-year-old rock of a church was not going to move easily. So Samuel started a Bible study with the leadership aimed at determining biblical principles applicable to the church today, and succeeded in turning things round. Our definition of an established church is based on the result of their study.

However, it would be just as ill-advised for TEAM Venezuela to impose change, or an external definition of an established church, as it was for Samuel Marcano in Dios Es Amor. So we are encouraging all of our churches to determine their own definition of an established church, trusting the Holy Spirit to guide them to a biblical definition. Based on that definition, the church can evaluate how it is doing compared with biblical principles.

The leadership in our church in Caracas has already spent a significant amount of time studying the biblical principles of the church. So we were able to do an effective evaluation in a day, where a newer church plant might want to spend weeks or months in the process, possibly during a Sunday School class. We identified key Bible verses in the following categories:

- Church leadership (e.g., Acts 13:1-3, 14:23, 20:28-31, 1 Tim. 3, 1 Pet. 5:1-4)
- Evangelism and mission (e.g., Matt. 28:16-20, Acts 1:8, 5:42, 8:4-5, 13: 1-3)
- Discipleship and Christian Education (e.g., Acts 11:26, Eph. 4:11-16, 2 Tim. 2:2)
- Fellowship (e.g., Acts 2:42-47, 11:22-30, Rom. 15:26, 1 Cor. 16:19)
- Worship (e.g., 1 Cor. 11:17-22, 14:40, Eph. 5:18-20, 1 Tim. 2:8, 4:13

As we studied the passages, we developed a list of characteristics of an established church. We then transferred those characteristics into an evaluation tool. (See sample evaluation at the end of this article.)

Questions should reflect the biblical principles of an established church that leaders discover from their own study of the passages related to the church.[4] The numeric values from the evaluation questions can be assessed many different ways. When we did the evaluation in our church, we took the average for each question and for the broader categories. We also counted up the "0s" and the "4s" for each question and each category.

It was interesting that in our case, the "4s" were spread across all categories, except for one. And the "0s" appeared in that same category. It was clear to everyone where we needed to devote our attention over the next months.

We're encouraging all churches to do such an evaluation, regardless of whether or not they are being considered as a potential impact church. We want all churches to be well established. In fact, as more churches become established according to biblical principles, it should multiply the number of impact churches. And when the Venezuelan church is capable of multiplying its own impact churches, TEAM will be free to leave Venezuela and invest its church planting resources in places where the gospel has yet to be proclaimed.

Endnotes

1. Church-planting missionaries in other cultures should be differentiated from church planters in the same culture who are planting churches with the intent to stay and pastor the church they've started. When Christ is glorified, both are valid.

2. TEAM Venezuela's definition of an established church was approved by TEAM Venezuela Annual Field Conference in Rubio, Venezuela, July 22-29, 1998.

3. The church is for all people of all classes. The reason for the criteria of an unreached middle and upper class is that the Venezuelans are for the most part doing a good job of reaching the lower classes. The church associations with whom we work have asked for our help in reaching the middle and upper classes in the cities.

4. A good example of verses and principles to be studied can be found in Rick Warren's *The Purpose Driven Church*, in the chapter on helping a church define its purpose.

References

Allen, Roland. 1962. *Missionary Methods: St. Pauls' or Ours?* Reprinted. Grand Rapids, Mich.: William B. Eerdman's Publishing Co.

Steffen, Tom. 1997. *Passing the Baton*. La Habra, Calif.: Center for Organizational Ministry and Development.

Warren, Rick. 1995. *The Purpose Driven Church*. Grand Rapids, Mich.: Zondervan.

Sample Evaluation

Please indicate a number after each statement on the line provided, based on the following criteria:

0: Our church has not yet thought about this.
1: Our church has talked about this, but we haven't done anything.
2: Our church has started to do something in this area.
3: Our church is advanced in this area.
4: Our church is in excellent shape in this area.

1. Worship

1.1 Our church meets together regularly for unified worship of God.
1.2 It celebrates regularly the Lord's Supper.
1.3 Our church is unified in prayer as the source of its power.
1.4 It maintains the centrality of the word of God in teaching and preaching.
1.5 Its members give unselfishly.

2. Discipleship and Christian Education

2.1 The leaders in our church study God's word together and help each other spiritually.
2.2 New believers receive immediate attention and are baptized and incorporated into the church as soon as possible.
2.3 Believers are discipled consistently with a balance maintained in the areas of Bible knowledge, character development, and ministerial skills.
2.4 The leadership takes responsibility for the ministerial development of its present and future leaders.
2.5 Men are trained to be the spiritual leaders in their families.
2.6 Older women train younger women in their roles as wives and mothers.
2.7 The members use their spiritual gifts for the mutual edification of the whole body.
2.8 Church discipline is consistently and lovingly applied to members who are in sin.

3. Evangelism and Missions

3.1 Our church's members are involved in relationship evangelism on a personal basis with the goal of reaching whole families.
3.2 It impacts the community through service and outreach.
3.3 It reproduces itself in new churches in unreached areas of its own city/country.
3.4 Our church is involved in sending missionaries to unreached parts of the world.

4. Fellowship with Other Churches

4.1 Our church is a model for other churches.

4.2 It provides resources for helping other churches.

4.3 It recognizes its interdependence with other churches and participates with them to further the cause of Christ.

5. Leadership

5.1 Men recognized as meeting the biblical requirements are chosen to lead the church.

5.2 The leaders assume responsibility for pastoring and maintaining sound doctrine.

5.3 The church willingly and faithfully submits itself to its spiritual leaders.

EPILOGUE 1

From Pioneer to Facilitator: Church Multiplication into the Future

Tom Steffen

In 1988, a new ad slogan emerged. The tagline read, "This is not your father's Oldsmobile." Fathers immediately knew they now belonged to a by-gone era of lost nostalgia. The younger generation was somewhat ambivalent about purchasing something that closely related to lost nostalgia, even if it was a newer model. Both generations were confused. In some ways, the same thing has happened with cross-cultural church planting—or to use my preferred term (Matt. 28:19-20; Acts 16:5; 2 Tit. 2:2): *cross-cultural church multiplication.*

In the mid to late 1990s I began to notice some not-so-subtle changes among students taking church-planting classes at the Cook School of Intercultural Studies at Biola University. Fewer were focusing on pioneer church multiplication. Instead, they wanted to focus on *facilitative* church multiplication.

Rather than heading to unreached people groups to start and multiply church-planting movements, they were headed to reached areas of the world where churches already existed. They were doing this to help existing followers of Christ reach the unreached. I was somewhat taken aback.

A host of questions filled my mind, beginning with those concerning the realities of the mission field.

- *Did former church planters fail to help weave church planting into the nationals' DNA?*
- *Did the nationals not understand that they were to reproduce new communities of faith?*
- *Was there no modeling by expatriates to show them how to do it?*
- *Or did the nationals just want to abdicate this particular role?*
- *Or worse yet, did they want nothing to do with this new role?*

I then began to question our training at home.

- *Why did these students feel the Holy Spirit was leading them to work with existing churches, rather than start new ones?*
- *Whatever happened to Romans 15:21, where we find Paul's ambition was to go where no one else had gone?*

- *Should we be training for the facilitative role as well as the pioneer role?*
- *Is the pioneer role over for those of us in the West?*
- *In relation to the selection process, what are the profile differences between pioneers and facilitators?*
  - *Are there different types of facilitators?*
  - *How long do facilitators remain on site?*
  - *Does the facilitator go through role changes like those of the pioneer?*
  - *What is their exit strategy?*
  - *Should one become a facilitator without first having planted a multiplying church?*
  - *Will transferring cognitive information alone be sufficient for nationals to go out and multiply churches?*
    - *Who models how to do it?*
    - *Will nationals conduct church multiplication (CM) beyond their own culture (CM1) to include CM2 (similar cultures) and CM3 (distant cultures)?*

I had more questions than answers.

Comparing Models

I began to notice that authors of a new model (what I now call the facilitator model) considered it far superior and speedier than what had taken place through the pioneer model. It is not ideal to take twenty years to plant a single church only to have the missionary leave. Rather, it is best to work with existing churches that will start multiple churches simultaneously in shorter time with less cultural baggage. The baton is in their hands from the beginning; thus, there is no need for expatriates to pass it on. For sure, "This is not your father's Oldsmobile."

But what is the new model? I certainly had no problem eliminating the cultural baggage, reducing the timeframe, or adding the multiplication aspect, as evidenced in *Passing the Baton: Church Planting that Empowers* (1997). So what was going on?

Then it hit me. We were talking about two very different and distinct types of church multiplication. To blur the two would only create confusion and contradiction. There was no need to declare one superior or speedier then the other, even if improvement was necessary for the first. So I began to try to distinguish the two, the results of which can be found in *The Facilitator Era: Beyond Pioneer Church Multiplication* (2011).

Pioneer church multiplication calls for individuals who can start something from scratch, and then turn it over steadily to the new followers of Christ in every area of ministry. Pioneers pass batons frequently until there are no other batons to pass; they then find a new role to play.

Facilitator church multiplication, on the other hand, calls for individuals who can build upon the foundation begun by pioneers by addressing some aspect of church multiplication that requires additional attention. They go to those who already possess numerous batons, but still lack others. They go to national communities of faith to serve, assist, coach, mostly leading from the back, sometimes alongside, and less frequently from the front.

Like pioneers, facilitators have something to offer. They too have other batons to pass along. Neither pioneers nor facilitators should feel guilty for what they have to offer since God is the one who gives spiritual gifts and the skill sets necessary to mature and multiply local parts of the universal Body of Christ.

The Need for Humility

Both pioneers and facilitators, however, must arrive with humble hearts. There is no room for an attitude of "serve us," only for service. It is not what one brings to the table that impresses God (after all, he is the one who gave it), but the respect and dignity by with which it is offered and delivered to others. It would also seem likely that expatriates would receive some batons from the nationals. Just as Paul made visits to churches to give them something, he often received something in return.

If such an exchange of batons takes place between expatriates and nationals, it is more likely that batons will be passed by nationals to others as they minister to those residing in CM1, CM2, and CM3 contexts. We must remember that every baton has a shelf life within the race of life. Therefore, all batons, no matter who holds them, should be ready to be passed along.

When batons are passed, subtraction does not result; rather, multiplication occurs. That is the way it works in God's economy.

Under the leadership of Rick Warren, Saddleback Church became the first church in history to send missionaries to all 195 nations in November 2010. Their new goal is to reach the 6000-plus unreached people groups. Expect Saddleback personnel to work through existing churches or start their own in the major gateway cities of the world in close proximity to these unreached peoples.

This begs the question: *how did the existing churches they wish to work with get there in the first place?* Many came into existence through the sacrificial efforts of Western missionaries. Philip Jenkins puts it this way: "Whatever their image in popular culture, Christian missionaries of the colonial era succeeded remarkably" (2002, 56). I would argue that the same is true of other mission eras as well. This helps explain the present move by westerners from pioneers to facilitators. It also begs the question: *can the 6000-plus unreached people groups be reached through short-termers alone?*

A Fourth Era: Reaching the Reached to Reach the Unreached

Some time ago, Ralph Winter brilliantly identified three eras of modern missions.

Era 1: William Carey focused on the coastlands.
Era 2: Hudson Taylor focused on the inlands.
Era 3: Donald McGavran and Cameron Townsend focused on unreached peoples.

With all the fast and furious changes swirling around us today, have we entered a fourth era?

I believe we have, and that we have moved beyond the leadership of Mc-Gavran and Townsend. We in the West have moved from predominately *reaching the unreached* to predominately *reaching the reached to reach the unreached.* Even so, that does not jettison pioneer church multiplication by any means. It just means fewer westerners will prioritize pioneer church multiplication.

For sure, "This is not your father's Oldsmobile." We must become clearer as to what our next car purchase will be, without unnecessarily criticizing the past, or completely abandoning or abdicating it. After all, there is something nostalgic about old cars that should never be lost. We must never forget that it is only God's Spirit that can bring such clarity and focus in the midst of the fog of spiritual warfare.

The tectonic change from one mission era to another should drive participants in the assemblies, agencies, and academies to seek guidance as never before from the director and initiator of missions, the Holy Spirit. There are many unknowns and challenges that lay before us (not to mention an array of different religions, cultures, and languages, a number of which still lack a complete Bible translation).

May the Holy Spirit give those ministering in this era the wisdom of Solomon, the ability to be shrewd as snakes like Joshua and harmless as doves like Rahab, the willingness to be humbled so as to become effective servants like Moses, the ability to become strategic planners like Joseph and Nehemiah, and the fortitude not to run like Jonah did when under pressure. And may he give us the boldness of Paul in the midst of suffering so that we would become accurate and adequate spokespersons of the message of grace so that Jesus Christ will be glorified and his local body multiplied, matured, and his universal Church completed.

References

Jenkins, Philip. 2002. *The Next Christendom: The Coming of Global Christianity.* New York: Oxford University Press.

Steffen, Tom A. 1997. *Passing the Baton: Church Planting that Empowers.* Rev. ed. La Habra, Calif.: Center for Organizational & Ministry Development.

_____. 2011. *The Facilitator Era: Beyond Pioneer Church Multiplication.* Eugene, Ore.: Wipf and Stock.

Church Planting in the 21st Century: Seven Developments

Craig Ott

The preceding pages have taken the reader on a journey through the diverse landscape of church-planting ministry from a cross-cultural perspective. The insights and guidelines are the fruit of decades of experience and reflection by seasoned church planters and missionaries.

Recent decades have ushered in some of the most dramatic changes in world history, encompassing technology, geopolitics, globalization, world religions, and the growth of Majority World Christianity. These changes will no doubt continue into the coming decades, having a profound impact on missions in general and church planting in particular.

In this closing chapter we will briefly explore seven developments facing cross-cultural church planting as we progress into the twenty-first century. These are more than passing trends and are likely to only intensify in the coming decades. Each presents promise and peril, demanding wisdom to maximize each opportunity for kingdom impact in the global planting of the church among the unreached and underreached.

Development 1: Church-planting Support Systems

By the close of the twentieth century there had been a veritable explosion of various support systems for North American church planters. These included church planter assessment, boot camps, training centers, internships, coaching systems, resources, books, conferences, and support networks. Never before had so many tools and aids been available to church planters, and they greatly increased the effectiveness and success rate of church plants.

Only recently have mission agencies and Majority World churches begun to develop similar systems and deploy church-planting coaches. In the past, they tended to rely solely upon the spiritual "call" of the planter and provide minimum practical training and supervision for the task of church planting. Fortunately, this is changing.

Of course, the challenge of cross-cultural church planting or church planting in Majority World contexts means that North American systems, strategies, and resources will need to be adapted. There remains no substitute for church planters to continue to place their ultimate confidence in the same Lord who said, "Apart from me you can do nothing."

But such systems, when appropriately adapted to the cultural context, will

244 Extending God's Kingdom: Church Planting Yesterday, Today, Tomorrow

prove to be a tremendous boon to increasing effectiveness of church planters globally. Mission agencies and national churches with a vision for church plant- ing and who want to be the best stewards of their personnel and resources will increasingly invest in such church-planting support systems.

Development 2: Short-term Missions and Church Planting

The short-term mission (STM) phenomenon of recent decades is nothing less than spectacular. Studies indicate that there are at least 1.6 million Ameri- cans annually traveling abroad on STM trips (Wuthnow 2009, 170). Add to this thousands more STM Koreans, Europeans, and other nationalities and the picture emerges of a veritable tsunami of STM volunteers impacting mission around the globe.

Assisting in church planting is second only to construction projects as the primary purpose of STM (Priest, Wilson, and Johnson 2010). STM has become an integral part of most local church mission programs and shows no signs of letting up. Sponsoring churches increasingly expect that STM teams partici- pate in efforts of their long-term missionaries. STM is the primary way send- ing churches partner directly with church-planting missionaries and national churches.

Yet long-term church planters continue to struggle with the question of how to make the most of STM. Some view STM as a distraction from the nor- mal day-to-day work of church planting. The energy and time necessary to plan for, host, and guide STM teams is formidable. Yet the potential for STM making significant contributions to church planting, if well planned, should not be underestimated. English camps, school programs, prayer walks, litera- ture distribution, music, and community service are just some of the ways STM can enhance church-planting ministry.

Conversely, poorly prepared and planned STM can be harmful. Not only are STM members poorly prepared, but there can be a tendency for members of a church plant to overly depend upon contributions of STM teams. For ex- ample, they may assume that evangelism is something STM teams do (not lo- cal believers), or that the church's existence is dependent upon resources that STM teams bring. Church planters must judiciously employ STM teams, on the one hand welcoming the opportunities, while on the other giving firm and clear direction so that they genuinely contribute to the health of the church plant and do not merely serve the interests of the sending church.

Some have begun promoting cross-cultural church planting employing STM teams alone, apart from the assistance of a long-term missionary church planter (e.g., Bessenecker on page 65 of this volume and Avant Ministries n.d.). The verdict is still out if such approaches will bear long-term fruit.

Typically, partnering with national church planters will be necessary. There is increasing awareness that traditional pastoral approaches to cross-cultural church planting are expensive in terms of both time and finances, and have rarely led to healthy indigenous church reproduction. Various approaches to itinerate and short-term church planting are likely to be a growing trend which holds considerable promise.

Development 3: Internationalization of Missionary Sending and Church-planting Teams

As the Majority World Church has grown and come of age, it has become a major missionary-sending force. Increasingly, international church-planting teams are formed with members from several continents. With the number of Majority World missionaries continuing to grow while Western missionary numbers plateau or even decline, internationalization will continue to increase (see Wan and Pocock 2009; Jaffarian 2004).

International partnership has become a non-negotiable in the world of modern missions. The challenge of learning to work together harmoniously with different nationalities, leadership styles, financial resources, and spiritualities is formidable (see Mackin 1992; Roembke 2000). Especially in church-planting ministries, the potential to demonstrate diversity in the Body of Christ and the universality of the Christian message is enormous. Cross-cultural church planters of the twenty-first century must be prepared to exercise great humility and devote the required energy to make international mission teams work effectively.

Development 4: Migration and Diaspora Church Planting

In recent years, human migration has become a growing focus of missiological study and research. According to a United Nations (2010) report, three percent of the world's population live in a country in which they were not born. Church planting among ethnic minorities and first-generation immigrants is not new. However, globalization has increased the opportunities and needs, and will continue to do so.[1]

Increasingly, communities composed of unreached or restricted-access people groups now exist in contexts where they can be easily reached with the gospel and where churches can be openly planted. On the other hand, as Christians migrate to live in locations unreached by the gospel, the potential for evangelism and churches planting arises.

This phenomenon presents an enormous opportunity for church planting among unreached and underreached populations. Whether it is mission to the diaspora or through the diaspora, intentionality and training are key to maximizing potential and effectiveness. Local churches are often blind to unreached diaspora communities in their midst, or if they are aware, they lack the cross-cultural skills to initiate ministry to them.

Similarly, students, laborers, businesspeople, refugees, and even retirees who relocate to places where few indigenous churches exist need training in cross-cultural skills and church planting to equip them for such ministry in foreign and sometimes hostile contexts.

Another growing trend is that believers in the diaspora (such as Chinese living in America) are sending missionaries back to their homeland to plant churches.[2] Yet diaspora churches often have little vision for reaching persons or people groups beyond their own ethnicity, thus missing opportunities.

Church-planting strategies and training will need to increasingly give attention to the potential (as well as the challenges) of diaspora ministry to maximize opportunities for the spread of the gospel and kingdom impact.

Development 5: Holistic Mission and Church Planting

Evangelicals have shown increased interest theologically, missiologically, and practically in holistic mission. Ministry to the whole person spiritually, physically, and socially has become a non-negotiable, especially for younger evangelicals. Most church planters, however, have focused primarily on evangelism and discipleship, with the hopes of developing more holistic ministries once the church has been established. This approach may need to change for two reasons.

First, *younger missionary recruits are less interested in purely spiritual ministry that does not integrate evangelism and discipleship in a natural way with ministry to the poor and disadvantaged.* They theologically and practically refuse to separate physical from spiritual need. Advancement of the Kingdom of God is the overarching concern which goes beyond church planting in the narrower sense.

Second, *to reach the masses in urban centers, as well as the rural poor, ministry must address the needs of the whole person and demonstrate the love of Christ to gain a hearing and to ultimately be effective in evangelism and discipleship.* This concern is not new to church planters. But as the gap between rich and poor increases, as globalization and migration magnify human need, church planters will need to be more intentional in developing holistic ministries. Creative ways must be explored by church planters to make holistic ministry integral to their task, partnering wherever possible with other ministries and planting churches that are a witness, sign, and foretaste of the Kingdom of God.

Development 6: The Uncertain Role of Western Missionaries in Church Planting

Since the collapse of the Western colonial system, the role of Western missionaries has been in flux, generally toward serving under or alongside national churches. The growth of the Majority World Church has led some to question the need to send Western missionaries altogether. More and more mission leaders are questioning the effectiveness of traditional approaches to missionary church planting.

Paying a Western church planter for ten or twenty years to plant one church is hardly efficient. In 1912, Roland Allen called for a different approach in his classic *Missionary Methods: St Paul's or Ours?* Allen's thoughts have been reiterated anew in fresh forms by others in this volume (see Kendall on page 45 and Ott on page 35) and elsewhere. For example, David Garrison's study *Church*

Planting Movements (2000 and 2004) dramatically promoted the idea of missionary church planters moving from being the primary planters to becoming more facilitators of church-planting movements.

This raises a question also discussed in Tom Steffen's *The Facilitator Era: Beyond Pioneer Church Multiplication* (2011). Yes, missionary church planters should aspire to become movement mobilizers, but can they do that if they themselves have not learned firsthand how to plant churches in the given culture? Without such experience they lack credibility.

The goal of moving from church addition (in the more traditional model) to church multiplication in the facilitator model will continue to be a concern of missionary church planting. But there are no shortcuts on the road to getting there. Partnership, humility, and teachability will remain foundational however the role of missionary church planter may evolve.

Development 7: Continued Need for Contextualization and New Forms of the Church

We live in a day when cookbook approaches to ministry and mission abound. One-size-fits-all strategies promising to reach the world appear regularly with much pomp and promotion. Indeed, many of these approaches and strategies have proven effective in *specific* contexts and under *definite* circumstances, which unfortunately do not exist everywhere. We do well to learn from them.

However, each church planter will need to study and assess the local context of his or her church plant or movement and carefully evaluate what methods will best fit the particular circumstances. This must be done in a spirit of openness so as not to reject potentially effective methods just because they are unconventional. One must also realize that different methods may reach different people in the same context and thus have equal legitimacy.

Furthermore, globalization has not—contrary to popular opinion—resulted in a homogenization of cultures (see Martell 2010, 89-104). This means that the need to contextualize ministry has not disappeared merely because young people almost everywhere like to eat at McDonald's and wear jeans.

Cross-cultural church planters will need to resist the temptation of the cookie cutter and abandon the quest for the silver bullet. Be it the house church, metachurch, megachurch, or multisite church, leadership styles, artistic expressions, social dynamics, and transformational ministry will need to engage the local culture in biblically faithful and culturally appropriate ways. No church planter can be spared this hard, and admittedly sometimes risky, work. He or she must go back to the biblical basics, while at the same time exploring together with local believers creative contextualization that fulfills biblical purposes and connects with the needs and concerns of the contemporary culture.

This last point brings us full circle: there is nothing new under the sun, just new arrangements. Church planters then, now, and in the future will only serve their divine calling well in utter dependence upon the power of the word of God and the guidance of the Holy Spirit. That has not, and will not, change.

The more the methods and guidelines in this book are linked with the timeless message and models we find in scripture, the more we must heed them in the future. The more they are bound to specific times and places, the more they will need to be judiciously evaluated and adapted to face the opportunities and challenges facing church and mission tomorrow.

This much is sure: the promise of Christ that "I will build my church" will not fail, and the privilege of humble human servants participating in that mission will not end until he returns.

Endnotes

1. For example, there were 34.5 million diaspora Chinese living outside mainland China or Taiwan in 1999. In the Americas, the Chinese diaspora grew 19.8% from 1998 to 1999 (Wan 2003, 35).

2. Go' International is an example of an agency sponsored by diaspora Chinese churches in America that has forty workers with ministries in forty regions of the world (Wan 2003, 38).

References

Avant Ministries. n.d. "Short Cycle Church Planting." Accessed March 7, 2011 from www.avantministries.org/short-cycle.html.

Garrison, David. 2000. *Church Planting Movements*. Richmond, Va.: International Mission Board of the Southern Baptist Convention.

_____. 2004. *Church Planting Movements: How God Is Redeeming a Lost World*. Midlothian, Va.: WIGTake Resources.

Jaffarian, E. Michael. 2004. "Are There More Non-Western Missionaries than Western Missionaries?" *International Bulletin of Missionary Research* 28(3):131-132.

Mackin, Sandra L. 1992. "Multinational Teams: Smooth as Silk or Rough as Rawhide?" *Evangelical Missions Quarterly* 28(2):134-140.

Martell, Luke. 2010. *The Sociology of Globalization*. Cambridge: Polity.

Priest, Robert J., Douglas Wilson and Adelle Johnson. 2010. "U.S. Megachurches and New Patterns of Global Mission." *International Bulletin of Missionary Research* 34(2):97-102.

Roembke, Leanne. 2000. *Building Credible Multicultural Teams*. Pasadena, Calif.: William Carey Library.

Steffen, Tom. 2011. *The Facilitator Era: Beyond Pioneer Church Multiplication*. Eugene, Ore.: Wipf & Stock.

United Nations. 2010. "International Migration and Development: Report of the Secretary-General." Accessed February 19, 2011 from www.gfmd.org/documents/65th-UNGA_Report-of-UN-Sec-Gen.pdf.

Wan, Enoch. 2003. "Mission among the Chinese Diaspora: A Case Study of Migration and Mission." *Missiology* 31(1):35-43.

Wan, Enoch and Michael Pocock, eds. 2009. *Missions from the Majority World*. Pasadena, Calif.: William Carey Library.

Wuthnow, Robert. 2009. *Boundless Faith: The Global Outreach of American Churches*. Berkeley, Calif.: University of California.